Explore th

# TANZANIA

*Authors:*
*Elke Frey, David Kyungu*

*An Up-to-date travel guide with 127 color photos*
*and 20 maps*

**First Edition**
**1998**

**Dear Reader,**

Being up-to-date is the main goal of the Nelles series. To achieve it, we have a network of far-flung correspondents who keep us abreast of the latest developments in the travel scene, and our cartographers always make sure that maps and texts are adjusted to each other.

Each travel chapter ends with its own list of useful tips, accommodations, restaurants, tourist offices, sights. At the end of the book you will find practical information from A to Z. But the travel world is fast moving, and we cannot guarantee that all the contents are always valid. Should you come across a discrepancy, please write us at: Nelles Verlag GmbH, Schleissheimer Str. 371 b, D-80935 München, Germany, Tel: (089) 3571940, Fax: (089) 35719430.

# LEGEND

| | | | | | |
|---|---|---|---|---|---|
| ✳ | Place of Interest | 🐘 | National Park | ▬▬▬ | Expressway |
| ■ | Public or Significant Building | ⇥ | International Airport | ▬▬▬ | Principal Highway (Mainly Asphalt) |
| ■ ⌂ | Hotel, Lodge, Camp | ⇥ | National Airport | ━━━ | Principal Highway (Mainly Unpaved) |
| ▨ | Market | ✈ | Landing Strip | ──── | Highway (Unpaved) |
| ✝ ☪ | Church, Mosque | **Mt. Meru** 4566 | Mountain Summit (Height in Meters) | ══════ | Provincial Road (Partly Paved) |
| ϡ | Hindu Temple | Marangu | Place Mentioned in Text | ──── | Secondary Road, Track, Path |
| ☋ | Water Source | ▬▬▬ | National Border | ┉┉┉ | Railway |
| 🏖 | Beach | A19 | Route Number | \18/ | Distance in Kilometers |

**TANZANIA**
© Nelles Verlag GmbH, D-80935 München
   All rights reserved

First Edition 1998
ISBN 3-88618-050-6
Printed in Slovenia

| | | | |
|---|---|---|---|
| **Publisher:** | Günter Nelles | **English Editor:** | Anne Midgette |
| **Editor in Chief:** | Berthold Schwarz | **Translation:** | Linda L. Kurz |
| **Project Editor:** | Elke Frey | **Cartography:** | Nelles Verlag GmbH |
| **Photo Editor:** | Kirsten Bärmann-Thümmel | **Color separations:** | Priegnitz, Munich |
| | | **Printed by:** | Gorenjski Tisk |

- X01 -

# TABLE OF CONTENTS

### *FEATURES*

## *GUIDELINES*

## *MAP LIST*

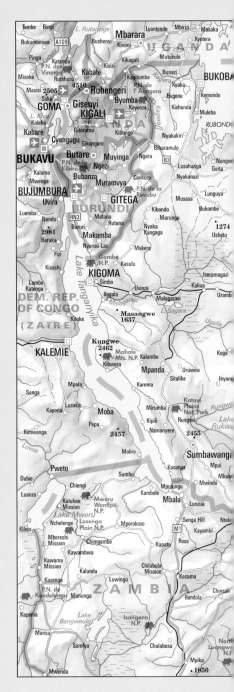

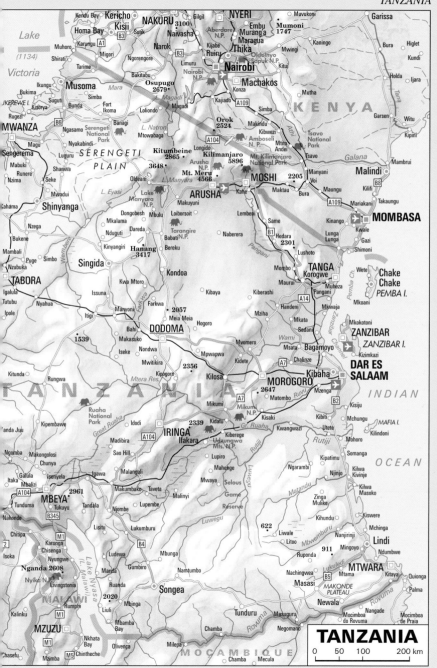

Lake Victoria (1134)

JKEREWE I.

Kendu Bay  Kericho  NAKURU 3100  Gilgil  NYERI  Muvukoni  Garissa
Homa Bay  Kisii  B3  Sotik  Naivasha  Aberdare N.P.  Embu  Mumoni 1747
Muhoro  Karungu  A1  Migori  Narok  Kijabe  Murang'a  Maragua  Mwingi  Kaningo  Bura  Higlet
Shirati  Ikungu  Tarime  Ngorengore  Limuru  Nairobi N.P.  Thika  Ruiru  Kitui  Holda  Kundi  Ijara
Musoma  Bakitabu  Osupugo 2679  Nairobi  Machakos  Mutha  K E N Y A  Ijara
Bukima  Suguti  Simba  Fort Ikoma  Loliondo  Magadi  Konza  Kajiado  Simba  Makindu  Garsen  Witu
Rugezi  Kisorya  Bunda  Banagi  A109  Kibwezi  Isavo National Park  Kipini
MWANZA  B6  Ngasamo  Serengeti National Park  Mtowabaga  L. Natron  Orok 2524  Amboseli N.P.  Mtito Andei  Tsavo  Galana  Mambrui
Magu  Nyakabindi  Kitumbeine 2865  Longido  A104  Mt. Kilimanjaro National Park  Malindi
Sengerema  Luguru  S E R E N G E T I  Oldeani  Arusha  Kilimanjaro 5896  Kilifi  B8
Mabuki  Runere  Shanwa  P L A I N  3648  Mt. Meru 4566  MOSHI  2205  Manyani  Voi  Maungu  Takaungu  Mariakani
Nzima  Seke  Mwadui  L. Eyasi  Lake Manyara N.P.  ARUSHA  Kahe  Maktau  Bura  A109  Mariakani
Kahama  Shinyanga  Dongobesh  Mbulu  Makuyuni  Loiborsoit  Lembeni  Same  Kinango  Kwale  MOMBASA
Nzega  Nduguti  Dareda  Tarangire N.P.  Naberera  B1  Hedaru 2301  Lushoto  Lunga Lunga  Gazi  Wete
Bukene  Ndala  Kinyangiri  Hanang 3417  Bereku  Shimoni  Chake Chake
Mambali  Puge  Simbo  Babati N.P.  Mombo  TANGA  Muheza  Pangani  PEMBA I.
Nzubuka  Singida  Kondoa  Kibaya  Kiberashi  Korogwe  Mkoani
TABORA  Kwa Mtoro  Handeni  A14  Mkwaja
Igalula  Issuna  Farkwa  Mziha  Mkata  Mkokotoni
Tutubu  Nyahua  Manyoni  2057  Hogoro  Sadani  ZANZIBAR
Ipole  Itigi  Meia Meia  DODOMA  Mvomero  Wami  Msata  Bagamoyo  ZANZIBAR I.
1539  Bahi  Makasuko  Nondwa  Mpwapwa  Kidete  Chalinze  Kizimkazi
Kitunda  Rungwa  Iseke  Mwitikira  2356  Kilosa  Kibaha  DAR ES SALAAM
Kipogoro  A7  MOROGORO  Mzenga  B2  INDIAN
T A N Z A N I A  2647  Matombo  Ruvu  Kisiju
Ruaha National Park  Mikumi  Mikumi N.P.  Kisaki  Kibiti  Mchungu  MAFIA I.
anda Juu  Kipembawe  Idodi  Kidatu  2339  Kiberege  Kwangwazi  Utete  Kilindoni
Ngomba  Makongolosi  Madibira  A104  IRINGA  Udzungwa Mts. N.P.  Mohoro
Chunya  Sao Hill  Ifakara  Lupiro  Gr. Ruaha  Rutiji  Somanga
Galula  Isenyela  Igawa  Malangali  Mahenge  Ngarambi  Kipatimu  Kilwa Kivinje
Itaka  Mbalizi  Makumbako  Taveta  Mwaya  Selous  Njinjo  Kilwa Masoko
A104  2961  Malinyi  Game  Matandu  Zinga  Kiswere
Tund.  MBEYA  Tukuyu  Tandala  Njombe  Lupembe  Reserve  Mulike  Kihundu  Mchinga
Nakonde  B345  Lisitu  Luwegu  622  Kihundu  Lindi
Chitipa  Karonga  Ludewa  B4  Lukumburu  Mbunga  Liwale  Litoo  Nanjirinji  Ndumbwe
Isoka  Chisenga  M1  Namtumbo  Ruponda  911  Mingoyo  MTWARA
Nganda 2608  Nyungwe  Manda  Gumbiro  Nachingwea  Mtama  Kitaya  Quionga
Nyika N.P.  Livingstonia  Ruanda  Masasi  MAKONDE PLATEAU  Palma
MALAWI  Rumphi  2020  Songea  Newala  Mocimboa do Rovuma
Kalinku  Liuli  Mbinga  Tunduru  Masuguru  Nangade  Mocimboa de Praia
MZUZU  M1  Mbamba Bay  Chamba  Negomano
Chasefu  Mzimba  Nkhata Bay  M5  Chintheche  Olivença  Milepa  M O C A M B I Q U E  Chamba  Mecula

## TANZANIA

0    50    100    200 km

# THE LANDSCAPE AND
# FAUNA OF TANZANIA

The landscape of Tanzania is overwhelmingly versatile. The Indian Ocean casts its breakers against 500 miles (800 km) of tropical coral reefs, white, palm-lined beaches and mangrove coasts. Powerful snowstorms sometiems powder the shining glacial ice and the dark volcano peaks of Kilimanjaro, which is after all, more than 19,000 feet (almost 6,000 m) high– the highest mountain on the African continent. The waters of Lake Tanganyika are crystal-clear and warm for the entire length of the lake (420 miles/676 km); countless shimmering cichlids swim through its upper regions, above a deep, unexplored crevice extending to a depth of 2,175 ft (663 m) below sea level: it is the longest and deepest lake in Africa and the second-deepest in the world. By contrast, Africa's largest fresh-water lake, the world's second largest, is flat and shallow as a saucer: Lake Victoria's immense surface is framed in a verdant, lake-irrigated landscape.

Millions of wild animals roam the savannas and grasslands in gigantic herds, seeking new grazing after the seasonal rains. The country is home to elephants, zebras, wildebeest and many other antelopes, as well as predators and a range of birds: no other African nation can boast such a wealth and variety of wildlife.

**Tropical Seasons**

Tanzania's northern border runs right through Lake Victoria, at a latitude of 1°

*Preceding pages: A cheerful farewell to the old year in Makunduchi. The lion knows that he's in no danger from the safari jeep. Left: A giraffe contemplates a photographer.*

south. For many hundreds of miles, the Ruvuma River marks the southern border, at a latitude of approximately 11° and 12° south, until it flows into the Indian Ocean. Tanzania, therefore, lies in the path of the sun's strongest rays: in the tropics, south of the Equator.

Everyone knows that it's hot in the Torrid Zone – the area, that is, between the Tropic of Cancer and the Tropic of Capricorn – but there are remarkable differences, particularly in a country as diverse and as large as Tanzania. Even in hot countries, the sun has different effects at different times and at different places in the course of a year. Between June 21st and December 21st, the vertical (and therefore most concentrated) rays of the sun "wander" from the Tropic of Cancer to the Tropic of Capricorn (23.5° north-23.5° south), thence to return to the north. March 21st and September 23rd see the worst heat waves crossing the equator.

The different positions of the sun have a decisive effect on temperatures in Tanzania. In the months when the sun's forces are concentrated on the northern hemisphere, it is comparatively cool: roughly between April and September. June and July are the coolest months. But what is "cool" in this tropical climate? A coastal community like Dar es Salaam has average temperatures of 75°F (24°C) in July; Arusha, the largest tourist town in the north, more than 185 miles (300 km) from the coast and 4,300 feet (1,300 m) above sea level, averages 63°F (17°C); while Mbeya, an important regional town in the south, at an approximate altitude of 5,600 feet (1,700 m) and more than 380 miles (600 km) inland, is about 55°F (13°C). Anyone who intends to visit Tanzania's lovely mountain landscapes during this period will encounter pleasantly warm weather during the daytime, but should bring warm clothing for the hours after sundown; and he or she will find no cause for complaint in the thick woolen blankets on his hotel bed.

However, if you're staying in the coastal regions or the offshore islands, you can forego the wool socks and cumbersome winter clothing: mild temperatures reign here even at night.

Between October and March, however, the sun's energy is focused on the area south of the equator, and it's now that it really gets hot along Tanzania's coast. In Dar es Salaam, the January mean temperature lies around 82°F (28°C), and, as it doesn't cool off much at night, this means that daytime highs are generally over 86°F (30°C), while at night the thermometer rarely drops lower than 75°F (24°C). In the highlands, too, the sun shines with greater force, banishing the disagreeable night chill. Arusha enjoys average temperatures of a pleasant 70°F/21°C (daytime mean temperature around 82°F/28°C, nighttime around 57°F/14°C); Mbeya, about 64°F/18°C (daytime around 73°F/23°C, nighttime about 57°F/14°C).

Of course, anyone planning to climb in the mountains should be prepared for special conditions: temperatures, of course, sink at higher altitudes. Use this rule of thumb: 12°F (6.5°C) for every 3,300 feet (1,000 m). Anyone who sits in Moshi at the foot of Kilimanjaro, 2,900 feet (890 m) above sea level, perspiring in temperatures of 77°F (25°C) in the shade, trying to catch a breath of breeze on a rooftop terrace and contemplating the white peak (while his ice cubes rapidly melt away in his lemonade), should bear in mind that the temperature up on top, amid the glaciers at an altitude of 19,344 feet (5,896 m), are several degrees below freezing, and at night sink even lower.

This heat wave vacillating back and forth between the two tropics doesn't only serve to bring high temperatures. It's also a tremendous flywheel for all of the earth's climate zones, which are ranged in broad belts around the globe, following the highest position of the sun .

At the point where the sun warms the earth most, it sets in motion tremendous masses of air, which rise, move off northwards or southwards at great heights, and, after "high flying" for 25 or 30 parallels, sink back down toward the earth. Part of this air is then drawn, near the ground, toward the wandering "thermal equator," there to become the northeast trade winds (north of this equator) or the southeast trade winds (south of it).

If you're in Tanzania during the hot season, therefore, when the great "oven" of the sun is focused over the southern hemisphere, you will probably feel northern or northeasterly winds (in Kiswahili, *kaskazi*). During the "cool" season, however, the winds come from the south (*kusi*). This reliable semi-annual shift in the wind's direction has been a boon to seafarers for centuries; and the European designations of these winds – *trade winds* in English or *Passat* in German (from the Portuguese *passar*, to move across) – reflect merchant shipping terminology. In fact, these trade winds have had a decisive influence on East African history for the past 2,000 years, for Arab, Indian, Indonesian and Chinese mariners took advantage of them to voyage along East Africa's coasts long before the Europeans found their way into these waters.

## Rain – Magic?

Not only is the sun a kind of flywheel for air currents in the tropics, but it ushers in, about four weeks after it reaches its highest position, the heaviest rains of the year, often in the form of violent thunderstorms. Since the sun is directly above Tanzania at two different periods in the hot season, the country generally experiences two periods of heavy rainfall every year. The majority of this falls around April/May (although in some parts of the

*Right: After a cloudburst in the streets of Stonetown (Zanzibar).*

country, it may come up to one or two months earlier), the height of the rainy season (in Kiswahili, *masika*); while November/December see a more moderate degree of precipitation during the lesser rains (*vuli*). During the hot season, however, cloudbursts occasionally crop up, leaving vast expanses of green landscape in their wake.

Between June and October, on the other hand, when the sun shines more strongly on the northern tropics, Tanzanian, south of the Equator, is mainly dry. Initially, in June/July, the "cool" season holds sway; the *masika* rains have just ended, and the vegetation is still fresh and green. Then the sun starts to come back into its own, and it gets hotter and hotter as the year progresses. The countryside gradually becomes parched until, in November, the long-awaited "lesser rains" finally arrive to clear the air and ease the scorching heat for a time.

If the rain were only as dependable as the earth's orbit around the sun, then the important position of "rainmaker" would never have developed in Tanzania. Rainmakers were chieftains or particularly knowledgeable persons who knew how to summon the rain when it was needed most. In general, this wasn't a question of magic: these experts understood quite a lot about weather phenomena, or, to be precise, about the natural indications of approaching rain. They observed the direction of the wind, humidity, birds, insects, plants, and the like, and, if they were especially sharp, began their rainmaking rituals only when there were clear signs of an approaching downpour, signs imperceptible to the uninitiated. Woe to the rainmaker unable to conjure up the promised rain! That could cost him his life.

Even the best rain magic is powerless if nature doesn't play along. Large areas of Tanzania receive very little precipitation, and what they do get can, unfortunately, be quite capricious. This is a great handicap to farmers, who need rain to fall in places where they have cultivated their fields, and at times shortly after they have sown their crops. Nomads have it

easier: they simply bring their herds to areas where rain has fallen and there is now good grazing for their livestock. Immense tracts of Tanzanian land unsuited to agriculture are thus productively used as pasturage.

Rain falls most abundantly and most dependably in higher, mountainous country, which is in direct contact with masses of damp air. However, only a few regions in Tanzania enjoy this advantage: the south and east flanks of the high volcanoes Kilimanjaro and Meru in the north of the country; the mountainous country, reaching altitudes of almost 10,000 feet (3,000 m), between Mbeya and Lake Nyasa in the south; and the chain of mountainous areas and isolated mountains which extends across the country, with interruptions, from the Usambara Mountains in the northeast to

*Above: Tea, corn, fruit and vegetables flourish in the highlands south of Mbeya. Right: Island-like rock remains, kopjes are reminders of long-vanished mountains.*

the southwest. The chain of mountains south of Bukoba on Lake Victoria receives extra moisture due to the east winds which sweep over the enormous lake. The coastal areas around the Indian Ocean, including the offshore islands, profit from the high humidity of the sea air, but this strip extends only around 30 miles (50 km) inland, and beyond it, this humidity is scarcely felt.

But in fact, this is one reason that Tanzania has retained so much of its wilderness and so many outstanding natural wonders: without adequate rain, people can do only so much to develop the land. Tanzania measures roughly 364,865 square miles (945,000 sq. km) in area (about the size of France, Germany and Switzerland combined; Texas and New Mexico together are only slightly larger), which makes it the largest nation in East Africa; yet, with 30 million inhabitants, it's also the least populous. The population is concentrated where there is the most rainfall; and the areas with little precipitation are nearly deserted.

## A Torn Continent

On a map of Africa, one thing that catches your eye is a kind of tear extending across the east of the continent, from the southern hemisphere to the north, continuing on through the Red Sea and thence, via the Dead Sea and the valley of the Jordan River, even on to Asia, visible in elongated valleys and chains of narrow lakes. Geologically speaking, Africa is ancient, and the earth's crust here behaves like a brittle ceramic plate. It no longer has the flexibility of "young" rocks, but has become hard and ruptured, while many former mountains have been eroded down to plains and plateaus.

In fact, Africa is only a fraction of what was once the more or less coherent continent of Gondwanaland. In the Mesozoic Period (about 150 to 100 million years ago), its component sections drifted apart, and are now broadly distributed all around the globe: they include Antarctica, Australia, South America and India. Only the large island of Madagascar shows any signs that it was once attached to Africa. All the others have gone their own way and altered almost unrecognizably, but their collective origin can be established by comparison of rocks or of traces of living nature (such as fossils which are common to all of the fragments of this former continent).

Much of Tanzania is comprised of now-leveled surfaces of this ancient continent. Its rocks are predominantly gneiss or granite, ground down over the ages to granular, crystalline debris that now covers the surface of the vast plains. As if to document the past, a few tenacious, uncorroded stones have held their own against wind and weather; today, these rise above the plains as large, rocky "islands," called *inselbergs*, or small, rounded *kopjes* (which means, in Dutch/Afrikaans, "little heads"). Most visitors to Tanzania encounter these in the Serengeti, the country's largest and most famous national park. Many tourists have to make a stop at the *Naabi Hill*

17

park entrance. This hill is a small *insel-berg*, or a large *kopje* if you like; within the park, the Seronera Hotel is even built into a group of *kopjes*. Granite hills dot the whole region east and south of Lake Victoria. *Bismarck Rock* at Mwanza harbor is one of the town's signature hallmarks. All the way in the south of Tanzania, in the Mtwara Region, the little district town of Masasi is surrounded by the scenic, legally protected *Masasi Hills*. The plain to the west is cluttered with oddly-shaped *inselbergs*.

As Gondwanaland broke apart – and even thereafter – the eastern edge of the African piece of the continent often sank under water and then rose to become dry land again. For this reason, a wide strip of land along the Indian Ocean, extending some 90 miles (150 km) inland, consists of marine deposits and coastal sediments. While there are no fossils to be found in

*Above: A view from the active volcano Ol Doinyo Lengai over one river-creased flank of the East African Rift Valley.*

the oldest parts of the continent, the relatively younger sections contain finds that are veritably astounding, such as the petrified giant dinosaurs and early mammals on Tendaguru Mountain in the Lindi Region in southeast Tanzania.

Limestone cliffs are still forming on the western edge of the Indian Ocean. Coral reefs are growing in the shallow waters off the East African coast. At low tide, level platforms of young coral lie exposed in places as breakwaters extending for miles before the islands and the mainland. In recent years, the land along the coast and on several islands has risen: coral limestone sometimes rises several feet above the surface of the ocean like a table top, while the sea continually eats away at its foundations.

But the most significant geological phenomenon in East Africa is the conspicuous trench in the east, mentioned above, running across the continent in a north-south direction, which first appeared some 20 million years ago: the *East African Rift Valley*. This is no linear cleft, but rather a whole series of gigantic crevices and steep valleys arranged like steps, leaping in height from barely 330 feet (100 m) to more than 6,000 feet (2,000 m). In the south of Tanzania there is only one deep chasm, Lake Nyasa; north of this, the rift forks into two clearly defined branches near Mbeya. The *Western Rift Valley* follows the line of the Rukwa basin and Lake Tanganyika, while the *Eastern Rift Valley* cuts a a wide arc through the middle of the country. In the south, it forms much of the broad valley through which the Great Ruaha flows, and defines the western flank of the Iringa Highlands. Many hundreds of miles further north, the rift forms the basin of Lake Eyasi. Only one shoulder of this trench is visible at Lake Manyara and on the eastern side of the Ngorongoro Highlands; farther north, the lowlands of Lake Natron again demonstrate a distinct trench form. From there, the rift continues on, studded with many smaller lakes, through all of Kenya as far as Lake Turkana.

Before this rift system developed in the area now known as Tanzania, there were none of the large lakes you see today. Lying as it does between the Western and Eastern Rift Valleys, the shallow basin of Lake Victoria is fed by the waters of all the rivers in the surrounding area, and has only one outlet, draining into the Victoria Nile. More than 20 million years ago, the spot occupied by today's lake was almost completely flat land, crossed by many rivers flowing from the east westwards toward the Congo and on to the Atlantic. Similarly, Lake Tanganyika's largest tributary, the Malagarasi, flowed uninterrupted westward to the Congo.

Then came the great upheaval. The Malagarasi managed to keep to its old course right through the deep chasm of Lake Tanganyika and take up its way again, via the Lukuga, Lualaba and Congo rivers, on the lake's western bank. Further north, however, the landscape was not only rent asunder, but magma flowed from the earth's interior, volcanoes erupted, and strata of ancient rock were suddenly thrust above the earth's surface. All of this blocked the westward paths of the rivers across the great plain (later Lake Victoria); they had nowhere to go but northward, flowing into the Nile and thence, ultimately, into the Mediterranean Sea.

Many of Tanzania's rivers only flow with water in the rainy season; a large part of their water runs into salt or soda lakes which have no outlets. Largest of these are the lakes Rukwa, Eyasi, Manyara and Natron; all of them fluctuate greatly in size depending on the season, and thus the volume of water borne by their tributaries. The remaining rivers, of which the largest are the mighty Rufiji and the Pangani, drain into the Indian Ocean. All the rivers that flow into Lake Nyasa ultimately take the same route: for the lake empties, at its southern extremity, into the Shire River, which drains via the Zambezi into the Indian Ocean. Tanzania is the only country in Africa from which water runs naturally into all three of the large oceans surrounding the continent.

## Landscape and Agriculture

The mighty rift through East Africa provided Tanzania not only with Africa's highest mountain, Kilimanjaro, but also with a number of other individual volcanoes and lava flows. Volcanic soil is quite fertile, and the high-altitude volcanic land, only slightly eroded, is favored by rainfall. Hence the most productive agricultural areas lie around Kilimanjaro and Meru, in the volcanic highlands south of the Ngorongoro region and in the south of the country, between Mbeya and Lake Nyasa.

Only about 10% of Tanzania's territory is classified as agriculturally productive; an additional 40% or so is regarded as grazing land. The country's national parks comprise about 4% of the country's surface: something under 16,000 square miles (40,000 sq. km). Apart from these strictly protected areas, which are closed to any sort of usage whatsoever – except for tourism – Tanzania has placed under protection an additional 42,000 square miles (105,000 sq. km) of game preserves, which may be used only according to certain rules and regulations. If you factor in the multitude of smaller marine, forest and special reserves, roughly 25% of the country is legally protected. The Tanzanian government is making a considerable effort to conserve valuable wilderness. At the same time, most Tanzanians are dependant on their country's natural resouces, as farmers, fishers, hunters and nomads, and it is no easy task to bring nature conservation into alignment with traditional ways of life.

Visitors from countries in which virtually every square foot of land is cultivated, citified or industrialized tend to experience Tanzania as an El Dorado of wild, open country, which can be experienced and marveled at both inside and outside the nature reserves.

With its pronounced seasons of dry and rainy weather, Tanzania's tropical climate brings out two distinct, seasonal characters in most of the country's landscapes, and fosters the *savannah* type of vegetation. And this encompasses quite a broad range of plant life.

Nearly half of the country (an area almost as large as France, or twice the area of New Zealand or the state of Colorado) is covered with *miombo*. Miombo is a sparsely wooded vegetation zone with tropical trees (mostly *Brachystegia* varieties), little underbrush, and soil that is often poor, usually covered with grass. The deciduous forest survives the annual dry season by shedding its foliage. The

grass, often as high as a person's head, withers. Yet even in the course of the dry season, this parched countryside awakens to new life: leaves begin to sprout, although during the first few days they possess no chlorophyll, and are instead brightly colored in hues of yellow, brown, pink and shades of red. Shortly before the rains, many trees blossom and their leaves turn green.

Often, the searing heat is such that the parched grass ignites and flames, together with the fallen leaves, into blackened ash. This causes hardly any damage to the trees, but is something of a burden to the indigenous smaller animals; on the other hand, quite a few pests are destroyed in the process. After a fire moves through a region, an astonishing metamorphosis takes place: in spite of months of dryness, fresh, green grass begins to push through the black layer of ash, even though not one drop of rain has fallen. Sometimes the farmers put this "natural miracle" to good use. At the height of the dry season, when their livestock finds little to feed on, the farmers set fires themselves, thereby providing fresh forage for their animals. In addition, poachers set a number of fires, both in order to lure game to the young grass shoots and to remove any cover in which it can take refuge.

Animal husbandry in miombo woodlands is possible only on a limited scale. Most miombo regions are infested by various types of tse-tse fly, which infect animals with the fatal disease *nagana*, for which there is no known remedy, and can also afflict humans with sleeping sickness, which, however, occurs only rarely and is curable. Wild animals are immune to this infection. Nature lovers can, therefore, see the prevalence of the tse-tse fly in Tanzania as something of a blessing, since it's a sure-fire method of protecting wilderness areas from the incursion of farmers. There's ample evidence to show that many parts of the country were

*Right: Well-camouflaged in its natural habitat, akudu roams in the miombo woodlands.*

populated in the 19th century that are now overrun with tse-tse flies and deserted. In the 19th and 20th centuries, in particular, the native population was decimated by slavery, tribal warfare, diseases "imported" by foreign colonists, famine, rebellions against colonial rule or resettlement to other regions. Their former lands were reclaimed by nature, with, as one of its manifestations, the tse-tse fly.

### Fauna of the Woodlands and Savannah

A great many of Tanzania's game reserves lie in miombo woodland. In these areas, limited hunting is allowed according to specified quotas; the largest is Selous Game Reserve in the southeast of the country. National parks with extensive stands of miombo lie in the central parts of Tanzania: Mahale, Katavi, Ruaha, Mikumi.

Typical woodland animals include the greater kudu (*Tragelaphus strepsiceros*),

an antelope weighing 375 to 550 pounds (170 to 250 kg), which is well camouflaged by its inconspicuous brown striped coat, or innumerable varieties of duiker (*Cephalophus sp.*), small antelopes of between 8 and 165 pounds (3.5-75 kg), who give the impression of crouching thanks to their short, slender forelegs.

Many animal species move freely between woodland and open savannah, a varied, park-like terrain, dotted with bushes and scattered trees, where, because the view is less obstructed, it's easier to observe them. In this way, animals that feed on grass as well as foliage are assured of always finding ample nourishment.

A common sight here is the African elephant (*Loxodonta africana*; in Kiswahili, *tembo* or *ndovu*), weighing in at 3.5 to 6.5 tons, the heaviest land mammal on earth. Its Asian cousin (*Elephas maximus*), found in, for example, India or Thailand, is not only considerably smaller – even around the ears – but also has only one prehensile finger-like append-

21

age at the end of its trunk instead of two, like the African elephant. For millennia, ivory has been a highly sought-after commodity, and it "grew" in great abundance in Africa's seemingly endless herds of elephants, in bulls and cows alike (unlike its Asian cousin, for whom tusks are a male prerogative), and achieving tremendous proportions: an African elephant's tusk can weigh more than 110 pounds (50 kg). Even today, poachers continue to decimate the pachyderm. In the 1980s, more than 110,000 elephants still lived in the Selous area; by the end of the century, their numbers have dwindled to about 25,000.

A five-ton elephant requires around 550 pounds (250 kg) of fodder and roughly 40 gallons (150 l) of water every day. Herds of elephants often roam many miles in order to fulfill their dietary requirements. This is becoming increasingly difficult for them, because humans also place ever-increasing demands on the land. While the elephants used to migrate regularly and often between Manyara and Tarangire Parks, the animals have recently been concentrating more in Tarangire Park, since the corridor of migration has been increasingly restricted by settlements and cultivated fields.

There's a danger to this: when elephants are confined to a limited area, they start to have a destructive effect on their habitat. If there's adequate space available to them, this effect is spread out over a greater area, and the vegetation can recover more easily.

Elephants occasionally stray over the borders of national parks and nature reserves and wreak havoc on farmlands in the vicinity; for, although they are by all accounts very clever animals, they still can't read the signs posted at the reserve boundaries...

*Right: Rhino, heed the warning of your tick-bird! Black rhinos and tick-birds in symbiotic harmony (Ngorongoro Crater).*

Weighing in at more than one ton, the black rhinoceros (*Diceros bicornis*), with its prehensile upper lip, feeds on foliage (the larger, grass-eating white rhinoceros, *Ceratotherium simum*, does not occur in Tanzania). Unlike elephants, rhinos are solitary animals. This alone is an impediment to future reproduction: these prehistoric-looking pachyderms, with one longer and one somewhat shorter horn (the shorter one is actually something more like a thickened shock of hair) on their "noses," have been so reduced in number by poachers that the animals have difficulty finding any mates whatsoever. To the misfortune of the rhino, these animals are also easy to hunt, since they are not only notoriously short-sighted but also take the same path to their watering-hole every day, in the firm but erroneous belief that no one can harm them. Man is its sole enemy, apart from the occasional predator that may pick up a young animal from time to time. The reason for the unchecked slaughter of rhinos is grotesque: powdered rhino horn is valued for its medicinal powers and as an aid to potency in East Asia, while in Yemen any man worth his salt has just got to have a dagger with a handle made of rhino horn. Rhinoceroses are well-protected in Ngorongoro Crater; and several were set free in the Serengeti in 1997 – there, each individual animal needs its own personal bodyguard.

*Askari wa kifaru*, guardian of the rhinoceros, is the Kiswahili word not for the armed wardens in the national parks, but for the tick birds (such as the red-billed oxpecker, *Buphagus erythorhynchus*), members of the starling family, whose hosts generously provide them with ample sustenance: ticks, tse-tse flies, and other parasites. These convivial birds don't confine themselves to rhinos, but also see to the personal hygiene of other large mammals of the savannah: buffalo, antelopes and zebras, as well as donkeys and cattle. They have even been observed

to warn their hosts in the event of danger, gathering on the back of an animal and hissing loudly to indicate, for example, the approach of a predator. This is in the birds' best interest, for the death of their host means for them that their restaurant is closed. Still, this has been of little help to the rhinoceros.

Hippopotamuses (*Hippopotamus amphibius*) can get to be twice as heavy as the black rhinoceroses. The word "hippopotamus" derives from the Greek for "horse of the river"; originally, one of the rivers in question was the Nile, where the animals were once common in the days of ancient Egypt (the German word *Nilpferd*, Nile horse, is more specific). However, with the rise in human population in the lower Nile valley, the animal was forced to yield pride of place, and moved to other areas of the country. In Tanzania it is often found even outside protected nature reserved – anywhere, in fact, where sufficient water is available. Groups of hippos may spend their days in lakes, rivers or in river deltas near the country's larger lakes. They generally remain submerged in water up to their eyes and ears, since this element is good for their skin, hairless and up to 3 inches (6 cm) thick. Tracts of wetland, as long as they are not swampy, are regarded as desirable farmland in Tanzania; and the hippos,which weigh several tons, can do considerable damage to such fields simply by ambling through them of an evening on their way to their feeding grounds. They feed mainly on grass.

Species of antelope such as the Bohor reedbuck (*Redunca redunca*) and waterbuck (common waterbuck, *Kobus ellipsiprymnus*; Defassa waterbuck, *Kobus defassa*) need to be near the water. This is especially true of the swamp-loving sitatunga (*Tragelaphus spekii*), which finds an ideal habitat in Rubondo National Park.

Crocodiles (*Crocodilus niloticus*) are also bound to the water. These reptiles, weighing up to one ton, are found in great numbers along the Rufiji River and on Lake Rukwa and are quite a common

23

sight in the freshwater rivers and lakes. Although they generally seem motionless and harmless, lolling about in the sun, they are exclusively carnivorous, and extremely dangerous hunters.

The other best-known hunters of the animal kingdom are mammals: the big cats, including lions (*Panthera leo*; in Kiswahili, *simba*), leopards (*Panthera pardus*; in Kiswahili, *chui*) and cheetahs (*Acinonyx jubatus*; in Kiswahili, *duma*). Although they share the same habitat and similar prey, their lifestyles and hunting methods differ greatly. Whereas lions live together in prides and their hunting success is the result of a cooperative effort (mostly on the part of the females), leopards are definitely loners, who can stalk other animals superbly and then drag even the heaviest carcass up into trees.

And while both of these great cats generally hunt at night, the cheetah hunts

*Above: Wild dogs gang up on a wildebeest in the Serengeti. Right: Only the male impala has horns.*

in the daytime, and its greatest advantage is its extraordinary speed. It generally preys on the herds of animals that graze on the open savannah and the grassy plains.

This seemingly endless, natural grazing land (most extensive in the Serengeti, but also present, to a lesser degree, in Tarangire National Park, Selous Game Reserve and other areas) is frequented in seasonal rotation by hundreds of thousands of wildebeest or gnu (*Connochaetes taurinus*), thousands of zebras (*Equus burchelli*) and herds of various types of gazelle: impalas (*Aepyceros melampus*), as well as Grant's and Thomson's gazelles (*Gazella granti* and *thomsoni*); in addition, there are African buffalo (*Syncerus caffer*), hartebeest (*Alcelaphus buselaphus ssp.*) and others.

Each year, millions of animals move across hundreds and thousands of miles of the African wilderness, seeking out whatever grazing is available following the rains. Since the animals generally feed on specific plants or parts of plants, you may see quite different species of animals grazing side by side on the same terrain; there is even room for the cattle of the nomadic Maasai. In places, these animals may be accompanied by large predators, or even such smaller ones as spotted and striped hyenas (*Crocuta crocuta*; *Hyaena hyaena*) or servals (*Felis serval*), but for the most part these predators remain in a their territory. Less territorial are the sociable African hunting dogs or wild dogs (*Lycaon pictus*); they follow the migrating herds and present a prime example of coordinated group behavior when they hunt.

Smaller, but extremely varied habitats are the *gallery forests* which line the rivers and dry river beds crisscrossing the savannahs and steppes. These form a refreshing change in the landscape, particularly during the dry season, when larger animals gather there, along with a variety of bird life.

Each habitat also has its own bird life. Rare species of flamingo, for example, live on the soda lakes; while birds of prey, like the bateleur eagle (*Terathopius ecaudatus*), are found almost everywhere in the country.

Anyone traveling to Tanzania to see the wealth of magnificent animal life in the savannahs and grasslands should consider the season. In the dry season (June-October), animals which reside in one fixed territory will concentrate around the shrinking watering-holes, and it's no problem to drive on most of the trails in the parks. When the rains come, the black clayey soil (in Kiswahili, *mbuga*) can render progress difficult, if not downright impossible; therefore, many parks are closed to visitors during the *masika*. Between the lesser and greater rains (roughly November-February/March) the countryside is wonderfully green in many places; and this is the best time to admire the vast migrating herds.

However, Tanzania has an abundance of other natural attractions on tap all year

round: the high mountains in the national parks of Kilimanjaro and Arusha, or the mountain forests in Udzungwa, Mahale and Gombe Stream national parks, as well as in the Uluguru and Usambara Mountains and the volcanoes in the Mbeya Region. The immense freshwater lakes, Lake Nyasa and Lake Tanganyika, are great for swimming, diving and snorkeling. Anyone dreaming of enchanted palm-lined beaches or of exploring the fascinating underwater world of coral reefs should plan to spend a few days on Zanzibar and/or Mafia.

With the help of experienced mountain guides, well-informed local chauffeurs and safari drivers in the national parks, diving instructors and the overwhelming number of knowledgeable, helpful residents, visitors to Tanzania can discover nature in a form that's been lost forever from most parts of our planet. Here, however, this natural wealth can still be found everywhere, in all its astonishing variety, at once a marvel and a challenge to anyone seeking to discover it.

# HISTORY AND CULTURE

The borders of the *United Republic of Tanzania* are a legacy of colonial times. England and Germany established "spheres of interest" in East Africa from 1886 to 1890 – without, of course, giving a thought to any interests the Africans might have had. At the same time, the Europeans curtailed the power of the Sultan of Zanzibar: his two large islands Pemba and Unguja became a British protectorate, while the Germans bought off him a strip of coast on the mainland opposite. Anything west of that, all the way to Lake Tanganyika, came into German hands. Their domain extended, in the south, to the Ruvuma River; in the north, to a boundary cutting across Lake Victoria, which then continued in a southeasterly line to the Indian Ocean – deviating only to curve around Mount Kilimanjaro, bringing that into German territory as well. After World War I, however, Germany lost its colony of German East Africa; Great Britain took it over from the League of Nations as a mandate, under the name *Tanganyika*. In 1961, the country became independent.

The tiny country of Zanzibar, 984 square miles (2,460 sq. km), consists of the two large islands of the former sultanate off the coast of East Africa. In 1964, it united with Tanganyika (roughly 377,200 square miles/ 943,000 sq. km) to become *Tanzania*.

## Early Trade Routes

The Indian Ocean has been an international body of water for more than 2,000 years. Intrepid mariners came westward across the ocean from Indonesia in the first millenium, landing at Madagascar.

*Left: An aid to the fortunes of Stone Age hunters? Cave drawing in the Sandawe region.*

Their most important contribution to African culture was the introduction of the banana, which developed here into a range of varieties and became an important staple of the local diet.

*Zanjistan* or *Zanzibar*, the Land of the Blacks, was the Persian name for the eastern side of the African continent, derived from its dark-skinned inhabitants (*zanj*). In the 9th century, Baghdad had risen to become the leading center in the Islamic world. Seafarers from the Persian Gulf and the southern coast of the Arabian peninsula imported luxury items for the monied classes of the Abbassid realm. East Africa had ivory, ambergris (secreted by sperm whales, used in making perfume) and, especially useful in transactions with East Asia, leopard skins and rhinoceros horn to offer. Two other wares lured the Persians and Arabs: mangrove poles for building houses in their almost treeless countries and – slaves. These were forced to work in the salt works in Basra and to drain the swamps of the southern Mesopotamian valley. Towards the end of the 9th century they revolted, and were successful enough that the slave trade from East Africa became relatively insignificant for hundreds of years, although it never completely died out.

For more than 1,000 years, well into the 20th century, Arabian, Persian, and later also Indian seamen dominated the northern Indian Ocean with their dhows, wooden ships with lateen sails. These sailors created a cultural exchange, as well as trade links, between India and the East African coast. The seasonal shifts of the trade winds are a downright invitation for this development. When the northeast trade winds blow (November-February), they propel the dhows from India to Arabia and further on to East Africa (the direct India-East Africa route takes anywhere from 20 to 30 days to travel). Between April and September, the southeast trade winds hold sway over the same area, fortunately veering southwest up near the Equator, providing the sailor with a fine southwest monsoon blowing from astern to convey him home.

East of India, the ships that sailed belonged to East Asians or to Arab traders who had settled in Asia. There is, however, also evidence that a Chinese ship put in at Malindi (Kenya) in 1420 and imported the first giraffe to China when it returned home. East Asia's precious goods, particularly silks and porcelain, often changed ships in India, generally either in Bengal, on the Malabar coast or Gujarat. Archaeologists have found Chinese porcelain at countless sites along the East African coast. Chinese porcelain bowls were often used as decoration, embedded in the tombstones of wealthy people or the walls of mosques in coastal towns.

### The Shirazi Period

The Arab-Persian merchants brought their culture to Africa. They introduced such plants as cotton and citrus fruits; as Muslims they erected mosques; they built houses of coral limestone – all unlike the indigenous Africans. These Bantu tribes dwelling along the coast supplied the towns with foodstuffs and established and maintained connections to the interior of the region. Over the years, the tradesmen and farming people of the coastal regions interbred; they became known as Swahili. Their language, Kiswahili, is a Bantu language, enriched with Arabic expressions.

Most of the major harbors lay on islands offshore, such as Kilwa, which was historically Tanzania's most important town in the period between the 12th and 15th centuries. It was also the center for trade of a new product on the East Afri-

*Right: A slave trek as seen through the eyes of African explorer David Livingstone in 1858.*

can market, highly coveted in Asia and Europe: gold. The Shona people in Zimbabwe, in the South African interior, mined and transported it to the coastal town of Sofala, opposite Madagascar. As the shifting trade winds did not travel so far south, it was necesssary to establish a kind of delivery service, with dhows, northwards along the coast.

If the "Kilwa Chronicle" is to be believed, Kilwa was, in the 11th century, one of the landing places for the seven ships of a noble Persian family from Shiraz. The head of the family and his six sons were established in the region between Manda (Kenya) in the north and the Comoro Islands in the south; Mombasa, in Kenya, and the island of Pemba were also terminuses for these Shirazi ships. Along the East African coast, the period before the 16th century is commonly referred to as "Shirazi time"; and the inhabitants of Zanzibar, who had already gained a foothold there by that period, call themselves *Shirazi*, although it is highly unlikely that all of the Muslim immigrants who arrived during that period actually came from Shiraz. From Kilwa, the Shirazi sultan Ali bin al-Hasan and his successors controlled the trade in gold.

### Portuguese Intermezzo

In 1497, the Portuguese navigator Vasco da Gama became the first European captain to round the Cape of Good Hope. In 1498, he showed up on the coast of East Africa, sailing past Kilwa and mooring at Mombasa. The Sultan's present to his guests – oranges, a fruit then little known to the Europeans – cured da Gama's crew, who had come down with scurvy. In the rival port of Malindi, Vasco da Gama took on an Arab pilot, who was able to command even this arrogant captain's respect through his local knowledge and navigational expertise. Without the aid of this Muslim, da Gama

would never have reached India so swiftly.

Lusting after gold, spices and Chinese silk, intolerant of anyone espousing a different religion than their own, and fanatically missionizing the Christian faith, these barbaric strangers were able to take control of East Africa in very short order. In 1505, they destroyed Kilwa and made Mombasa their most important harbor, equipping the port with a formidable fortress. As a result, international trade bypassed the Tanzanian coast.

It gradually revived, however, as Portuguese fortunes began to wane. There were never actually very many Portuguese in the land of the Swahili, and they had their hands full enough in Asia with competition from other Europeans: French, Dutch and Englishmen. One city-state after another along the coast withdrew from Portuguese control, and with a little help from the Omanis, from the southeastern Arabian peninsula, even Mombasa fell in 1698, after a three-year siege.

## Oman's Presence in East Africa

Until 1891, the Sultanate of Oman controlled most of the East African coast. In 1840, Sultan Seyyid Said (1804-1856), who was an active businessman, moved his headquarters to Zanzibar, thereby risking a split from his mother country (1856). He had sound economic reasons for this move. Zanzibar was the most important trading port for the coastal ships that had taken on their cargoes at the termini of caravan routes: Tanga, Pangani, Bagamoyo, Kilwa, Mikindani, and others.

Trade with the interior had increased dramatically, for a number of reasons. Ivory and rhino horn were still as much in demand as ever; in addition, there was suddenly a large market for a kind of "goods" that had played a subordinate role for hundreds of years: slaves. As East Africa was slumbering in a kind of torpor during the Portuguese occupation, the Europeans had introduced plantation farming to the tropical regions of

America, and imported West African slaves to work there. It wasn't until the second half of the 18th century that comparably labor-intensive production began off the coast of East Africa, on French estates in the Indian Ocean. From a plantation-owner's point of view, it was only logical that the French should start to bring in slaves from nearby South and East Africa for their sugar-cane plantations on Mauritius.

The market for slaves was also growing in Arabia, and soon the Sultanate of Oman/Zanzibar found itself in need of cheap labor, as well. In the 1820s, some estate-owners had begun cultivating cloves on Unguja and Pemba; the work was carried out by slaves. In a very short time, Zanzibar had become the world leader in the production and export of cloves.

*Above: Cloves remain Zanzibar's main export and a staple of its economy. Right: Australopithecus goes about his business—in a museum diorama.*

Apart from the enormous profit from the trade in slaves, cloves and ivory, there was another factor contributing to the trade boom in the island kingdom. The East African interior opened up as a market for European and American industrial products: wire, glass beads, iron hoes, cotton fabric, and, soon enough, for rifles and liquor as well. European and American consulates were established on Zanzibar. Along with the Arab nobility and the Europeans, Indian bankers completed the picture of Zanzibar's upper class, while Christian missionaries began to censure the thankless lot of the slaves who had been imported from the mainland.

**Early Cultures and Tribal Migrations**

What had been taking place on the continent during the preceding hundreds and thousands of years? Historical relics of the kind found along the Swahili coast – stone houses, travelers' reports, chronicles, finds of coins – are almost

nonexistent in the interior before the mid-19th century. The prehistoric evidence, however, extends much further back into the past: scientists have found them in the footsteps of man's early ancestors (*Australopithecus afarensis*), capable of walking upright on two feet, in Laetoli or in finds of bones and tools stemming from *Australopithecus robustus boisei*, *Homo habilis* and *Homo erectus* in nearby Olduvai Gorge. An immense accumulation of stone tools from Isimila, near Iringa, proves that this area was also settled between 100,000 and 60,000 years ago.

Hundreds of rock drawings, believed to have been executed by a people of hunters between 3,500 and 800 years ago, demonstrate striking similarities to paintings of the Bushmen in Southwest Africa – especially those in Dodoma and Singida Regions. Researchers noticed that there are two tribes which live only in this part of Tanzania, the Sandawe and Hadzabe, whose language (*Khoisan*), contains the so-called "clicks" characteristic of the Bushman languages. Fur-

thermore, there are still hunter-gatherers among the Hadzabe. From this, it's infered that bushmanoid peoples were once more prevalent here, but that Bantu tribes moving in from the west either assimilated them or forced them to move to South Africa. The Bantu were farmers who cultivated bananas, among other things, in the fertile, rainy parts of the country, and were already knowledgeable in iron production as much as 2,000 years ago.

They were not the only immigrants. North of the Hadzabe hunting-grounds on lake Eyasi are the settlements of the Iraqw (*Mbulu*), a people who came in from the north even before the Bantu invasion. The Iraqw speak a Cushitic tongue, a language they have in common with peoples from Ethiopia and Somalia.

In Engaruka, a bit north of the fertile Mbulu plateau, stone irrigation systems and house foundations bear witness to a mysterious, long-forgotten people, who, until about 300 years ago, practised sophisticated cultivation of their fields and gardens. No one knows where they went nor why they disappeared.

The fourth Tanzanian language group, Nilotic, is thought to have originated in Sudan. Nilotic-speaking peoples may have reached northern Tanzania at the same time as the Bantu, and they, too, understood the fine art of forging iron implements, including weapons. They were for the most part cattle-herding nomads, at home in the grassy plains and open savannah. The Barabaig people, now also resident on and around Lake Eyasi, belonged to this category. They had to hold their ground against the Maasai nomads, also Nilotic-speaking, who had been migrating into the area since the 16th century. Not until the 19th century were the warlike Hehe (Bantu farmers) in the middle of the country able to check the Maasai's further southward migration.

Maasai in their traditional garb, the women with shorn heads, adorned with colorful glass beads, and the young men of fighting age, the strikingly adorned, creatively coiffed *moran*, never fail to impress visitors – so much so, that this "exotic" folk has become a popular tourist attraction. The self-confident Maasai make the most of their appeal, asking princely sums from tourists who want to take their pictures. Their remarkable persistence and fearlessness gain them respect; although the *moran* also make themselves unpopular when, on their raids, they occasionally steal their neighbors' cattle.

More than 90% of Tanzania's inhabitants are of Bantu origin, or, rather, speak a Bantu language, since the word "origin" implies an ethnic relationship that often doesn't exist. For centuries, Africans of different ethnic origins and language groups have been wandering all over the continent. Immigrants were constantly learning from settled residents, and vice versa. Time and again the newcomers mingled with the long-established indigenous population. African tribal divisions were well shaken up in this process. Tanzania has roughly 120 different "tribes" – smaller linguistic and cultural units – and not one of them dominates the present scene.

There have, however, been recurrent conquests and struggles for power, the most notorious in the 19th century. The tribes more likely to take the lead were those which were well-organized and in possession of the newest technology. The *Yao* in southeast Tanzania were active in inland trade with the hoes and weapons they forged, and even participated in the ivory trade, which extended further afield. As a result of their excellent contacts with the coast, they converted to Islam. The other African peoples feared them as slave hunters; the Europeans, as bitter opponents of "Christian" colonial rule. And they used firearms very early on.

Bitter battles with many tribes were caused by the sudden invasion of the Ngoni, who pushed northward from Zululand in South Africa within only a few decades and reached southern Tanzania in 1840. Their short spears and tall shields were superior to the other tribes' weapons – at least until those other tribes, such as the Sangu in the south and the Hehe in the middle of the country, had adopted these innovations themselves. The Ngoni founded centralist, tightly organized realms east of Lake Nyasa, and, at the beginning of the 20th century, were to prove themselves bitter guerilla fighters against the German colonial rulers.

The Nyamwezi, closely related to their Sukuma neighbors to the north, had extensive expertise as merchants. Many Nyamwezi worked as long-distance traders; their routes stretched over half the continent, from the east coast to the

*Right: The Maasai are some of the most recent immigrants to East Africa.*

Congo basin. They traded in copper from Katanga (Congo), salt from Uvinza, iron-mongery and naturally ivory, which they brought to the harbor towns on the eastern seaboard.

### Ivory and Slaves

The demand for ivory and slaves had grown so much since the beginning of the 19th century that the Nyamwezi could not keep up with it. Arabs and Swahili merchants exploited their experienced colleagues' knowledge of the trade routes: they hired Nyamwezi as porters and organized their own caravans, often with the financial backing of Indian bankers. Sometimes a caravan included more than 1,000 people! Using draught animals to transport the goods was out of the question, since the tse-tse fly prevailed in many parts of Tanzania even then.

There were no clearly defined roads from the coast into the interior; the caravans simply proceeded wherever it was possible. In the rainy seasons, this depended on fords; in the dry season, on watering-holes, as well as on the supply of food, which had to be purchased from the various tribes encountered along the way. Another decisive factor was the toll which some chieftains imposed on passing travelers. Sometimes, a caravan had to detour to avoid belligerent conflicts between other tribes. A trek from Bagamoyo on the coast to Ujiji on Lake Tanganyika (a good 800 miles/1,300 km) took at least three months. The most important town on the way was Unyanyembe (Kazeh, Tabora), where Arab and Indian merchants had been established since 1820. From here, the caravan routes branched off, leading to the kingdoms on Lake Victoria and on the northern and southern shores of Lake Tanganyika.

Beyond this lake there were regular slaving expeditions and ivory hunts, extending far into the rain forests of the Congo basin. It was here that, in the second half of the 19th century, Tippu Tip, the infamous Arab slave trader from Zanzibar, ran his own private, well-organized merchant empire, ably assisted by his sons.

Although Zanzibar's slave market was officially shut down in 1873, covert slave-trading lasted well into the 20th century. Understandably, there was no offical tally kept on this traffic in human beings in East Africa, but it's estimated that there were 1 to 3 million transactions between 1770 and 1896. European nations had abolished slavery by the first decades of the 19th century, which only gave added urgency to the appeals from Africa of slavery's most famous opponent, the Scotsman David Livingstone.

This doctor and missionary, who was well-versed in African matters, set off from Mikindani on the southern Tanzanian coast to explore anew the source of the Nile in 1866; by the end of the decade, he had vanished without a trace in the African interior, and was presumed dead. The journalist Henry Morton Stanley tracked Livingstone down in Ujiji on Lake Tanganyika in 1871 on a search and discovery mission, which was a media spectacle from the very outset. Stanley's reports in the *New York Herald* and the books about his adventures in Africa were very popular in Europe and America, as were the writings of other "discoverers" like Speke, Burton or Baker (who made their "discoveries" on well-known caravan routes, aided by porters and professional guides). These reports are among the most detailed descriptions of the conditions in East Africa at that time, although they contain many misunderstandings and tenacious prejudices, some of which persist to this day.

**German Reich Against British Empire**

These adventure stories spurred colonial competition and were taken as a challenge by unscrupulous daredevils, such as the German Carl Peters. In 1884, acting on his own initiative, Peters had begun duping individual East African chieftains into believing that the German emperor would protect them in the future, if they would only set their signature to a document – which in fact signed away the rights to their land. Only a few years later, when after discussions with England the borders of the new colony of "German East Africa" had been established, the Africans were forced to recognize that what they had agreed to amounted not to protection, but to bloody and brutal supression of revolts when individual tribes rose up against the new rulers. The most well-known uprising, and the one with the most serious consequences, was the Maji Maji War of 1905. In Kiswahili, *maji* means "water"; in this case, a magician discovered a "holy water" that brought good harvests, fertility and success in hunting and was believed to counteract black magic and disease and to make people immune to the musket-balls of European firearms. The tidings of this miracle water spread like wildfire from tribe to tribe over hundreds of miles in the southeast of the country, representing the first time that so many different tribes had been united in the belief in a single, common idea: to get rid of the troublesome intruders in their country. But the *maji* did not live up to expectations. Fighting, systematic destruction of the villages and the three-year famine that ensued wiped out an estimated one-third of the population in the southeast. Large areas of land that had once been settled were reclaimed by the wilderness.

In "peaceful" parts of the country, plantation cultivation was on the rise, of products such as sisal, rubber, cotton, coffee. German colonists settled in the Usambara Mountains and around Kilimanjaro; and two railway lines from the coast – Tanga-Moshi in the north and Dar

*Right: The eastern segment of the Dar es Salaam-Kigoma railway wasn't completed until 1910.*

es Salaam-Kigoma in the middle of the country – opened up the interior. In 1914, the railway line to Lake Tangayika had just been completed when German East Africa was drawn into World War I – with considerable losses for the African mercenaries employed by both Germans and British. The wily retreat tactics of the German colonial force under General von Lettow-Vorbeck continued until 1918, in Northern Rhodesia.

Germany lost the war and its colonies. Great Britain administered Tanganyika as a League of Nations mandate. Compared with the British colonies Uganda and Kenya, both blessed with a greater wealth of natural resources, Tanganyika was initially able to develop more independently. Especially in areas favorable for agriculture (such as the Chagga on Kilimanjaro, the Haya of Bukoba, the Sukuma of Mwanza), farming cooperatives existed very early on.

A new generation of young, self-assured Africans started to call for justice and their right to have some say in their country's government, and defended themselves against one-sided measures taken by the European government. July 7, 1954 saw the founding of TANU (Tanganyika African National Union). Its president was the teacher (in Kiswahili, *mwalimu*) Julius Nyerere.

### Independence and Socialism

On December 12, 1961, Tanganyika became the first East African nation to gain independence. TANU was a convincing African movement, which insisted on independence (in Kiswahili, *uhuru*). Furthermore, Great Britain may have found it relatively easy to let go of its protectorate: several agricultural projects had failed, there were few natural mineral resources, and the number of white settlers was small compared to that in Kenya.

The colonial boundary outlined a political unit, something with which the Africans had virtually no experience: the immense country of Tanganyika consisted of 100 tribes with widely differing cultural backgrounds, for which there was no established system of common government. Having devised the infrastructure to serve its own purposes, the colonial administration had left behind a pile of unsolved problems. In tiny Zanzibar, which became independent in 1963, class differences between Arab landowners and landless tenants and workers escalated in 1964 until the sultan was overthrown and there was a massacre of the Arab population. In the same year, Presidents Nyerere and Karume decided on the union of Tanganyika and Zanzibar, Tanzania.

Under the guidance of TANU chairman and President Julius Nyerere, the nation began to try to set itself to rights in the 1960s, still with only vague objectives, and struggling with the powerful influence of its colonial legacy. In 1967, the *Arusha Declaration* set forth clear guidelines for the future: Tanzania's new political course included equal opportunities in education and income, elimination of special privileges, and a break with foreign capital and community. Large sectors of the economy came under state control, particularly major firms and banks. More significant was the reorganization of the agricultural sector, livelihood of 90% of the population. *Ujamaa* (family community) was the slogan of Tanzanian socialism under Julius Nyerere. In African families, it is understood that all members have a responsibility to support one another. The new plan was to extend this tradition of mutual aid to all the inhabitants of a village. Therefore, the rural population was to be consolidated into larger *Ujamaa* villages. Such central communities could be supplied with water, schools, shared farm machinery, warehouses and other modern facilities much more easily than widely scattered hamlets.

*Right: "Father of the Nation" – Julius Nyerere and his wife.*

At the beginning, these principles aroused immense enthusiasm among Tanzanians and also inspired many foreign investors, both in the west and the east. But in this enormous, underdeveloped country, there were bound to be obstacles to realizing these grand, nationwide goals. In some cases, the suitability of the locations of the new villages had been insufficiently researched, and when it became clear that the whole establishment of the *Ujamaa* villages was proceeding slowly, there was a certain degree of forced resettlements. Functionaries of the ubiquitous Party, represented in the most remote parts of the country (the mainland TANU and Zanzibar's ASP, or Afro-Shirazi Party, merged in 1977 to form the united party CCM or Chama cha Mapinduzi, the Revolutionary Party of Tanzania), often enjoyed special privileges – the stated ideals of equality were evidently hollow phrases. Dependence on foreign capital rose rather than sinking. As in other socialist states, criticism was also suppressed in Tanzania in the 1970s: newspapers came under state control, and many a dissident landed in prison.

In the same decade, Tanzania was unfortunately forced to struggle with other, unforeseeable difficulties. All over the world, oil prices soared, while world market prices for agricultural products (sisal, coffee) fell. Severe drought struck the country. The EAC (East African Community), established with Uganda and Kenya with such high hopes in 1967, foundered in 1977. In 1978, Ugandan dictator Idi Amin's soldiers invaded northeastern Tanzania and provoked Tanzania's army into marching on Uganda, which led to the fall of the reign of terror there, but also created a bottomless pit in Tanzania's budget.

Because of his active commitment to establishing justice in all of Africa, as well as his exemplary modesty, *Mwalimu* Julius Nyerere became known as "the conscience of black Africa." Tanzania granted asylum to South Africa's ANC (African National

Congress), for example, until the collapse of apartheid in 1992. On the home front, many of his compatriots did not consider the *Mwalimu* flexible enough to correct the failings of the *Ujamaa* policy and to allow more democracy in the country. Nyerere may not have done justice to all the difficult tasks that confronted him, but Tanzanians still see in him the "father of the nation" (*baba ya taifa*), and they acknowledged their respect for him by continuing to elect him president at five-year intervals until he retired in 1985. He accomplished the impossible: creating a national identity for a territory that had been randomly carved out of the map of Africa. Aids to the process were a single national language, Kiswahili; the rotation of official posts throughout the entire country; and an education policy which was consistent from the very start.

### Reforms for the 21st Century

Although it was clear that the *Ujamaa* policy had failed and that there were dis-advantages to government control in nearly every sector, reforms didn't get underway until the mid-1980s.

In 1985 Ali Hassan Mwinyi, the former president of Zanzibar, became Nyerere's successor. At this point, the presidency was limited to two terms of office; private industry was again permitted, not least through pressure from the International Monetary Fund; and, in 1992, Parliament agreed to abolish one-party rule. The shift away from socialism is clearly apparent. Tanzania's economy is on an upswing; still, there are a number of social issues for which the country is still seeking solutions.

The CCM was victorious in the country's first multi-party elections in 1995: since it had existed for decades, it was better organized than the new parties that opposed it. Former foreign minister Benjamin Mkapa became president. Although it has embarked on a definite policy of reform, the CCM is still going to have to pay much more attention to the competition of other parties in the future.

37

# Guests And Hosts

Tanzania has a distinctive tradition of tourism. One of the most famous visitors to the country, Ernest Hemingway, immortalized the luxurious life of hunting parties in such works as *The Green Hills of Africa* and *The Snows of Kilimanjaro*. Even today, such hunting expeditions still take place, and, indeed, make considerable contributions to Tanzania's state coffers, since big-game shooting can bring in several thousand dollars per animal.

A modern *safari* (in Kiswahili, the word means trip or journey) into the African wilderness, where animals can be observed and photographed, still evokes the spirit of the luxurious expeditions of the big-game hunters. You need a vehicle which is equipped to drive in difficult conditions, and a driver who knows his way around and can also recognize, and name, the plants and animals. A cook is usually included, who is, as a rule, a man of many talents: he organizes the food, loads water and fuel, packs the camping equipment, cooks, does the washing-up, puts up and takes down the tents, and even helps to repare the car if necessary. Tourists are perfectly happy to be cared for so thoroughly; they would be rather helpless if left alone, without their Tanzanian guides, in this gorgeous but unfamiliar wilderness. If you prefer not to camp out, even under such deluxe conditions, the best-known national parks also boast well-appointed hotels or luxurious permanent tent camps which are every bit as fine as the hotels.

Even the ascent of Kilimanjaro proceeds in the height of comfort, with guides, porters, and cooks on hand. Many a *mzungu* (white person; plural: *wazungu*), used to carrying his own gear and toting tent, cooking utensils, food and water in his own backpack, can only shake his head at the sight of others doing his "dirty work."

In the famous national parks, guests are to enjoy the incomparable presence of nature on the one hand, and be waited on in style on the other. This brings in foreign currency, creates jobs and helps to keep up the national image, all understandably desirable in a country with rather limited resources. Tanzania is deliberately doing everything it can to avoid becoming a cheap holiday destination for mass tourism.

For decades, the hotels along the coast of the Indian Ocean, between Tanga in the north and the island of Mafia in the south, were overshadowed by those in the nature reserves. That situation has taken a sudden turn for the better since the liberalization of Tanzania's economy, especially since the mid-1990s: Tanzania has begun to interest tourists in search of beaches and sun. The island of Zanzibar is the most powerful magnet, as it boasts picture-postcard beaches, an fascinating underwater world and lush spice gardens, in addition to historic buildings, carefully renovated witnesses to its past. Here, a wide range of hotels and guest houses, and legion offers for cheap flights, compete for the tourists' attention. On the mainland, the coastal communities of Kunduchi and Bagamoyo also offer beach pleasures, and are heavily frequented by weekend visitors from Dar es Salaam. Quieter and more secluded are Mafia island, Ras Kutani and Pangani, which also offer high-quality hotels.

The third pillar of Tanzania's tourist trade was not at all planned as such: the enormous remainder of the country. Unspoiled, it offers little in the way of trained service, nor of tarting-up for tourists; but can promise warm, open, sincere inhabitants, a magnificent range and variety of scenery, and predominantly bad

*Left: Helpful Tanzanian guides facilitate the ascent of Mount Kilimanjaro.*

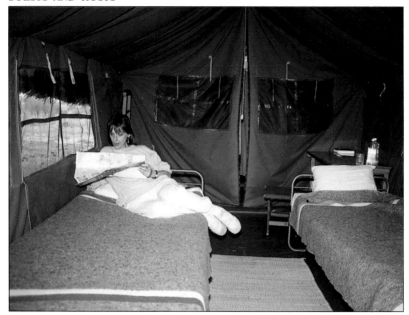

roads. The country is poor, but its infrastructure is rapidly improving: from Dar es Salaam, you can now travel easily to the neighboring countries of Malawi, Zambia and Kenya by bus on newly-paved roads. Trains are relatively punctual, while cruises on the large lakes and along the coast are a memorable experience. There is an increasing number of typical *gesti*, small hotels provided with the bare necessities: mosquito netting over a bed with a foam mattress and hand-washed bed linens. Don't count on much more in the way of furnishing in older *gesti* in remote areas, however, newly-built houses usually offer several rooms, complete with shower and toilet. At times, in some places, electricity or running water may be lacking; in which case you'll be provided with kerosene lamps and water buckets. Here, the

*Above: Experiencing the wilderness with kid gloves in a luxurious camp. Right: Sopa Lodge, a luxury hotel in Tarangira National Park.*

foreign guest (*mgeni*, plural: *wageni*) lives as the Tanzanians do, rather than in some tourist ghetto.

*Kilakabila* one young hotelier programmatically calls his new *gesti* on an island in Lake Victoria. Anyone who understands the Kiswahili word feels personally included: it means "every tribe." A guest who enters his name in the large guest register (*kitabu ya wageni*) at the reception of a simple *gesti* must provide quite a bit of personal information: from his or her name (*jina*), through where he is coming from (*kutoka*) and where he is headed (*kwenda*), down to the room rate (*bei ya chumba*), and, finally, a signature (*sahihi*). Many other details are wormed out of the guest, as well, which you can easily deduce from the other entries, even if you don't understand Kiswahili: nationality, date, room number, and the like. But most *wazungu* hesitate at the entry for *kabila*. Whereas Tanzanians conscientiously register their tribal affiliation into the book – Chagga, Makonde, Maasai or any of the other 100-plus

tribes, most foreign visitors do not quite know what to do and just leave it blank. This is not incorrect, but some have in all seriousness – or perhaps in fun – entered "Texan," "Scot," "Saxon," if their home is the United States, Great Britain or Germany. In a sense, their claim is perfectly accurate. They belong to a special group of people in their country, which differs froms neighboring cultural entities in history, culture, characteristics, and in dialect. They are somewhat proud of their home, without feeling in any way superior because of that. This feeling of belonging to a certain group and identifying with its people and culture is something to keep in mind when speaking of "tribes" in Tanzania. Here, you won't find problems like those tearing apart Tanzania's western neighbors Burundi and Rwanda (declared "tribal hostilities," but actually resulting from rebellion against social injustices), or the fear of being outnumbered by the superior strength of an especially large tribe (such as the *Kikuyu* in Kenya). There's no basis

for this kind of problem in Tanzania, simply because of the sheer number of tribes and the absence of any single one that plays a clearly dominant role.

One unifying factor in Tanzania's identity is the national language, Kiswahili. This *lingua franca* of East Africa is also understood by the populations of Tanzania's neighboring countries. It is consistently used in Tanzanian schools, administrative offices and in public, although many families will habitually speak their tribal language at home. Anyone who wants to travel overland in East Africa will have an easier time if he or she picks up a few Kiswahili expressions. A rudimentary knowledge will gradually develop in the course of his travels: there's always time and opportunity to learn. Traveling in outlying areas by public transport, which often means antiquated buses or pick-up trucks, proceeds *polepole*, slowly. You're never alone when you're waiting for hours at some local bus stop, and conversations just sort of start up...

41

The farther you get from tourist centers and asphalt roads, the more rarely an area is visited by *wazungu*, the more welcome is anyone who brings news from far away. The children generally discover the visitor first and, uninhibited as children are, they gleefully call out: "*Mzungu!*" (white person!). Some schoolchildren, as often as not, will pipe up with "*Good morning, teacher,*" regardless of the time of day; others utter a respectful "*Shikamoo!*" In rural areas, people often greet passers-by and then pause for a short chat. If you want to visit a particular site in a remote community, or even simply embark on a short walk through the open countryside, it's best to call on the village headman first.

A proper, thorough greeting is an essential element of Tanzanian etiquette; a direct approach is not appreciated. First,

*Above and right: The greeting "karibu" – in relaxed mode from schoolchildren in Igawa (Mbeya Region), or in more restrained form from a nursing student in the Moshi District.*

a person established harmony with the person he's greeting: *Hujambo?* How are you? or, literally: Have you got any problems? Answer: *Sijambo!* No, I haven't got any problems (although there might be the odd problem lurking about, but that is not expressed until later)! *Habari gani?* What's up (literally: What news is there)? *Nzuri.* Good (perhaps it is not so good, but there is time enough to speak of that later). *Habari za leo?* What's up today? Literally: News from today? *Nzuri! Habari za kazi?* How's your job (news from your job)? *Nzuri* or *njema* (good), then *salama* (peace), and with that, greetings are ended (especially in coastal areas). It's a good idea to have a few of these expressions on hand when addressing someone, be it an acquaintance or a stranger, a policeman in the street, a civil authority in his office – any time you're starting a conversation. Elderly or high-ranking people are greeted with *shikamoo* (a derivation of: "I hold your feet"), to which they reply with *marahaba* (welcome). The greeting *jambo* (hello) is rather more casual, but it is frequently used with foreigners, if only because they are not thought to be familiar with the ritual greeting phraseology (a frequently accurate assumption).

Politeness and self-control are simply matters of good form in Africa, as is correct clothing. But what is correct, when you so often see someone on the streets dressed in rags? However, anyone who has so much money that he can afford a flight to East Africa (even the cheapest ticket is beyond the means of many Tanzanians) is expected to look well-groomed from head to toe. Short trousers or skirts, sloppy dress, or skimpy beach attire beyond the actual premises of a beach area are all seen as indications of boorish behavior.

Many Tanzanians have fixed preconceptions about the *wazungu*; the common notion is that they have virtually unlimited financial means and a good education. This generalization is understandable, since most of East Africa's foreign visitors over the past 150 years have been missionaries, doctors, merchants, consultants, or other specialists – in short, people who indeed possessed specialized and considerable knowledge and whose money, from the point of view of the Tanzanians, seemed to flow freely and limitlessly from an unknown source.

All of the Kiswahili words for money are taken over from other languages. *Fedha* ("silver") comes from Arabic; the Portuguese introduced *pesa* with their own "peso," the Germans bequeathed *hela* ("Heller"), and the Tanzanian currency is called "shilling" – a European word with centuries of tradition. Tanzania is one of the African countries which received large amounts of financial aid since its independence; unfortunately, one unintentional result of this is a sense of financial dependence. A tourist who has scraped together his savings to finance a trip to Africa and is unpleasantly surprised by unexpectedly high prices in Tanzania, confronted with a local an-

nouncing *naomba hela* ("I beg for money"), is confronted head-on with this dilemma, and the misconception that all white people are wealthy.

Foreign travelers in Tanzania often have trouble with the relaxed attitude toward time. The word "punctuality" does not exist in Kiswahili. On the other hand, it can be pleasant to hear, instead of a clear but incontravertible "No!" (*hapana*), a friendly *labda kesho*, "perhaps tomorrow."

Like other former socialist states, Tanzania is having to rethink many things after a long period of state control which had a deadening effect on initiative and work attitudes. It would be crass prejudice on the part of the visitor to pass judgment on the Tanzanians without taking into account the constraints and habits that resulted from this system. The best way to assess the intelligence, wit and involvement of people in Tanzania is to socialize with them. The word *karibu* (literally, "near"), come here, welcome! is, in Tanzania, an invitation to do just that.

# ON SAFARI IN THE NORTH

**SERENGETI / NGORONGORO
MANYARA / TARANGIRE
ARUSHA / MT. MERU
KILIMANJARO / MOSHI
PARE AND USAMBARA
MOUNTAINS**

## TOURIST ATTRACTIONS IN NORTHERN TANZANIA

Kilimanjaro, Africa's highest mountain; Serengeti, Tanzania's largest national park; and Ngorongoro Crater, a breathtaking natural setting for appearances of the so-called *Big Five*: these three highlights are renowned the world over, and are the main visitor attractions of northern Tanzania.

Tanzanian environmental protectionists and people in the tourist field are proud of these natural treasures, yet realize that there's a danger that nature may start to defend itself against the influx of visitors. There are plenty of instructive negative examples in neighboring Kenya, right on the other side of the border; those in charge of tourism in Tanzania would prefer not to make similar mistakes. They generously delineated the whole region from the western border of the Serengeti to the Usambara Mountains in the east – a distance of more than 370 miles (600 km) – and christened it the *Northern Circuit*. The three most famous sights lie within this area, as well as many other attrac-

*Preceding pages: Daily life among the Maasai in the Ngorongoro region. Wildebeest in flight. Left: An elephant performs its skin-care regime in Tarangira Park.*

tions too good to miss – offering a wide range of choices is an effort to relieve the burden of the most frequented spots.

In addition, tourism authorities "invented" the *Southern Circuit*, meant to divert visitors from focusing solely on the north and draw attention to the abundance of natural beauty in the center and south of the country. Prices are another means of distributing the tourists more evenly: since the beginning of 1997, the entrance and overnight fees have been raised in the parks in the north, lowered in the south.

Fortunately, people were able to recognize the problem of overburdening the environment while there was still time to take action. The degree to which it has been solved, however, depends largely on the attitude, and cooperation, of visiting tourists. Tour operators know that many customers are primarily concerned with getting top value for their dollar, so they present packages offering as many sights as possible in the shortest period of time. Anyone who judges a safari's value in terms of how many parks he sees or how many miles he covers, or who measures its success by the number of photos he took – a kind of modern hunting fever – will probably, in his haste, overlook many wilderness treasures. Take your time, or *polepole*, the East Af-

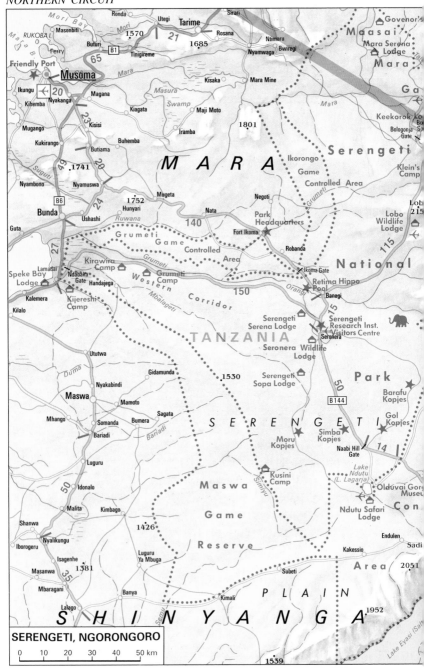

**SERENGETI, NGORONGORO**

0    10    20    30    40    50 km

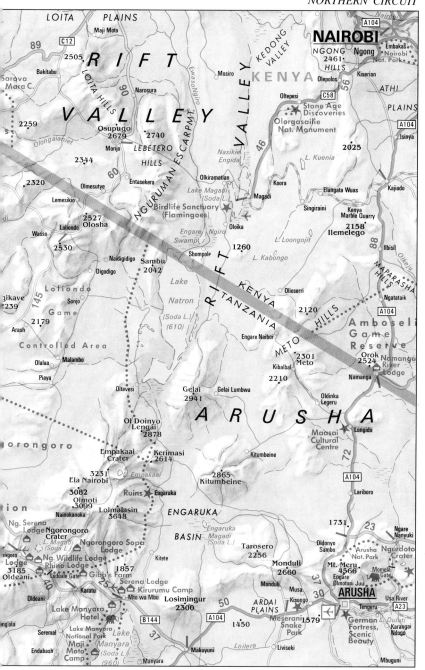

LOITA    PLAINS

Maji Moto

RIFT

89  C12

2505

Bakitabu

NAIROBI

NGONG  Ngong
2461
HILLS

Embakaš
Nairobi
Nat. Park

KEDONG
VALLEY

Mosiro

KENYA

Olepolos

Kiserian

ATHL

Sarova
Mara C.

Narosura

Oltepesi

C58

56

Stone Age
Discoveries

PLAINS

2259

VALLEY

Olorgasailie
Nat. Monument

A104

Osupugo
2679
Morijo

2740

LEBETERO
HILLS

Nasikie
Engida

46

L. Kuenia

2025

Isinya

2344

60

Entasekera

Olkiramatian

Koora

Elangata Wuas

Kajiado

2320

Olmesutye

Magadi

Singiraini

Kenya
Marble Quarry

Lemesikio

Birdlife Sanctuary
(Flamingoes)

Oloika

2158
Ilemelego

88

Ilbisil

2527
Olosha

Engare
Swamp

Ngiro

1260

L. Loongojit

Wasso

Loliondo

2530

Naidigidigo

Sambu
2042

Shompole

L. Kabongo

MAPARASHA
HILLS

Lake

Olioserri

A104

jikave
2239

Loliondo

Sonjo

Game

Natron

KENYA

2120

Ngatataik

Amboseli
Game

Arash

2179

(Soda L.)
(610)

TANZANIA

Olongalapiet

METO
HILLS

Reserve

Controlled  Area

Engare Naibor

2301
Meto

Orok
2524

Namanga
River
Lodge

Olalaa

Malambo

Piaya

Oltevesi

Kibalbal

2210

Namanga

Oldinka
Legeru

72

Longido

Gelai
2941

Gelai Lumbwa

ARUSHA

orongoro

Ol Doinyo
Lengai
2878

Kitumbeine

Maasai
Cultural
Centre

Empakaai
Crater

Kerimasi
2614

2865
Kitumbeine

A104

3231
Ela Nairobi

Empakaai

Engaruka

Lariboro

3082
Olmoti
3099

Ruins

ENGARUKA

1731

23

Ngare
Nanyuki

Nainokanoka

Lolmalasin
3648

BASIN

Engaruka
Magadi
(Soda L.)

Oldonyo
Sambo

Arusha
Nat. Park

Ngurdoto
Crater

tion

Ng. Serena
Lodge

Ngorongoro
Crater

Kitete

Tarosero
2256

Momela
Gate

ongoro
Lodge

Ngorongoro Sopa
Lodge

Monduli
2660

Mt. Meru
4566

3185
Oldeani

Ng. Wildlife Lodge
Rhino Lodge

L. Magadi
(Soda L.)

1857

Monduli

Musa

Engare
Olmotoni Juu

ARUSHA

Ludoale Gate

Gibb's Farm

Serena Lodge

Kisongo

Usa River
A23

Karatu

Kirurumu Camp

37

30

Tengeru

Oldeani

25

Mto wa Mbu

Losimingur
2300

ARDAI
PLAINS

1579

German
Fortress,
Scenic
Beauty

Dulıtı
Karangai
Ndogo

ng'ola

Lake Manyara
Hotel

50

Meserani
Snake
Park

Seremal

Lake Manyara
National Park

Lake

B144

A104

1450

Maji
Moto
Camp

Manyara

(Soda L.)
(960)

Makuyuni

Loilera

Liviseki

Mbuguni

Endabash

Manyara

rican catchword, is good advice for a safari-goer: taking it will enable you to see, hear and experience more!

## A World-Famous Wilderness

In the huge area between the eastern tract of the East African Rift and Lake Victoria, the game population has undergone frequent changes in the course of the 20th century. One inglorious chapter was European visitors' uncontrolled passion for hunting in the first half of this century: white hunters were known to shoot as many as 100 lions on a single safari, and even be proud of having disposed of these "harmful" predators in a more or less heroic fashion.

In 1929, a sizeable game reserve of 96 square miles (250 sq. km) was set up in the middle of what is today the Serengeti.

*Above: Bernhard Grzimek, famous lobbyist for African wildlife. Right: The gregarious zebras like to bathe daily after they finish grazing.*

In the 1950s, this developed into a national park: a strip of land between Lake Victoria in the west and the eastern margin of the volcanic massif, where the Ngorongoro Crater is located. At that time, little was known of the animals populating this wilderness. No one had ever counted them, and there were only vague ideas of their habits and migratory movements, unsupported by any scientific proof. Between 1957 and 1959, the German zoo director Professor Bernhard Grzimek and his son Michael researched the behaviors of several species of the larger mammals; by systematically flying over great areas of the reserve, they were able to take a census of sorts, and they also looked into the feeding habits of some species. Their findings led to a restructuring of the borders of the reserve. Moreover, the international publication of their investigations, in book and film form, bearing the dramatic title *Serengeti Shall Not Die*, brought the region so much publicity and popularity that this, the world's largest habitat for plains animals, is still, decades later, profiting from this attention.

## Classified Ecosystem

In the three decades following Grzimek's significant studies, many researchers have focused on animal and plant life in this area, and have thus been able to observe notable changes. One example: in 1957, the Grzimeks counted a population of 100,000 white-bearded gnus or wildebeest. In the 1990s, their numbers were estimated at 1.3 million. The nature reserve has to come to grips not only with the changing requirements of animals, but also those of human beings. To the north, in the Tanzanian Region of Mara, the lands around its borders are increasingly being converted to farmland. Some of the wild animals' grazing land is also used by the nomadic Maasai and their herds. Some of the inhabitants of the wil

derness cultivate their land. There are still poachers at large. And, finally, the number of tourists is rising.

Organizing such a complex nature reserve to the satisfaction of all concerned – animals, plants, humans – involves at best a series of ongoing compromises that continually have to be revised. The reserve is structured in the following manner:

The heart of the area is **Serengeti National Park**, 5,678 square miles (14,763 sq. km) in area, a strictly protected region in which any and every kind of for-profit use – hunting, farming, or animal husbandry – is strictly forbidden. The park's characteristic hooked shape comes from an 87-mile (140-km) east-west panhandle; from north to south, it measures 118 miles (190 km). Along its northern boundary, the park meets the Kenyan border and the adjacent **Maasai Mara Game Reserve** in Kenya. There are three nature reserves adjacent to the park's western border, as the park is not large enough to accommodate the wanderings

of its huge herds of migrating animals (however, if one were to confer upon these reserve areas the protected status of a national park, one would have to resettle the inhabitants elsewhere): both the controlled zones **Ikorongo** and **Grumeti** in the Mara Region and the **Maswa Game Reserve** in the Shinyanga Region.

To the east is the second large nature reserve, in which land cultivation and use is permitted, albeit according to strictly enforced regulations: the **Ngorongoro Conservation Area**, measuring 3,150 square miles (8,200 sq. km). To the north, another controlled zone of about 1,540 square miles (4,000 sq. km) extends up to the Kenyan border: the **Loliondo Controlled Area**, where the protection status is not quite as strict. All of these parks and reserves, to a greater or lesser degree, play a part in the migrations of unimaginable numbers of animals every year.

What use is it to the traveler to be able to distinguish between the different types

of nature reserves? For many, it's a matter of money: in Serengeti National Park and the Ngorongoro Conservation Area, the charge is US $25 for each 24 hours you remain on the premises, as well as at least US $20 for a tent site. Some tour operators have realized that there is a market for travelers who like to watch their budget, and they undertake tours outside the "expensive" areas, or at least arrange overnight stays outside these areas. For example, there are no entrance fees on a trip to Lake Natron (in Loliondo Controlled Area), and the camping costs there are minimal; by contrast, due to the fees set by the state, a visit to Serengeti is much more expensive.

## SERENGETI NATIONAL PARK

The Maasai word *siringet* means "wide country," but that does not adequately de-

*Above: The cheetah, fastest big cat in the world, hunts its prey in broad daylight. Right: When the sun sets, the nocturnal hunters come into their own: here, fleeing buffalo.*

scribe the multifaceted landscape of the Serengeti National Park. The rivers there come out of the 10,000-foot (3,000 km) Ngorongoro Volcanic Highlands and flow westward to Lake Victoria (3,720 feet/1,134 m above sea level). Serengeti has no volcanoes of its own; rather, it is a plain, an almost completely eroded rocky landscape. In many places bizarre, rounded "islands" of granite and gneiss, also called *kopjes* (Dutch/Afrikaans: "little heads"), rise above the plains, while sediment drifts across the plains to form the soil.

The vegetation in the center consists of open acacia woodland, with denser woodland to the north and west. Gallery forests grow along the rivers. The best-known areas of vegetation are the expanses of grassland in the south and southeast, which gave Serengeti its name (there are also less extensive grasslands in the western corridor). This is the "wide country," where millions of wild animals graze in a regular yearly rhythm. The most noticeable "wanderers" are the **wil-**

debeest (other names: brindled or white-bearded gnu, *Connochaetes taurinus*), staggering for their numbers alone (more than a million, as mentioned above). Other grazing animals that also migrate in great numbers are the **Burchell's zebra** (*Equus burchelli*, about 200,000) and the **Thomson's gazelle** (*Gazella thomsoni*, about 250,000). Among the migrating antelopes are **topi** (*Damaliscus korrigum*) and **eland** (*Taurotragus oryx*). It is difficult to determine the number of predators who move, when it suits them, with the herds: **lions** (*Panthera leo*), **cheetahs** (*Acinonyx jubatus*), **wild dogs** (*Lyxon pictus*), and **spotted hyenas** (*Crocuta crocuta*), as well as countless **vultures**.

## Millions of Animals in Circulation

The yearly rains regulate the course of nature. During the dry season (June to October) the grass withers, and the animal population disappears almost entirely from the vast grasslands. As soon as the rains have begun (in November) everything flourishes once again, whereupon the herds return and graze large areas down to the roots. If it rains here again, allowing the grass to regenerate, the animals graze here again; if, however, more rain fails to materialize, the animals are forced to go wherever they can find forage. In the Serengeti area and the adjoining reserves, the annual cycle generally runs along the following lines:

In the permanently green biotopes of the Kenyan Maasai Mara and the surrounding area, the animals linger from September to the beginning of November. When the rains begin in November (progressing from the south to the north), the grass grows in the great southeastern steppes of the Serengeti and in the adjoining western segment of the Ngorongoro reserve. It is often the zebras who begin migrating in great herds, with long lines of wildebeest (gnus) trailing behind. Wishing to reach the southern expanses of green as fast as possible, they generally move quickly across the border zone of the east Serengeti/west Loliondo region. By December they have reached their destination, the short-grass plains ( on the eastern edge of the Serengeti/west Ngorongoro). Here the zebras foal well into January, while in or around February the wildebeest calve. The March rains, which are usually heavy, keep the grass green and also replenish the all-important watering-holes, the small rivers and shallow waterholes. From April on, the grazing area shifts westward into the long-grass plains and toward the middle of the Serengeti. Between May and July, you can still expect occasional thunderstorms, especially in the western part of the Serengeti; the rivers are full, guaranteeing sufficient water; and there's ample feed available on the small grassy plains in the Western Corridor of the Serengeti, where the herds now make their way. In July and August, they continue their migration northward into the Grumeti and Ikorongo reserves, until, around September, they have come full circle and returned to the green Maasai Mara. This immense annual circulation, with numerous stops, doesn't have an exact, scheduled "timetable": all progress depends on the chance of rain.

## On Safari in the Serengeti

The Serengeti has more to offer than just the sight of the migrating herds of larger animals. It has also a range of natural habitats, undisturbed by human settlement, and is therefore the permanent home of a host of other animals.

A tourist who wants to experience nature directly won't confine himself only to *game drives*, on which he can observe the animals from the safety of a motor vehicle during the daytime, but will also spend the night in a tent, with merely a layer of fabric separating him from the

*Right: Lush gallery forest along the Seronera River.*

vastness of the wilderness and its unfamiliar sounds. The park administration has set up a good two dozen campgrounds in the Serengeti area. Visitors can choose between two kinds: public campsites (US $20 a night per person), which you have to share with other visitors, and special campsites (US $40), which are booked in advance for an individual or a group, guaranteeing that you'll be alone there. Generally, the campgrounds are provided with neither water nor sanitary facilities, but are simply places in the wild. They are sensibly distributed throughout the park, so that visitors can experience different landscapes and the flora and fauna particular to each, as well as observe, from different points, the highlights of the annual migrations.

The campgrounds at **Kirawira** and **Hembe** on the **Grumeti River** in the **Western Corridor** are well suited to the observation of migrating herds in June and July, and are good for *game drives* all year long (best time is June-October). **Black and white colobus monkeys**, and a wide range of **birds** live in the gallery forests along the river, and there are especially large **crocodiles** on the banks. Stationary wildebeest, topi, **giraffes** and **buffalo** graze on the smaller plains of black cotton soil (Kiswahili: *mbuga*).

In the **north**, from the camps around **Lobo**, you can see the animal life of the hilly woodland, including **buffalo**, **elephants**, **klipspringer** (*Oreotragus oreotragus*), and the migrating herds during the dry season from August to November (best time: June to December, but visits are possible all year round; tourists rarely visit this area, mainly because the border to Kenya at Bologonja is closed). **Klein's Gate** enables visitors to enter Serengeti year-round via the Loliondo Controlled Area.

A number of campsites are located in the **center of the park**, near the **Seronera River**, which flows all year round. Here, there are a number of different

habitats side by side, which present a broad spectrum of animals: giraffe, buffalo, topi, Grant's and Thomson's gazelle, **impala** (*Aepycerus melampus*), **Cook's hartebeest** (*Alcelaphus buselaphus cookii*), **common waterbuck** (*Kobus ellipsiprymnus*), **hippopotamus** (*Hippopotamus amphibius*), **warthog** (*Phacochoerus aethiopicus*), **dikdik** (*Rhynchotragus sp.*), **olive baboon** (*Papio cynocephalus*), **vervet monkey** (*Cersopithecus aethiops*), **rock hyrax** (*Procavia capensis*), **lions** dozing under low-limbed trees, **leopards** resting on acacia branches; crocodiles, **serval cats** (*Felis serval*), and an abundance of birdlife. The center of the Serengeti is worth a visit all year round, especially during the dry season from June to October as well as in January and February. There is a **Visitors' Center** with informative exhibitions. There's an especially dense network of tracks around Seronera: drivers must never leave the roads or tracks, and excursions on foot are not allowed.

The **park headquarters** is no longer situated in Seronera, but outside the park's borders, further northwest in **Fort Ikoma**, where there's an old fortress from the days of the Germans; it is a good 13 miles (20 km) away from **Ikoma Gate**, the exit to the Mara Region and toward Musoma.

There are two campgrounds at **Naabi Hill**, at the eastern park entrance, which are ideal for the observation of the **short-grass plains**, where millions of migrating animals graze between December and April. Naabi Hill is a very noticeable *kopje* in the seemingly endless plain.

Four campsites are surrounded by the diverse scenic beauty around the **Moru Kopjes** in the **long-grass plains** northwest of Naabi. The park administration released some black rhinos (*Decirus bicornis*) in this area in 1997, and intends to guard them well enough to shield them from poachers.

You'll need a park guide if you want to visit the spectacular *kopjes* **Barafu Kopjes** and **Gol Kopjes**, northeast of

57

Naabi. The main road between Naabi and Seronera runs through the **Simba Kopjes**.

Six campgrounds managed by the Ngorongoro Conservation Area are located on **Lake Ndutu** (also called Lake Lagarja), a temporary salt lake with a wide range of habitats, surrounded as it is by forest, savannah and grasslands. One of the wildebeests' migratory routes as they travel between the Serengeti and Maswa areas takes them through this shallow lake. Many wildebeest calves are born here in the first few months of the year. December to May is the best time to visit Lake Ndutu and the surrounding area.

Not everyone is enthusiastic at the prospect of sleeping in a spartan tent. For this reason there are also comfortable lodgings distributed throughout the different landscapes of Serengeti National

*Above: Clouds over the Ngorongoro Crater part to reveal the Lerai Forest and Lake Magadi. Right: Excellent service at the Simba campsite.*

Park. In the center, there are luxurious hotels such as **Seronera Hotel**; south of that is the **Serengeti Sopa Lodge** at the **Oldoinyo Rongai** rock; the **Serena Lodge** lies in the northern part of central Serengeti; **Lobo Lodge** and the luxury tent camp **Klein's Camp** are in the northern sector of the park; the simpler **Ndutu Lodge** on the lake of the same name is in the south; and on the border of the Maswa Game Reserve is the luxury tent camp **Kusini**. For the Western Corridor there are the luxury tent camps **Kirawira** and **Grumeti Tented Camp** within the park; outside the park, but near **Ndabaka Gate**, the western park entrance, is **Kijereshi Camp**. Situated directly on Lake Victoria, **Speke Bay Lodge** is but a few minutes' drive on a good asphalt road from this entrance.

## NGORONGORO CONSERVATION AREA

The world-renowned volcano **Ngorongoro** is visited by 160,000 to 200,000

tourists every year. They enjoy the luxury of four hotels with a view of the crater: **Sopa Lodge**, **Wildlife Lodge**, **Crater Lodge**, **Serena Lodge**. In addition, there's the **Rhino Lodge**, which doesn't actually have a view of the crater, as well as the beautifully situated **Simba Campsite**. Camping in the crater is forbidden. There are Maasai settlements and pasturages outside the caldera itself.

From these four luxury hotels and from several observation points you look out over an almost unreal landscape: the steep rim of a crater rises to altitudes of 7,200-7,900 feet (2,200-2,400 m) around the mighty caldera, the base of which lies about 2,000 feet (600 m) deeper. At the center of this crater is the light-colored edge of the soda lake, **Lake Magadi**, which varies considerably in size, depending on the season. Running toward this are rivers, their banks picked out with lines of trees; while a few small, dark green patches of forest and swamp stand out against the lighter grasslands. This 105-square mile (260-sq km) bowl-shaped center of this extinct volcano is a multi-faceted biotope. And it is unique. More than 25,000 large mammals live in this comparatively small area; where the widely divergent habitats in a very confined space create a wealth and diversity of wildlife which you would otherwise be able to see only on a number of long game drives through the wide open spaces of the Serengeti. With luck, you will be able to sight all of the *Big Five* – elephant, rhino, buffalo, lion and leopard – during a single visit.

### In the Crater

There's something powerfully tempting about the prospect of a chance to see a cross-section of East Africa's animal life in a surprisingly short time. But many visitors begin to question their decision during the cautious drive down **Seneto Descent Road**, the one-way access road into the crater, for, rather than being alone in the wilderness, one is merely a link in a long, unbroken chain of four-

wheel-drive vehicles. Alas, there are plenty of people eager to feast their eyes on this wondrous sight, declared a World Heritage Site by UNESCO in 1978.

The drivers are well familiar with this problem, however, and, while the tourists are still taking in their first sight of the crater floor near the bushes and trees of **Seneto Springs**, and distracted by their first glimpses of animals, perhaps buffaloes or elephants, the vehicles generally spread out quickly and skillfully throughout the area.

The animals tend to gather at watering-holes (which are, therefore, also attractive to predators!). This means that the **Goose Ponds** are generally rewarding observation spots for tourists; during the wet season, you can also see plenty in the **Mandusi Swamps** as well as the small

*Above: The daily crowds in the Ngorongoro Crater: 25,000 large animals and some 200,000 tourists a year. Right: The Maasai warrior proudly sports heavy jewelry and an elaborate coiffeur.*

ponds scattered throughout the area. There are a few crater cones within the caldera, and you have a good view of them in the north from the top of **Engitati Hill**, which stands about 200 feet (60 m) above the crater floor; the ascent of the **Silalei** in the east is much more difficult.

The **Munge River** has its source on the neighboring volcano **Olmoti**, at an altitude of almost 10,000 feet (3,000 m), and has cut into the northeastern edge of the Ngorongoro. Near its course stand the weather-beaten remains of the walls of a farm which the German farmer Adolf Siedentopf ran until 1914: he kept as many as 1,200 cattle, and also raised ostriches.

At **Ngoitokitok** Springs, a popular picnic spot, you will probably meet up again with other tourists. The water of the spring flows into the **Gorigor Swamp**, where you're virtually certain to catch a glimpse of some of the hippopotamuses at **Hippo Pool**. **Lake Magadi**, the soda lake, is well-frequented by flamingoes. A track circumnavigates **Lerai Forest**, crossing several small river beds near the crater rim: it's a good place for bird-watching. Above the forest, **Ascent Road**, another one-way road, winds back in a series of switchbacks up to the rim of the crater; it can get quite muddy in wet weather.

### Crowds in the Crater

Experienced drivers generally do their best to show visitors as many animals as possible. In light of the great variety of animal life here, it is interesting to note which animals you *won't* find in the crater: giraffes, topis and impalas. Nor, evidently, is there adequate space for elephant families; a few bulls may find their way down into the crater, but the cows and calves stay outside, in the woodlands beyond the crater rim.

Most of the animals of the caldera now live here permanently, as migrations to the outside are growing increasingly difficult. The crater itself comprises only 3% of the total surface of the Ngorongoro Conservation Area (NCA), and the surrounding area is controlled in a variety of ways: open to use, but protected. Around 25,000 Maasai live here and graze their animals, as well as farming a little. The woodland on the western and southern sides of the highlands has been recognized as playing an important role in supplying water, so it has to remain free of human interference. From the south, farmlands and coffee plantations are moving up to encroach on the park boundaries. And the number of tourists runs into the hundreds of thousands.

### Volcano Highlands

The **volcano highlands** and the area around them have been the home of man and beast for millions of years. This, too, is unique: nowhere else in the world is there proof of established settlement over such a long period of time.

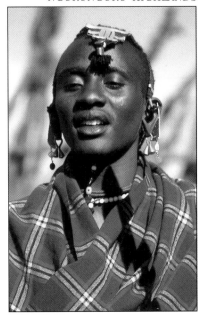

The row of volcanoes that runs north-south around the Ngorongoro Crater is not very old, geologically speaking. The youngest among them, **Ol Doinyo Lengai**, is still active – and stands beyond the northern boundary of the Ngorongoro Conservation Area. All the rest are extinct. The oldest of them lie in the south: **Lemagrut**, **Sadiman** and **Oldeani** are green, symmetrical mountains, some rising as high as 10,000 feet (3,000 m).

Volcanoes came into being here because, 20 million years ago, a long crack opened up for the first time in this part of Africa's rather old continental crust. You can still make out this fissure along the west bank of **Lake Eyasi**, in the far south of the NCA: it's a very noticeable "wall" about 3,300 feet (1,000 m) high and more than 50 miles (80 km) long. An additional rift, scarcely 2 million years old, created the steep incline west of **Lake Manyara**. The wooded volcanic highlands begin above the top of its high slope. In the north, the young **Kerimasi** volcano conceals this fissure, which then runs westward from Ol Doinyo Lengai and the soda lake, **Lake Natron**, all the way into Kenya.

These volcanoes, today extinct and greatly eroded, were once much higher – Ngorongoro was supposedly once as high as Kilimanjaro is today – and much better at trapping precipitation. In the shelter of their western flanks, the Serengeti stretched out into endless steppe, rich in animal life, watered by rivers and lakes from the highlands, much as it does today.

Time and again in the course of millions of years, the prevailing east winds carried the volcanic ash from eruptions to the west, covering large portions of the earth surface and thereby "conserving" the conditions of that particular moment. Therefore some of earth's earliest history lies beneath the many layers of volcanic deposits.

### Phoenix from the Volcanic Ashes – Olduvai and Laetoli

Sometimes lucky chance can uncover long-concealed evidence of the distant past. A *korongo*, a river bed, dry for most of the year, extends from Lake Ndutu (Lake Lagarja) towards the highlands and seeps away into the **Olbalbal Swamps** in the **Ngata Salei** grasslands west of the volcanoes. Over the last 30,000 years, the river has cut deep into older rock strata and this gorge is the habitat of many sansevieria (a kind of agave), which the Maasai call *oldupai*. Geologists were the first to explore this **Olduvai Gorge**; in 1931, they were joined by two archaeologists, a married couple named Louis and Mary Leakey. The Leakeys were to make one of the world's most important finds relating to the evolution of mankind.

*Right: The layers of stone in the Olduvai Gorge reveal important stages in the evolution of human life.*

There is a small **museum** near the gorge 4 miles (6 km) from the main road between Ngorongoro and Serengeti, which shows the finds and illustrates the steps in man's development. Long ago, 1.7 million years in the past, there were, presumably simultaneously, two representatives of humanoid species, one of them, *Australopithecus robustus boisei*, with a smaller brain, the other, *Homo habilis*, a larger one. The former died out over a million years ago. *Homo habilis* didn't survive, either, but he is believed to have used rudimentary stone tools and it is possible that he was an ancestor of *Homo erectus*, who fashioned more sophisticated tools about 1.2 million years ago.

A look in the gorge reveals the succession of the different-colored layers of sediment that have built up over the last 2 million years. If you would like to see the actual sites where human and animal bones, as well as stone implements, were discovered, you'll have to take a local guide.

In 1978, Mary Leakey managed to make another sensational discovery a mere 12.5 miles (20 km) away from the Olduvai Gorge. In a 3.5-million-year-old layer of ashes from the Sadiman volcano she found, in addition to animal tracks, the footprints of a bipedal ancestor of the human race. Three members of the species *Australopithecus afarensis* must have walked along there at that time. However, you needn't go out of your way to visit this site near **Laetoli**, since it was carefully sealed by scientists in 1996, after they had made copies of the footprints for museums and research purposes.

### The Many Tribes of Volcano Country

It is not easy to establish which people have lived in the Serengeti and the plateau around the crater during the last few

centuries. But a notably large number of different tribes are now settled in this fertile volcanic landscape.

The Maasai were the most recent "owners" of the Serengeti and the crater region (in the meantime their rights are being curtailed by higher state interests, to the benefit of tourists). Presumably they drove the Tatoga tribes, also nomads, toward the south. However these nomads, also known as the Barabaig, defended themselves so admirably against the warlike Maasai that the aggressors dubbed them *Mangati* ("esteemed enemy"). The Barabaig live as nomads or farmers to the east and south of Lake Eyasi, and are now being pressured from other quarters: the expansion of large state-owned wheatfields in the southern foothills of the volcano plateau is encroaching on their territory.

While the Barabaig and Maasai are Nilotic tribes, the Mbulu people, or, as they call themselves, the Iraqw, are of Cushitic origin. This people seems to have been farming land on the higher levels of

the crater and to the west of Lake Manyara for hundreds of years, and the Maasai forced them further south onto the **Mbulu Plateau**. The last larger community before **Lodoale Gate** (also "Loduare"), the entrance to the NCA, is **Karatu**, the center of the fertile, intensively cultivated land of the Mbulu. Here, in addition to a campsite and very simple *guest houses*, you'll find the stylish hotel **Gibb's Farm**.

Yet another people which lives in the vicinity of Lake Eyasi call themselves Hadza, but are known to others as Tindiga. They are one of only two tribes in Tanzania whose language contains the so-called "clicks," a characteristic otherwise found in the South African Bushman languages (the other Tanzanian tribe is the farming Sandawe in the Dodoma Region). The Hadza are hunter-gatherers. This fact has not only whetted ethnologists' appetites for knowledge, but has also aroused the tourists' curiosity, and some tour operators include a visit to the Hadza on their itineraries.

To reach them, drive to **Mang'ola** above Lake Eyasi, set in verdant surroundings. Allow an hour and a half for the drive, which is well over 30 miles (50 km) from Karatu. After a sharp curve to the right on the main road to the Ngorongoro Crater, a track branches off to the left, 4.5 miles (7 km) west of Karatu, to the village of **Oldeani**, which lies on the eastern slope of the volcano of the same name. However, you don't actually pass through this village, but pass it at a distance of about half a mile (1 km). From here, the route leads you southwest through plantations, then through varied savannah bushland with very few settlements.

About 4.5 miles (7 km) before you reach Mang'ola, whitened stones edging the track mark the entrance to **Chemchem Camp**. The name indicates that it

*Above: Maasai herds graze near the Ol Doinyo Lengai. Right: The sacred mountain of the Maasai is Tanzania's only active volcano.*

lies near a spring. Tall, dense trees, a small marsh and the bubbling water lure countless birds here. The level lawn is ideal for tenting, and the scenery is pure paradise.

Each visitor can decide for himself whether he would like to have the local guide show him "genuine" hunter-gatherers. Nearby (a 20-minute walk from the campsite; you can also drive there), the loosely woven round huts of the Hadza stand at the ready, their inhabitants already waiting for the visitors, to give a demonstration of the use of bow and arrow and collect money. The true hunter-gatherers usually live hidden in the woods.

### Ol Doinyo Lengai – On Foot to the Sacred Mountain

Park officials are giving serious consideration to the question of how to reduce car driving in the park and offer visitors walking safaris. With NCA guides, you can take hiking tours lasting

from four to five days to Oldeani Volcano; even better known, however, are the hikes from Ngorongoro Crater to the Maasai "Mountain of God": **Ol Doinyo Lengai** (*ol doinyo* = mountain, *ngai* = God). You can arrange to have a car pick you up there.

Outside the NCA, mere tracks lead to the mountain, passing through lonely regions, and difficult to traverse during the rains. From June to August, at the beginning of the dry season (June to October), it can be quite cool in the crater highlands; toward the end of the dry season, however, it is very hot around Ol Doinyo Lengai, and the tracks become extremely dusty. In the mountains, you may encounter unexpected downpours; and the high-altitude hiking trails can lead through thick clouds, which block the view. The facilities in the *special campsites* generally amount to little or nothing, yet an overnight stay costs US $40. Anyone who isn't frightened off by the prospect of such adversities will be rewarded with an unusually delightful tour through

an ever-changing natural countryside and Maasai villages.

Starting-point for a hike to the crater highland is the village of **Nainokanoka** at the foot of the volcano Olmoti. At Lodoale Park Gate, you pay the entrance fees for your entire sojourn on the NCA premises (US $25 per person per 24 hours) and camping fees. From here, you can count on a two- to three-hour drive (a good 28 miles/45 km; you pass Sopa Lodge after 18.5 miles/30 km) from the gate over the densely forested eastern rim of the Ngorongoro Crater to the campsite in the village. The short hike to and from the 9,840-foot (3,000 m) high edge of the crater takes about an hour. The Munge river, which waters the Ngorongoro, has its source in the Olmoti caldera.

It is customary to hire a donkey and driver in Nainokanoka, so that you don't need to carry your own equipment (US $10 per person and animal).

The path takes you through Maasai villages in the short-grass plains of the **Bulbul Flats**, where not only the Maasai cattle and goats graze, but also wild animals such as zebras and wildebeest. A campsite lies near the village of **Bulati**, 6 miles (10 km) north of Nainokanoka. After that you begin the ascent to the western rim of **Empakai Crater** (also Embagai or Empakaai), its 10,500-foot (3,200-m) high brim circumnavigated by what used to be a road (total circumference 20 miles/32 km). There are several spots here suitable for tenting. The caldera has a radius of about 2.7 miles (5 km) and contains woodland and a lake. Count on at least four hours for a detour down into the crater.

From the northern edge of the crater you descend through lush tropical woodland; on a clear day, Ol Doinyo Lengai (altitude: 9,442 feet/2,878 m) and Lake Natron are distinctly visible. The fields of the village **Naiyobi** lie below the woods, another place to pitch a tent (the whole trip from Bulati to Naiyobi takes about 6-7 hours).

After about 2 hours you have reached the escarpment of the East African Rift (another tent-site), in sight of the symmetrical peak of the sacred mountain. Then you descend the slope through a field of loose volcanic debris. To reach the car that's waiting to pick you up, you have to walk a few miles further northward, over the dry plains.

## Lake Natron

Few people actually climb the sacred mountain: the loose volcanic ash, its steepness and the daytime heat make this mountain tour something less than a pleasurable outing, and it takes at least ten hours. If you do essay it, make sure you bring a lot of water! A local guide is also advisable.

All year long, the clear water of the **Ngare Sero** (also Engare Sero) moves through the hot, parched plains, which run out northwards into **Lake Natron**, located at an altitude of 2,000 feet (610 m). It plunges over several waterfalls from the escarpment down through a narrow ravine; there's a campsite by the point at which it exits onto the plains (**Kamakia Campsite**; 2 miles/3 km further north is **Sengo Campsite**).

These river arms are an astounding sight in the dusty desert; you can cross them at suitable fords. The southern peripheral zone of Lake Natron is still fed by the Ngare Sero, and its fresh green is the result of the toothbrush bushes growing there (*Salvadora persica*; its twigs, cut off, make very good toothbrushes). It is inadvisable to venture very far out onto the marshy ground, where numerous varieties of birds (such as the avocet and other Limicolae) find food in the freshwater zone. Where other animals shy from the discomfort of the hot brine (more than 100°F/40°C), flamingoes have specialized in the algae of the alkaline lake. They hatch their eggs in August, and thanks to the fact that their living conditions are unbearable to other animals, have virtually no enemies.

A rough track veers off west through the plains to **Malambo** (camping possible), further west you reach the Serengeti at Klein's Gate; north, near the Kenyan border lies **Loliondo**, the major village of the nature reserve of the same name.

## Engaruka

While working your way east on the rocky track out of the East African Rift, cast a glance back over the broiling, arid valley at inaccessible Lake Natron shimmering to the north and at the barren, furrowed peak of Ol Doinyo Lengai jutting up into the southern skies – the latter an uncertain entity, since no one knows when it will next start discharging ashes or fiery lava. Next, you reach a vast expanse of wide-open grassland. If it has rained, everything is vibrantly green, providing grazing land for Maasai herds as

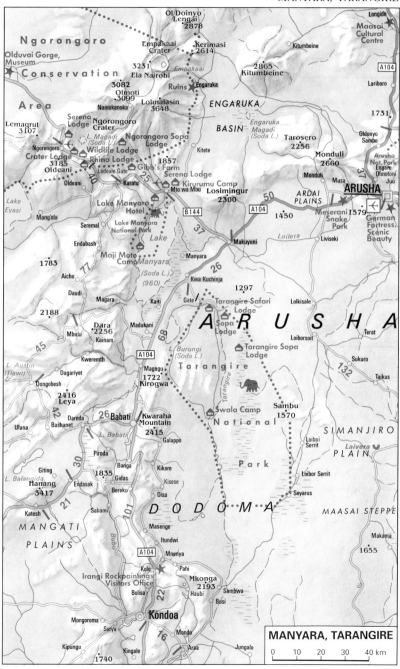

**MANYARA, TARANGIRE**

0   10   20   30   40 km

well as for wildebeest, zebras and gazelles. Small, overgrown volcano cones divide the landscape; their larger "colleagues" in the distance, **Gelai** and **Kitumbeine**, both more than 9,200 feet (2,800 m) high, are covered with trees. When visibility is good, you can see dark, lofty Mount Meru (14,980 feet/4,566 m) and even the snowcapped peak of Kilimanjaro (19,344 feet/5,896 m) in the east.

The track forks here: it is about 47 miles (75 km) southeast to **Monduli**, around 43 miles (70 km) south to **Mto wa Mbu**. The former route draws close to Kitumbeine; the latter approaches, then veers away from, the steep flank of the rift, and the volcanic plateau towers over it all. Marking its northeastern end is the volcano **Kerimasi**, which is young, but extinct. A first flush of plant cover is slowly taking hold on its scarred, furrowed slopes.

You cross **Engaruka Basin**, a savannah devoid of any grass, with only a scant growth of thorn bushes. The **Engaruka River** flows down from the volcano plateau all year round, finally trickling away in the broad depression. The only larger community on this stretch of road lies at the foot of the mountain and seems, from afar, like a great, beckoning oasis: **Engaruka**.

This spot has been luring people here for many hundreds of years. Nowadays there are houses as well as irrigated fields and gardens lying in the plains. Many are surrounded by dead thorn bushes or living fences of the smooth branches of a euphorbia tree (giant milkwort; *Euphorbia tirucalli*) to guard them from the grazing animals. Up until 300 years ago an unknown tribe dwelled here in seven villages a bit further up the slope. They farmed the land below their houses and at

*Right: Characteristic traits of the dwarf flamingo include its pink feathers and dark red beak.*

the edge of the plains, land divided up into neat right-angled plots, irrigated by a system of canals. The inhabitants built houses, field walls and canals out of stones.

No one can say where these people came from and why they gave up this settlement, which seems, from the evidence, to have flourished. The Maasai who penetrated into this area around 1700 generally preferred to trade for agricultural products rather than force the farming communities out. It is also unclear where these people went, since there are no parallels of this kind of irrigation culture anywhere else in East Africa.

You can reach the site and visit he stone foundations of the round houses, the level, rectangular field plots framed with low walls of dark lava, and the remains of the canal system by driving through the village up to the school (500 feet/150 m before that you cross the Engaruka River at a sandy ford; there is a campsite). The site with the ruins begins directly behind the school buildings; it covers a surface of 8 square miles (20 sq. km) of bushland with plenty of trees. You also encounter many wild animals there, such as giraffes.

## LAKE MANYARA NATIONAL PARK

A little way east of the village **Mto wa Mbu** the track from Engaruka joins the Arusha-Ngorongoro tourist route, heavily travelled by Land Rovers and small buses. Its name is identical with that of the river, which bubbles plentifully from the plateau all year round: it means "Mosquito River," appropriately enough, since there's certainly no lack of mosquitoes! A few decades ago an irrigation oasis emerged here, populated by inhabitants from all parts of Tanzania. You can purchase vegetables and fruit from the local gardens at a large market. There is an additional market for souvenirs, closer

to the road, so that passing tourists cannot miss it.

Not only do the river and the ground water allow the community's tall, shady trees, fields and gardens to thrive, but they also keep the northern edge of a flat, long, outstretched depression here so wet, that a dense, natural forest grows there. This hollow is named for that practical euphorbia which the inhabitants of Engaruka use to protect their plants from herd animals; the Maasai let them grow as a protective hedge for their flocks and call them *manyara*.

At an altitude of 3,150 feet (960 m) above sea level, **Lake Manyara** more or less fills the depression, depending on how much water comes down in the numerous little rivers from the Mbulu Plateau or how long and searing the dry season is. The water falls down from the west, from the high wall of the escarpment of the East African Rift that runs along the entire length of the foreland.

The foot of the escarpment and the western half of the lake make up the 127-square mile (330-sq. km) **Lake Manyara National Park**, more than two-thirds of which is taken up by the lake. The flank of the escarpment in the west is nearly 3,300 feet (1,000 m) high, and its monumental proportions, together with the seemingly immeasurable vastness of the land in the east, make the location of the park exceedingly appealing. You can gaze upon this peerless scenery not only within the park itself, you can also get a bird's-eye view during the slow drive up the rocky road from Arusha to Ngorongoro, which serpentines up from the plains to the Mbulu plateau; or, even better, you can spend the night on top, right at the edge of the rift. There are three hotels to choose from: **Lake Manyara Hotel**, **Serena Lodge** and the luxury-tented camp **Kirurumu Tented Lodge**, ardently devoted to nature conservation, which also offers room to pitch your own tent.

You can make out the park's various landscapes from the heights: woodland in the north, where ground water keeps the

soil wet; the shimmering edge of the lake, sometimes lined with flamingoes; acacia woodland; grassland, as well as gallery forests along the short streams.

A main track winds roughly 30 miles (50 km) on the narrow strip of land between lake and escarpment to the southern end of the park, where you have to turn around, as the only entrance to the park is in the north. A variety of animals can be observed in the different habitats: in the woods, for example, there are baboons and blue monkeys (*Cercopithecus mitis*); in the grassland, where occasional wild mango trees (*Tabernaemontana usambarensis*) and doum palms (*Hyphaene ventricosa*) stand scattered in the plain, zebras, impalas, buffalo and warthogs; in the ponds and rivers, hippos.

South of the humid woodlands begins a varied landscape of acacia savannah.

*Above: Lions in trees: a hallmark of Manyara National Park. Right: Character actors of the savannah: baobabs in Tarangira National Park.*

Here, a great attraction awaits visitors: lions dozing serenely in the shade, up in the branches of the umbrella trees. If many tourists are disappointed not to have encountered these predators at their unusual resting-places, their own impatience may be at fault: the lions are not trained animals who perform on command when camera-toting visitors happen to show up in their territory. However, some of the lions have, in fact, given up their former tendency to climb trees.

Elephants, giraffes, reedbuck, waterbuck, banded mongoose, and an immense number of birds, such as the elegant crowned cranes, can be observed between the towering mountain wall and the lake shore. Two hot springs (*maji moto*) are located in the south of the park, and south of these there is a luxury-tented camp.

The park administration has three campsites and bandas for visitors near the park gate. The best time to visit is during the dry season, from June to October, and in

January and February. Even when it has rained, the park is quite lovely, but after heavy precipitation on the plateau the streams that run down from it are often so swollen that you sometimes can't cross them at all. Under such conditions, you can only visit a small area of the northern part of the park. Here, however, in the woods and the surrounding area, you can go on hiking safaris.

## TARANGIRE NATIONAL PARK

The **Tarangire** River has its source in the mountains of Kondoa, which are the southern continuation of the volcanic plateau. It flows northward through the **Maasai Steppe**, a vast are of low rainfall, and ends in the depression of **Lake Burungi**, not far from the southern tip of Lake Manyara. For most of its course, it runs through **Tarangire National Park**, which, measuring 1,000 square miles (2,600 sq. km) in area, created in 1970. Large areas in its northeastern and southern sectors have been declared game

reserves (**Lolkisale**, **Simanjiro** and **Mkungunero**), as have the savannahs in the north by the Kenyan border (**Mto wa Mbu** and **Lake Natron Game Controlled Areas**), areas which the herds of the nomads share with wild animals. Like the Serengeti, Tarangire Park is but the heart of a much larger region, in which the game migrates from place to place in search of suitable pastures.

At the peak of the dry season, between August and November, Tarangire Park is the lifeline for the animals who dwell in this extended area, especially the river and its adjacent wetlands; at this time, the herds of the Maasai are banished from this park, just as they are from the Serengeti. As soon as the lesser rains commence in November/December, the zebras foal and the wildebeest calve; the animals remain within the park during the short dry period in January/February. However, when the main rainy season follows in March, the surrounding areas turn green, and many animals leave the reserve, heading north and east. Towards

71

the beginning of the dry season they gradually return: in June the elands, Beisa oryx and elephants, in July the zebras, wildebeest and buffalo.

Considering the variety and abundance of its animal life, it is amazing how seldom this park is visited, especially since it is only a two hours' drive from Arusha. Follow the excellent asphalt road west via **Makuyuni** (where most of the tourists turn off onto the poorer road to Ngorongoro Park), and continue on toward **Kwa Kuchinja**, where you'll see signposts toward the park entrance (another 4.5 miles/7 km). It is equipped with three "public" and nine "special" campsites, as well as **Sopa Lodge**, **Tarangire Safari Lodge** and **Swala Tented Camp**.

Lying at an altitude of 3,600 feet (1,100 m), this park consists mainly of flat, level landscape in which even low hills seem like significant landmarks. It

*Above: Baboons demonstrate their family life for photographers – but may also attack when they're in the mood.*

consists mainly of acacia woodland, with such plants as umbrella thorn (*Acacia tortilis*), whistling thorn (*Acacia drepanolobium*), and fever tree (yellow-barked acacia, *Acacia xanthophloea*); characteristic is the baobab (*Adansonia digitata*). Borassus palms (*Borassus aethiopia*) also grow where sufficient water is available.

Not all the animals participate in the annual migrations; some are permanent residents, such as impalas, lesser kudus, Grant's gazelles, or giraffes. The park is also famous for its pythons, which have the habit of wrapping themselves around tree branches.

The park administration has covered the park with tracks for round-trip tours which take in all the different habitats. Those in the north are more frequented, and rarely does a visitor stray into the lonely south. A hiking path is planned near the campsite **Gurusi** ("wood") in the center of the park.

## ARUSHA

**Arusha** is the absolute hub of tourism in Tanzania, and, furthermore, lying at an altitude of 4,530 feet (1,380 m), is favored with a pleasant climate. Still, the town does not act the smart tourist resort; rather, it is an up-and-coming center of trade and administration, where tourists can stay overnight, organize their safari, change from one mode of transportation to another, arrive or depart. Almost as many visitors land at **Kilimanjaro International Airport,** 28 miles (45 km) from Arusha, as they do in the Tanzanian metropolis Dar es Salaam; the **Inland Airport** at the western edge of the town is serviced by both scheduled and chartered flights. Two-thirds of Tanzania's tourists come over the Kenyan border; the main port of entry is the border town **Namanga**, roughly 85 miles (140 km) from Kenya's capital Nairobi and 65 miles (105 km) from Arusha.

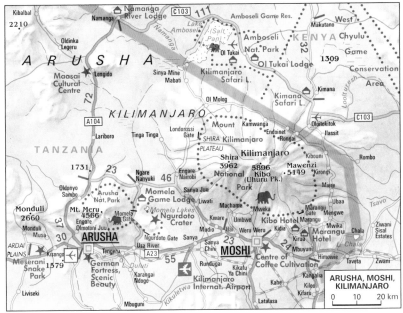

The town's is located in ideal proximity to a large number of national parks (Arusha: 18.5 miles/30 km; Tarangire: 70 miles/115 km; Manyara: 75 miles/120 km; Kilimanjaro: 75 miles/120 km; Ngorongoro: 100 miles/160 km; Serengeti (Seronera): 220 miles/350 km). About 100 tour operators have offices here.

Capital of the region, Arusha has approximately 200,000 inhabitants, and is the market center for the intensive agricultural cultivation of the fertile lans around it. Arusha has special significance in Tanzania's recent history: on Feb. 5, 1967, the *Arusha Declaration* laid out the guidelines of Tanzanian socialism. The town was also the site for meetings of the (now-dissolved) East African Community (EAC). The Arusha International Conference Center (AICC) is still a meeting-place for experts and politicians, who are also able to take advantage of the town's relatively large range of hotels.

In the north, **Mount Meru**, the country's second-highest mountain at 14,980 feet (4,566 m), towers above Arusha to the north with its green flanks and its dramatic peak, and sends down several rivers which form pleasant divisions between the town's various quarters. Along with the remains of the old German **boma** (part of it is a **museum** of natural history and ethnology), administrative offices, banks, Forex offices, the **main post office**, most of the travel agencies and several hotels, the smaller, but significant part of the city center lies on the narrow ridge between the deep-cut valleys of the **Themi** and **Naura Rivers**. On and around the three parallel streets **Boma**, **India** and **Goliondoi**, as well as in the **AICC**, located a mere 500 feet/100 m further north, tourists can compare exchange rates, souvenir prices and safari offers as well as meet others like-minded travelers who are looking for safari partners. The efficient new **Information Office** of the **Tanzania Tourist Board** (TTB) in Boma Street gives advice about licensed tour operators and much, much more.

Boma Street ends in a traffic circle with a **clocktower**. East of Themi Bridge, **Old Moshi Road** proceeds through a luxuriantly green neighborhood of villas with an adjoining golf course. Broad **Moshi Road** forks northward at the modern **Impala Hotel**, linking up with the main road to Dar es Salaam-Nairobi. At something of a remove from this highway are the generous grounds of **Hotel Mount Meru**, containing spacious gardens and a swimming pool; this complex is frequented by many tour groups. Campers can find a large campsite on the continuation of Old Moshi Road, 2 miles (3 km) further east.

The Naura River cuts the second part of Arusha's core off from the first: A network of right-angled streets lies west of its deep, green ravine, between the shopping street **Sokoine Road** and **Makongoro Road**, with, in the middle, the lively **market** (well worth a visit), and close by the busy **bus station**, almost opposite the **stadium**. There are any number of simple, inexpensive hotels along **Stadium Road** and in its vicinity (William's Inn, among others).

Set between Meru's precipices and those of several other smaller volcanoes, the scenery of the coffee plantations and various other places of intensive farming surrounding Arusha is quite alluring – a good reason to find lodgings outside the town, if you have your own vehicle or are not put off by the taxi fares.

### Arusha National Park

Before you can set out from Arusha on a longer safari, there is sometimes a period of one or two days of forced inactivity, which you may not care to spend in the city. There are some very popular guided day-tours into the surrounding rural areas, both nearby and farther away:

*Right: Arusha's bustling heart: the market at the city center.*

to the villages of the Arusha or Meru on the slopes of Mount Meru, to the Maasai in **Monduli** or **Longido**. On hikes you can observe plants and animals and learn quite a lot about the local population's traditional use of nature.

**Arusha National Park** (18.5 miles/30 km from Arusha; drive 12.5 miles/20 km towards Moshi/Dar on the main road and turn north – the turnoff is signposted Ngare Nanyuki – after **Usa River** village) is especially suited for a day-trip: measuring 53 square miles (137 sq. km) in area, the park is not large, but it is comprised of a wealth of different landscapes at altitudes of between 4,900-14,980 feet (1,500-4,566 m). It encompasses the towering crater of Mount Meru in the west and the watery scenery of Momela Lakes in the northeast, while the southeastern sector is quite taken up by the Ngurdoto volcano crater. Small volcano peaks, swamps, and the grassland with the slightly pretentious name of Serengeti Ndogo ("little Serengeti") complete the variety in Tanzania's second-smallest national park.

A through road crosses the park south to north and links the main road Arusha-Moshi with a town that lies north of the park: Ngare Nanyuki, named for a river which has its source in the Meru Crater (in the Maasai language *Engarenanyokie* means "brown water"). You can enter the park from the south or north by **Momela Gate**, as well as from the southeast by **Ngurdoto Gate**.

Tall, dense woods line the edge of **Ngurdoto Crater**; buffalo, warthogs and waterbuck are the undisturbed tenants of its caldera. The crater floor is off-limits to tourists, but several excellent lookout points are signposted along the track at the crater rim; from them, you can take in views of the crater or of the surrounding countryside, with Kilimanjaro and Meru, or even observe the wildlife in the forest, such as the black-and-white Colobus monkey (*Colobus abyssinicus*).

In contrast, **Momela Lakes** lie in more open country and serve as a home to hippopotamuses and an abundant avifauna, including countless flamingoes, as well as many migratory birds between October and April. Around the lakes, you can observe waterbuck, reedbuck, bushbuck and buffalo. An especially lovely background is a given when clear weather conditions permit a view of snowcapped Kilimanjaro in the northwest.

Not far from Momela Gate, well-appointed **Momela Lodge** is an nice place for a noontime break with a view of Mount Meru.

## MOUNT MERU

Meru's horseshoe-shaped crater gapes to the northeast and takes up almost the entire western sector of the park. A track for four-wheel-drive vehicles leads from Momela Gate (4,920 feet/1,500 m) to **Miriakamba Hut**, at an altitude of 8,248 feet (2,514 m), but after the first few miles it is pretty rough – hiking might be preferable. Because of the wild African buffalo, an armed gamekeeper is required for hikes and for climbing Meru.

With Kilimanjaro so near, many mountain hikers "look down on" Meru, 4,265 feet (1,300 m) lower. That is unfortunate, since Meru has magnificent views to offer, in addition to providing an ideal opportunity to get in shape and get acclimatized for the "Kili" ascent.

The mountain tour generally takes four days and begins at Momela Gate. On the first day, it takes off through ever-changing woodland, with wild animals, waterfalls and occasional vistas of Kilimanjaro, up to Miriakamba Hut (a 3,300-foot/1,000-m difference in altitude; 6 miles/10 km long, roughly 5 hours).

You need about three hours for the 2.5-mile (4-km) hike to **Saddle Hut** at 12,300 feet/3,570 m (with impressive views into the crater and at the summit), the hut lies on the saddle between the main volcano and **Little Meru**. For a side-trip from the hut to this 12,533-foot

75

(3,820-m) secondary peak you should count on 2 hours there and back.

On the third day it is best to get going as early as 2 a.m., in order to see the sun rising behind Kilimanjaro from the top of Meru. Many people don't even notice until they're on their way back down how extremely exposed the path is, balancing as it does on the narrow crest between the steep drop on the bowl side of the crater and the cliffs on the outer side. The views are unsurpassed: west as far as the Ngorongoro crater plateau, south to Arusha and the expanses of the Maasai Steppe, east to the highest mountain in Africa. If you are in a hurry, you can descend to Momela Gate the same day, though that will give you little leisure to take in the beauty all around.

Be wary of offers for a "cheap" climb up Meru through the forested areas from the west or north side, which enables you to avoid the park fees. Not only is this illegal, but also exceedingly dangerous.

*Above: On Mount Meru, clouds irrigate the lush foliage of the mountain rain forest.*

## KILIMANJARO NATIONAL PARK

In the year 1849, when the missionary Rebmann reported seeing a snow-covered mountain in East Africa, no one believed him. Snow at a latitude of 3°S, so near the equator – back then, the experts thought it impossible. For the native population, the mysterious glacial peak of **Kilimanjaro** has always been a reality, since in clear weather conditions, it can be seen from an astounding distance: from Nairobi in the north, for example, 125 miles (200 km) distant, or from the southwest, right across the Maasai Steppe, from the mountains of Kondoa, 155 miles (250 km) away. From up close this highest mountain of Africa appears tempting, especially from its north or south side: the massif of this huge twin-peaked mountain, almost 60 miles (100-km) long, seems to grow gradually out of the plains. Its western peak, the white, gently rounded **Kibo** (19,344 feet/5,896 m), is the higher of the two. The **saddle** forms a long, level sweeping line between it and the lower, dark, wildly rugged **Mawenzi** (16,893 feet/5,149 m) in the east.

The first Europeans to conquer Kilimanjaro were the German geologist Hans Meyer and the Austrian alpinist Ludwig Purtscheller in 1889, only after many others before them had failed. Geologists did not thoroughly investigate the summits until the 1950s; in 1984, two adventurers succeeded in reaching the highest spot with their bicycles; and now, towards the end of the 20th century, the park administration is pondering how best to control and regulate the floods of tourists on the mountain so that no more that 58 visitors reach the top on any given day. A rapid development!

No less swift have been the changes all around the lower slopes of Kilimanjaro. As long as they can remember, the Chagga tribe has inhabited the heights between 2,200 feet and 4,600 feet (700 m-1,400 m) and has farmed coffee, bananas, millet, taro and forage grass in the shade of the trees, keeping their livestock in barns. Their ingenious system of irrigation, combined with fertile soil and ample rainfall, has kept their population high. However, the number of inhabitants has more than tripled in the second half of the 20th century, so that they now farm as far as 6,600 feet (2,000 m) up the slope into the wooded area, but also downwards toward the foot of the slope. Forest land is decreasing, and with it, also their water reserves, so that it is becoming more and more difficult to farm all the plots on the slope satisfactorily.

The forest reserve, consisting of indigenous vegetation and forested parts, starts from 4,600 feet (1,500 m) in the south and east, and from 5,500 feet (1,800 m) in the drier north and west of the Kilimanjaro slopes and reaches as far up as 8,900 feet (2,700 m). From this altitude, Kilimanjaro National Park expands, with its interesting "exotic" flora, such as giant groundsels or giant lobelia which grow best at altitudes of 8,900-13,000 ft (2,700-4,000 m).

Three larger volcanoes form the elongated massif of Kilimanjaro. They lie in a row, running from southeast to northwest; Mawenzi and Kibo are joined by the 12,998-foot (3,962 m) **Shira** in the west. Its crater is more heavily eroded and lava emissions from Kibo have destroyed its northern rim, making it less noticeable. Shira and Mawenzi are judged to be roughly the same age. Mawenzi has quite a distinctive shape: its rocky outcrops are the heavily-weathered remains of its vent. Anyone wishing to conquer it must be an experienced mountain climber, bring his own equipment and – this goes for all "normal" hikers on any route in the national park, as well – enlist the services of a licensed agency. Solo runs or climbs without mountain guide and porters are not permitted.

Kibo, the youngest, is presumed to be a dormant volcano. Sunk into its snow- and glacier-covered top is a small, almost circular crater, **Reusch Crater**, with, almost concentrically at its middle, a smaller ash cone with a vent opening, which emits sulphur vapors and hot water.

**Uhuru Peak** (known, until 1918, as *Kaiser-Wilhelm-Spitze*) lies a good half-mile (1 km) south of that; at an altitude of 19,344 feet (5,896 m), it's the highest point in Africa. Of the thousands who have climbed "Kili" (roughly 12,000 a year), only a fraction have gone all the way to the top; most take the Marangu route and are contented with Gillman's Point.

### Marangu Route

The easiest way to the top – and the only one equipped with huts – begins and ends at Marangu on the eastern slope of Kilimanjaro and takes five days (four overnights). This is the one chosen by 90% of all hikers; not all of these intend to climb Kibo. Many are content to climb to the first or second hut.

The village Marangu is about 25 miles (40 km) from the district town **Moshi**, where any number of agencies are resident and where there is a good choice of hotels. You can book your tour either here or in the hotels in Marangu, if you haven't already done so in Dar, Arusha or abroad. Public buses run frequently to Marangu and take about an hour. The park entrance **Marangu Gate** is located 3 miles (5 km) above the village.

The hikers' path begins at 6,500 feet (1,980 m). On the first day, it proceeds 4.5 miles (7 km) through dense, tall mountain forest to **Mandara Hut** at an altitude of 8,860 feet (2,700 m).

The second day's hike is 7 miles (11 km) long and takes you out of the woods into more open landscape dominated by giant heather. In this area you can make a

*Above: Snow in the tropics – Kilimanjaro from the southeast. Right: The giant groundsel grows at altitudes of 10,000-13,000 feet (3,000-4,000 m) and can withstand extremes of heat and frost.*

side-trip to **Maundi Crater** (signposted). The weathered tips of Mawenzi make a dramatic backdrop for this small parasitic volcano, overgrown with herbs and bushes. This is also the day on which you first sight Kibo. Towards **Horombo Hut** vegetation becomes scarce; you've reached an altitude of 12,140 feet (3,700 m).

On the third day, you cover a distance of 6 miles (10 km) through the largely barren saddle to **Kibo Hut**, at a height of 15,400 feet (4,700 m). On your way you pass the last watering-hole, bearing a sign: **Last Water**. In other words, fill'er up! The upper level of the mountain is low on rainfall, furthermore the naked rock is very porous, so you won't encounter any running water up here. Instead of vegetation there is a varied "rock landscape" with bizarrely-shaped volcanic boulders, snowy Kibo in front of you, and dark and rugged Mawenzi behind you – provided, of course, that visibility is good. But it could easily be that you find yourself hiking through the clouds; it might rain or even snow.

Nights are exciting in Kibo Hut: The warmly-dressed hikers set off between two and three in the morning and in the dark they toil roughly 3,300 feet (1,000 m) up the steep, serpentine path to Gillman's Point (18,635 feet/ 5,680 m). Here at the outer crater rim, after an arduous climb, you watch the sun rise behing Mawenzi, and many a hiker hastens to climb down again. Up here it is ice cold - usually at least 55-70°F (30-40°C) colder than at the base of the mountain - the air is thin, and therefore you get exhausted easily. Nevertheless, a word of advice to all those spared the headache which sometimes goes with this terrain: walk on *polepole* (slowly) through this tropical world of snow and ice, along the gentle incline of the crater rim with its grand views, on to the very highest place of Africa, to **Uhuru Peak** – one of the unforgettable experiences of a Kili ascent.

When coming down on the Marangu route hikers generally overnight in Horombo Hut, unless it is full, then they struggle on to Mandara Hut; those with more stamina make it all the way to Marangu Gate, where there are likewise accomodations.

### Rongai Route

The road from Machame, which bypasses Kilimanjaro, half-way uphill to the east, is fully developed as far as the village **Rongai** (several buses a day from Himo), making Kilimanjaro accessible from the north side, a possibility little used for a time. On the **Rongai Route** you overnight in tents; the caves formerly utilized when passing this way should no longer be used by tourists. On the saddle, the Rongai Route links up with the Marangu Route short of Kibo Hut. You spend the third night in Kibo Hut, then you climb to the summit. The way back follows the Marangu Route.

The Rongai Route is quite lovely and hardly more difficult than the Marangu Route, but you must do without the comfort of the huts and you have a longer drive to your starting-point (about 43 miles/70 km from Marangu). Many may find it advantageous to camp out and avoid the many mountain climbers on the lower stages of the Marangu Route.

### To the Shira Plateau - and Further

On the west side of Kilimanjaro the park administration has developed various hiking possibilities from **Londorossi Gate** (7,380 feet/2,250 m; 47 miles /75 km from Moshi). To reach the gate drive along the main road Moshi-Arusha; at the little village of Hai (part of the area called Boma ya Ng'ombe) the road to Sanya Juu turns north from the main road. One of the abovementioned possibilities is a demanding climb up to the peak by the Shira Route (overnight in tents) through the **Western Breach** of the Kibo crater, if you do not prefer to go round south of the crater, in order to take advantage of the easier approach to the peak from the east via Barafu; the descent can follow the Mweka Route.

The other gives you a chance to spend up to three days on Shira Plateau (about 13,000 feet/4,000 m high) even without a mountain guide and porters and wander freely on the two paths laid on there; overnight in tents. A drive and a parking lot 3 miles (5 km) above the entrance make access easier. Open to the north, Shira's wide crater offers delightful hikes in a setting of giant lobelias, giant groundsels and heather as well as unusual views of Kibo and of the wide open country to the north (Amboseli Park) and west (Mount Meru).

The drive to Londorossi Gate, located above the forestry-workers' settlement, constitutes a trip to the country in itself. Via **Engare Nairobi**, still at the foot of the mountain in the dry savannah, drive east to **Simba Farm**, first through deciduous forest, then through dense pine forest; at the forest's edge and in forest nursery areas, there is intensive vegetable cultivation. Buffalo, elephants, elands, dikdiks and black and white Colobus monkeys all frequent these wooded areas.

Driving around Kilimanjaro in a four-wheel-drive vehicle further north and east, you enter the **Kitendeni Corridor**, a nature reserve created to allow the wild animals free access between Kilimanjaro and Amboseli Parks. Population pressure is making severe inroads into the land that was originally set aside for the animals, but from August to October migration movement can most likely be observed there. With a jeep you can get through to Rongai further east, from there, circumnavigating the eastern side of the mountain on a wide road all the way round to Marangu. Plan on 155 miles (250 km) for the whole trip around the Kilimanjaro massif via Moshi.

*Right: We made it! Arriving at the highest peak in Africa just in time for the sunrise.*

## Southern Routes

Three "camping routes" to Kibo are available on the southern slope. The ascent follows the **Machame Route** (gate at 5,900 feet/1,800 m) or the **Umbwe Route** further east (gate 4,600 feet/ 1,400 m); generally chosen for the descent is the steeper **Mweka Route**, the most easterly route, which also passes by the renowned *College of African Wildlife Management*. All three of these routes involve camping. As on the Shira Route, you can climb the west face, which places rather greater demands on a climber, or you can travel south around the crater and reach **Stella Point** on Kibo (18,850 feet/5,745 m; 30 minutes from Gillman's Point) from the eastern side along the **Barafu Route**.

The routes on the southern slope are more taxing than the Marangu Route, but the landscape has much more to offer and they are not so overrun; Machame Route takes longer (6 days) and so it gives you more time to get acclimatized to high altitude conditions.

## Lake Chala

The exclave **Lake Chala** on the Tanzanian/Kenyan border is under the rigorous protection of Kilimanjaro National Park. After days of privation on Africa's highest mountain, you might welcome a bit of rest and relaxation at this 2-square-mile (5-sq.-km) crater lake (15 miles/ 25 km from Himo).

## MOSHI

Even someone who does not originally intend to climb the highest mountain in Africa might change his plans, as soon as he has enjoyed the view of Kilimanjaro in **Moshi**, perhaps from the roof-terrace of a hotel or at the YMCA swimming-pool. Moshi's greatest visual attraction is the mountain. The town itself, at an altitude

of 2,900 feet (890 m), and therefore noticeably warmer than Arusha, is a significant center for the *Chagga* farmers in this extremely densely settled agricultural part of the country, especially for marketing the high-quality *Arabica* coffee grown there.

The town center is small and neat, tucked in between the bus station, the through road Arusha-Dar es Salaam and the **market**, overflowing with fresh tropical fruit and well worth a visit. Here there are any number of inexpensive lodgings for tourists, and also most of the travel agents, whose clients mainly wish to climb Kilimanjaro. Banks and foreign exchange agencies are found near the **clock tower**.

Long-distance buses depart from Moshi daily for Nairobi, Tanga, Dar es Salaam, as well as for the villages around Kilimanjaro, the Pare and Usambara Mountains. Rail transportation is of less interest to tourists: There is but one connection a week to Dar es Salaam, and it is by night.

## PARE MOUNTAINS

About 15 miles (25 km) east of Moshi the main road to Dar es Salaam bends sharply south, while the turnoff to the east leads off to the Kenyan **Tsavo National Park** and Mombasa via Himo. At Himo a side road turns off for Marangu (7 miles/11 km).

Compared to Kilimanjaro's dimensions, the non-volcanic summits of the **Pare Mountains**, east of the road, seem unimpressive at first. The steep western slopes stretch out almost in a straight line from north to south. A pre-colonial caravan route followed along the foothills, originating in the valley of the East African Rift, from Lake Natron and areas further north, and ending on the coast in Pangani or Tanga. Railway and road are the mountains' modern-day escorts. The mountains and plains of the dry Maasai Steppe lie to the west – although, as the Pare Mountains shadow it from rain, the area often seems withered and shriveled to those driving along the main road.

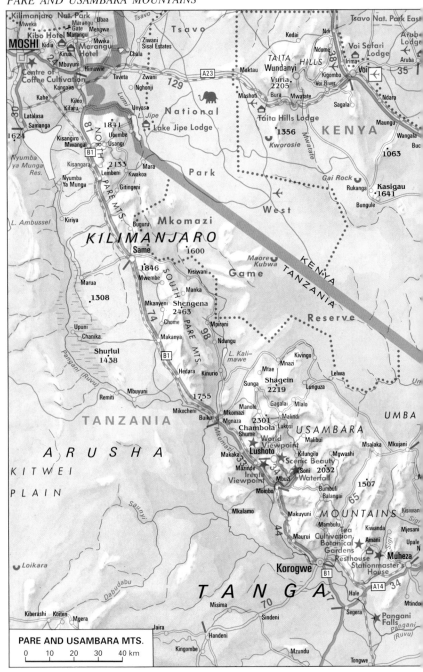

PARE AND USAMBARA MTS.

0   10   20   30   40 km

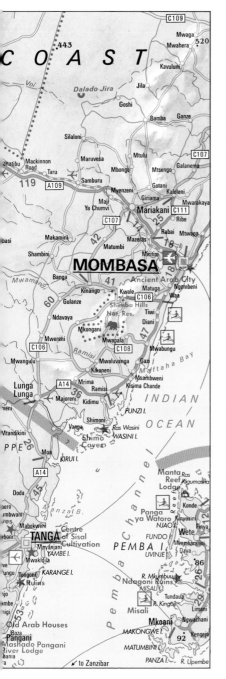

From **Mwanga** a road winds upward into the **North Pare Mountains**, and at the top you can't help but notice how lushly verdant and how intensively farmed this mountainous country is. Most of the rain comes from the east; the country to the west of the great main road has to rely on irrigation. For this purpose, and also to generate electricity, a dam was built and a lake created on the **Pangani**: **Nyumba ya Mungu** ("House of God").

Near the district town of **Same**, a narrow strip of plain separates the North from the **South Pare Mountains**, which reach much higher altitudes than the northern counterparts. The 47 miles (75 km) from Same to the southern tip of the mountains, to **Mkomazi**, go quickly on the asphalted main road, but between the two towns you can also take an eastern route around the mountains, on 62 miles (100 km) of poor road with ever-changing views, which for stretches runs along the border of the **Mkomazi Game Reserve**, which merges into Tsavo Park on the Kenyan side.

## USAMBARA MOUNTAINS

Near Mkomazi, the plains of the Mkomazi River form the border with the Pare Mountains. It is here that the **Usambara Mountains** begin. The Usambaras have been inhabited for more than 2,000 years. The Shambaa tribe has made its home here for centuries; traditionally, it placed its settlements on the mountain ridges, while the slopes were reserved for fields, planted with bananas, corn, millet, yams and cassava. This was evidently a strategic choice, necessary for defense in the numerous tribal feuds. Around 1740 a powerful chieftain, Mbegha, united the Shambaa. Peace, however, was not to endure, It was not a lasting peace; the tribe had plenty of trouble with slave hunters and, later, toward the end of the 19th century, European colonists, especially Germans.

The mountains appear unapproachable with their cliffs, protruding spurs and

slopes rising almost vertically from the base, where the main road passes.

The market town **Mombo** is the best place to find passage into the interior of the mountains. A paved road leads to the district capital of **Lushoto** (20 miles/32 km). Up it goes in serpentines and switchbacks, commanding views of the orderly fields of sisal on the plains. Then the road winds through narrow valleys to **Soni**, where the river of the same name creates an impressive waterfall. The slopes are densely planted, the steepest flanks wooded, and the air is quite pleasant at this altitude. Small wonder that Europeans liked to settle here during the colonial era. The Germans called Lushoto "Wilhelmstal." Several colonial buildings still stand.

The surrounding countryside is ideal for hiking. To get a feel for it, take the

*Above: Seeking advice in a hospital in the Moshi district. Right: The Amani Nature Reserve also contains tea plantations which you can visit on the Tea Factory Tour.*

one-hour path to **Irente** (the road from the town center past the Mandarin Hotel), where you can gaze down from a rocky lookout (**Irente Viewpoint**), 3,300 feet (1,000 m) high, over sisal plantations, the railway line and main road, and far over the mountains and the plains towards the Maasai Steppe. You can even tent just a few yards away. More famous is the vista from **Jiwe la Mungu** ("Stone of God"; also known as **World Viewpoint**), near Shume, some 20 miles (32 km) from Lushoto.

Accompanied by a local guide (ask in guest-houses and hotels or at the Green Valley Hotel at the bus station), you can take a range of eventful day tours or even tours of several days' length to explore the land and people of the Shambaa.

More remote regions of the Usambara Mountains still boast remnants of the original woodlands; near **Mazumbae** (15 miles/25 km from Lushoto), you can visit the forest reserve, if you are accompanied by a forest ranger. Some areas are being reforested. In **Magamba Forest Reserve** there are signposted hiking trails and two

cozy colonial villas for overnighting (roughly 10 miles/ 15 km from Lushoto).

### Amani

**Korogwe** presents another passage into the Usambara Mountains from the main road Arusha-Dar es Salaam. A number of roadside stands offer plums, cherries, apples and other fruit from the interior. In Segera, a good paved road branches off toward Tanga, and from that yet another side road veers off in **Muheza** into hill-country.

This southeastern sector of the Usambara Mountains is lower than the northern segment, but no less difficult of access: the route leads over steep, rocky roads and through narrow valleys. Until 1880, when the first colonial settlers arrived, the area was covered in dense tropical jungle; but the new arrivals, wanting to put in coffee plantations, cleared the jungle in many places, and the Germans built a railway from Tanga to **Kisiwani** at the foot of the mountains in

1891, to transport the wood. And although the tracks have long since been removed, the old train station, the half-timbered **station-master's house** still stands and was painstakingly renovated in 1997.

Here, where the railway ends at an altitude of 1,300 feet (400 m), marks the beginning of steep mountainous country, covered in dense stands of tall trees. Indigenous trees grow alongside such imported varieties as jackfruit trees, teak, oil palms and many others. The native flora of the Usambaras is quite varied and many plants are peculiar to this area, since this mountain region has been isolated from other regions for millions of years. Best-known plant here is the **Usambara violet**, bred from a relation of *Saintpaulia confusa*, today found hidden in Usambara forests.

There are quite a few "foreign" trees between the train station and the town of **Amani**, 7.5 miles (12 km) away. These exotics date back to the German colonial era. In 1893 a health resort was built in

85

Amani, whose altitude of 3,000 feet (900 m) makes for a much more pleasant climate than that on the coast around Tanga, where many Germans resided. A small **Botanic Garden** was laid out in an endeavor to smarten up the settlement. In 1902 the Germans established the Amani Institute of Biological and Agricultural Research, and German farmers planted extensive fields of rubber trees, sisal, tobacco and sugar cane. After 1916 this research and experimental agriculture continued under the British. Today the complex houses the National Institute of Medical Research (NIMR), which runs the comfortable, rustic **resthouse**.

**Amani Nature Reserve** is the most varied and best-developed hiking area in Tanzania. It extends over 48 square miles (126 sq. km): more than 40% of this is woodland, more than 30% farmland of the 11 surrounding villages, and a good 20% tea plantations. Nine signposted hiking trails and three circular auto routes have been selected and described by the team of the *East Usambara Catchment Project*; all 12 routes are outstanding. The park headquarters lies near the **Sigi River**, not far from the historic train station, on the Muheza-Amani route.

Don't be put off by the poor road conditions! The following are only a few of the many sightseeing routes available. **Sigi Spice Garden**: 1- to 3-hour hike through palm gardens, a fruit and spice garden near the park entrance; **Tea Factory Tour**; **Kwamkoro Forest Trail**: a circular route nearly 6 miles (10 km) long, leading from the rest house through varied woodland, with occasional glimpses of *Saintpaulia confusa* in its native habitat.

Walking the **Derema Trail** is a day trip which starts out with a steep ascent from the rest house, but rewards you with fantastic views all the way to the Pangani estuary on the Indian Ocean as it leads past woods, tea plantations, villages and historic sites.

## ARUSHA
Area Code 57
### Accommodation in Town
*MODERATE - double rooms 75 US$ and over:*
**Impala Hotel**: Old Moshi Rd. (around half a mile/1 km from clock tower), Box 7302 Arusha, tel. 2962, 7083, 8448-51, fax 8220; most modern large hotel in Arusha, in-house travel agency, many travel groups, comfortable rooms. **Novotel Mt. Meru**: Nairobi Rd., Box 877 Arusha, tel. 2711/12, 2717, 8804, fax 8221, 8502; international large hotel; shops, tour operators, a number of good restaurants, large garden with swimming pool, many tour groups, rooms need renovation. **New Arusha Hotel**: Old Moshi Rd., near clock tower, Box 88 Arusha, tel. 8541/3, fax 8085, centrally located, many businesspeople, beautiful park.
*MODERATE - double rooms below 75 US$:*
**Eland Motel**: Nairobi Rd., Box 7226 Arusha, tel. 7868, fax 8468. **Equator Hotel**: Boma Rd., Box 3002 Arusha, tel. 8410/2, fax 4379; centrally located, quiet; large rooms, renovation planned for 1998. **Golden Rose**: Stadium Rd., Box 361 Arusha, tel. 8861, 7959, fax 8862; near bus stand, bar, restaurant. **Hotel A.M. 88**: Makao Mapya, Box 1045 Arusha, tel. 7873, 7168; near bus stand, quiet side street. **Ilboru Safari Lodge**: More than a mile/2 km north of the city center, signposted on Nairobi Rd.; Box 8012 Arusha, tel. 7834; small hotel. **Maasai Safari Centre**: From Nairobi Rd., start as if going to Ilboru Hotel, turn right after 400 yards/300 m, proceed another 300 yards/200 m; Box 1549 Arusha, tel./fax 8535; well-tended garden, fantastic views of Mount Meru, six rooms with shower and toilet, connected to a small tourism training institute. **Mezza Luna Hotel**: Moshi Rd, (near to Impala Hotel), Box 14365 Arusha, tel./fax 4381; large restaurant and garden (Italian food); few, but modern rooms.
*BUDGET*: Arusha has about 100 guest houses and simple hotels, often with shared bathrooms and toilets.
**Hotel Splendid**: Kikuyu St., tel. 2125; near the market; small hotel, professional staff, rooms with bath and toilet. **Kilimanjaro Villa Guest House**: Azimio St. (between the market and Uhuru Monument), tel. 8109; centrally located, quiet, shared bathrooms. **Naaz Hotel**: Sokoine Rd. (near clock tower), Box 1060 Arusha, tel. 2087, centrally located, quiet, restaurant and shop on lower floor, breezy terrace on 1st floor, some rooms with bath and toilet. **The Outpost**: Serengeti St. (turns off from Old Moshi Rd., signposted), Box 11520 Arusha, tel. 8405; mansion in beautiful garden, 1 mile/1.5 km from clock tower, spartan rooms, expensive; ideal campsite. **Williams Inn**: Makao

Mapya, near Hotel A.M. 88, simple, clean rooms with shower and toilet, good value, includes breakfast. **YMCA**: India St., Box 658 Arusha, tel. 6074, 6097; centrally located, shared bathrooms, overpriced, but popular meeting place, cafeteria. Many simple hotels north of bus stand and around the stadium.

*CAMPSITES:* **Masai Campsite**: Old Moshi Rd., 2 miles/3.5 km from the clock tower, Box 6130 Arusha, tel./fax 8299; spacious premises, well-guarded, hot showers, restaurant, bar, travel agency, car repair. **Olasiti Garden & Camp**: Oljoro Rd., Box 8026 Arusha, tel. 8705, 3651, south of Dodoma Rd., signposted, in attractive, well-tended garden, tennis courts. *Small-sized campsites:* **Kinyoro**, next to Equator Hotel on Themi river, in the gardens of the **Maasai Safari Centre** and **Outpost**.

### Accommodation Out of Town

*MODERATE:* **Dik Dik Hotel**: 12 miles/20 km on Moshi road, Box 1499 Usa River, tel. 57-8498; beautiful setting with garden, swimming pool, restaurant. **Mount Meru Game Lodge**: 12 miles/20 km on Moshi road; Box 751 Arusha, tel. 8106, fax 8268. **Mountain Village Lodge**: 9 miles/15 km east of Arusha, Box 376 Arusha, tel. 2699; beautifully located near Lake Duluti, former coffee farm, restaurant, campsite, horseback riding. **Ngare Sero Mountain Lodge**: 9 miles/15 km on Moshi road, Box 425 Arusha, tel. 3629, fax 8690, lovely villa on a lake, in well-tended park, swimming pool. **Tanzanite Hotel**: 7.5 miles/12 km on Moshi road; Box 3063 Arusha, tel./fax 8459, Usa River 169.

### Restaurants

All the larger hotels have their own restaurants. *AFRICAN*: **The Barracuda**: Boma Rd. tel. 2823, bar and grill. **B.O.T. Club**: Makongoro Rd., delicious *ugali*, pleasant ambience. Small, cheap restaurants and fast food near market: Somali Rd., Market St., Sokoine Rd.

*CHINESE:* **Shanghai**: Sokoine Rd. (near Meru post office), tel. 3224. **Everest**: Old Moshi Rd. (east of Themi bridge), tel./fax 8419. **Mandarin**: Serengeti Rd., tel. 7844.

*ITALIAN:* **Mezza Luna**: Moshi Rd., tel. 4381, pizza and pasta in pleasant garden.

*INDIAN:* **Shamiara**, in Pallson's Hotel, Market St., tasty Northern Indian food (*biriyani* etc.).

*ETHIOPIAN:* **Ethiopian Restaurant**, Old Moshi Rd.; specialty: *injera*.

*BAKERIES:* **Hot Bread Shop**: Sokoine Rd. (near clock tower). **Mac's Patisserie**, apple strudel, croissants, rye bread, cappuccino etc.

### Transportation

*PLANE:* International flights: **Kilimanjaro Airport**, 30 miles/50 km towards Moshi on perfect asphalt road. **Domestic airport**: Dodoma Rd., 3 miles/5 km west of Arusha; daily flights to Dar es Salaam, several flights weekly to Mwanza and Serengeti.

*BUS:* To Nairobi, there are several (expensive) **shuttle buses** from Mt. Meru Hotel/Riverside, Sokoine Rd.; cheaper buses depart from the bus stand, e.g., by Arusha Express. Several buses a day to Dar es Salaam, Tanga. Daily departures to Mbeya via Chalinze; daily service to Dodoma, Singida, Mwanza via Babati. Three departures weekly for Mwanza and Musoma via Serengeti; foreigners have to pay 25 US$ at each park gate (NCA und Serengeti). Frequent service to Moshi.

### Tourist Information

**TTB** (Tanzania Tourist Board): Boma St., Box 2348 Arusha, tel. 3842/3, fax 8256; professional service, Mon-Fri 8 am-4 pm, Sat 8.30 am-1 pm.

### Tour Operators

There are some 100 tour operators in Arusha which organize safaris, climbs on Mt. Meru and Kilimanjaro, etc. TTB keeps an updated list of licensed tour agents. The larger ones, which mainly organize safaris for clients who have booked their tours before they arrived in Tanzania, or, on the spot, at fairly *HIGH PRICES*; are: **UTC** (Goliondoi Rd., Box 2211 Arusha, tel. 8844, fax 8222), **Ranger Safaris** (AICC, Ngorongoro Wing, Box 9 Arusha, tel. 3074, 3023, fax 8205), **STS** (Sokoine Rd., Box 1369 Arusha, tel. 8715-7, fax 8209), **Leopard Tours** (Novotel Mt. Meru, Box 1638 Arusha, tel. 8442-3, fax 4131), **Abercrombie & Kent** (Sokoine Rd., Box 427 Arusha, tel. 8347, fax 8273). In addition to these, smaller, and no less professional tour operators offer tailor-made safaris, on the spot, to individual tourists, according to their desires. *MEDIUM PRICES*: **Easy Travel**: Joel Maeda Rd., Clocktower Centre, 2nd floor (next to main post office), Box 1912 Arusha, tel. 3929, fax 7322, professionals for any tours to Tanzanian parks; airlines and shipping agents; another office at Dar es Salaam. **Equatorial Safaris**: AICC, Serengeti Wing, 4th floor, Box 2156, tel. 7006, fax 2617, approved safari programs in the *Northern Circuit* and Zanzibar/Pemba/Mafia. **Flycatcher Safaris**: Haile Selassie Rd. 50, Box 591 Arusha, tel. 6963, fax 8261, customized tours all over Tanzania; luxury-tented camp on Rubondo Island. **Hoopoe Adventure Tours**: India St., Box 2047 Arusha, tel. 7011, 7541, fax 8226; very experienced, nature-loving team, for individual tours in the *Northern Circuit* and all over Tanzania. Their campsite and luxury-tented camp *Kirurumu* up from Lake Manyara is ideal for safaris and hiking tours. **Nyika Treks & Safaris**: AICC, Ngorongoro Wing, 1st floor/151, Box 13077 Arusha, tel./fax 3384; in addition to standard safaris, they offer more unusual destinations, such as the

Pare Mountains. **Scan-Tan Tours**: AICC, Serengeti Wing, 3rd floor, Box 2611 Arusha, tel. 4135, 6691, fax 4133, 8170; wide choice of standard safaris, but also tours to rarely-visited areas: Lake Eyasi, Lake Natron, Engaruka. **Shidolya Tours & Safaris**: AICC, Serengeti Wing, 3rd floor, Box 1436 Arusha, tel. 8506, fax 8242. **Tropical Africa Trails**: Masai Campsite, Old Moshi Rd., Box 6130 Arusha, tel./fax 8299; hiking and trekking tours off the beaten track.

### Park Authorities

**Ngorongoro Conservation Area Authority**: (Arusha Branch) Makongoro Rd., Box 776 Arusha, tel/fax 3339; head office: Box 1, Ngorongoro Crater, tel. 57-6091. **TANAPA (Tanzania National Parks)**: AICC, Serengeti Wing, 6th floor, Box 3134 Arusha, tel. 3471, fax 8216.

### Museums, Exhibitions

**Natural History Museum**: Boma Rd., open 7:30 am-6 pm. Entr. fee 1 US$/500 Tsh.; human evolution as demonstrated by the most important finds in Tanzania. Copy of footprints from Laetoli. Collections are being enlarged. Guided group tours by appointment: Box 2160 Arusha, tel. 7540. **Arusha Declaration Museum**: Makongoro Rd., next to Uhuru monument; 9 am-5:30 pm. Tanzanian history. **Meserani Snake Park**: Dodoma Rd., 16 miles/25 km from Arusha.

### SERENGETI, NDUTU
#### Accommodation

*LUXURY:* **Seronera Wildlife Lodge**: center of Serengeti and **Lobo Wildlife Lodge**, 50 miles/80 km further north, reservations: Novotel Mt. Meru, Box 877 Arusha, tel. (57) 2711 or TAHI; Box 96 Dar es Salaam, tel. (51) 322 12, fax (51) 116609. **Serengeti Serena Lodge**: 16 miles/25 km north of Seronera, Serena Lodges & Hotels, Arusha, tel. (57) 6304, fax (57) 4155. **Serengeti Sopa Lodge**: 12 miles/20 km south of Seronera; Sopa Lodges, Box 1823 Arusha, tel. (57) 6886, fax (57) 8245. *MODERATE:* **Ndutu Safari Lodge**: reservations: Gibb's Farm, Box 2 Karatu. *LUXURY-TENTED CAMPS:* **Grumeti Tented Camp**, in the Western Corridor, and **Klein's Camp**, in theNortheastern Serengeti, reserv.: ConsCorp, Sokoine Rd., Arusha, tel. (57) 8078, 3303, fax (57) 8268. **Kirawira Camp**: Western Corridor, on Grumeti River, reserv. see Serena Lodge. **Kusini Tented Camp**: some 40 miles/60 km south of Seronera, near border of Maswa Game Reserve, Mashado Central Reservations, Box 14823 Arusha, tel. (57) 6585, fax (57) 8020. **Kijereshi Tented Camp**: near Ndabaka Gate, Box 190 Mwanza, tel. (68) 40139. **Speke Bay Lodge**: On Lake Victoria, 9 miles/15 km from Ndabaka Gate, Box 953 Mwanza, fax: (68) 41726.

*CAMPSITES:* TANAPA has seven public campsites (20 US$) and 19 special campsites (40 US$).

### NGORONGORO
#### Accommodation

*LUXURY:* **Ngorongoro Crater Lodge**: for reservations, contact ConsCorp, Sokoine Rd., Arusha, tel. (57) 8078. **Ngorongoro Serena Lodge**: Arusha tel. (57) 6304. **Ngorongoro Sopa Lodge**: Box 1823 Arusha, tel. (57) 6886. **Ngorongoro Wildlife Lodge**: Box 877 Arusha, tel. (57) 2711.
*MODERATE:* **Rhino Lodge**: Box 16 Ngorongoro Crater, tel. 21, reservations also through NCAA office at Arusha.
*CAMPSITE:* **Simba Public Campsite**: Reservations at Lodoare Gate or apply in writing to the Director NCAA, Box 1, Ngorongoro Crater.

### KARATU-MANYARA
#### Accommodation

KARATU: *MODERATE:* **Gibbs Farm**: north of Karatu, Box 2 Karatu; stylish building surrounded by coffee plantations. *BUDGET:* **Safari Junction**, **Kudu-Karatu**: bungalows and *CAMPSITES*, southwest of Karatu. In town, very simple guest houses.
ABOVE LAKE MANYARA: *LUXURY:* **Lake Manyara Hotel**: On top edge of escarpment, for reservations see Ngorongoro Wildlife Lodge. *MODERATE:* **Lake Manyara Serena Lodge**: On top edge of escarpment, for res. see Ngorongoro Serena Lodge. *LUXURY-TENTED CAMP:* **Kirurumu Tented Lodge**: On top edge of escarpment, panoramic views of Manyara NP, in bush country with rich birdlife; camping permitted, good cooking, res. Hoopoe Adventure Tours, India St., Box 2074 Arusha, tel. (57) 7011, fax (57) 8226.
**Mto wa Mbu/Manyara National Park**: In town, simple guest houses; outside the park, TANAPA offers group accommodation; inside the park, there are several special campsites and bandas. *LUXURY-TENTED CAMP:* **Maji Moto Camp** in southern part of park, near hot springs, res. ConsCorp, Sokoine Rd., Arusha, tel. (57) 8073, fax (57) 8268.

### TARANGIRE
#### Accommodation

*LUXURY:* **Tarangire Sopa Lodge**: Res. Box 1823 Arusha, tel. (57) 6886, fax (57) 8245. *MODERATE:* **Tarangire Safari Lodge**: Bungalows and tented camps, res. Box 2703 Arusha, tel./fax (57) 7182. *LUXURY-TENTED CAMP:* **Swala Camp**: Western part of park, Mashado Central Reservations, Box 14823 Arusha, tel. (57) 6585, fax (57) 8020. *CAMPSITES:* TANAPA has three public campsites near the park entrance and nine special campsites in a range of diverse habitats in the northern section of the park.

## ARUSHA NATIONAL PARK
### Accommodation

*MODERATE:* **Momela Lodge**: near northern park entrance, res. Simba Safaris, Joel Meada Rd., Box 1207 Arusha, tel. (57) 3509. TANAPA maintains *MOUNTAIN HUTS:* **Miriakamba Hut** (sleeps 48) and **Saddle Hut** (sleeps 24) for climbers to Mount Meru, and four special campsites.

## MOSHI
Area Code 55
### Accommodation

*MODERATE:* **Key's Hotel**: north of YMCA; Box 933 Moshi, tel. 52250. *BUDGET:* **Moshi Hotel**: near clock tower; Box 1819 Moshi, tel. 3071. **Moshi View Hotel**: South of market, Kiusa St.; Box 13, Moshi, tel. 50993, new, rooftop terrace. **New Castle Hotel**: Mawenzi Rd., Box 2080 Moshi, tel. 53203, rooftop with panoramic view of Kilimanjaro. **New Kindoroko Hotel**: Mawenzi Rd., Box 1341 Moshi, tel. 54054, rooftop terrace, excellent views. **The Coffee Tree**: Inside KNCU building near clock tower, Box 3032 Moshi, tel. 55040; slightly run-down, cheap, restaurant with perfect views of Kilimanjaro. **YMCA**: Box 85 Moshi, tel. 52362; shared bathrooms, cafeteria with splendid views of Kilimanjaro.

### Tour Operators

For tips on how to compare prices for Kilimanjaro climbs, see "Safari....," p. 24. **AfriGalaxy Tours & Travel**: CCM Building, Taifa Rd., Box 8340, tel. 53666. **Kilimanjaro Guide Tours and Safaris**: Rengua St., Box 210 Moshi, tel. 50120. **MJ Safaris International**: THB Building, Box 9593 Moshi, tel./fax 52246. **Mauly Tours & Safaris**: Near bus stand, Box 1315 Moshi, tel. 50730. **Shah Tours & Travels**: Near bus stand, Box 1821, tel. 52370. **Trans Kibo Travels**: Inside YMCA, Box 558, tel./fax 52017. **ZARA Travel**: Inside Moshi Hotel, and Rindi Lane, Box 1990 Moshi, tel. 54240. More agents: Check hotels in Marangu.

### Transportation

*BUS:* Several departures a day to Nairobi, Dar es Salaam, Tanga. Frequent service to Himo, Marangu, and constant service to Arusha.

## MARANGU
### Accommodation

*LUXURY:* **Capricorn Hotel**: 2 miles/3 km from Marangu; Box 938 Marangu, tel./fax (55) 51309; small convention hotel in beautiful park.
*MODERATE:* **Kibo Hotel**: Box 102 Marangu, tel. 4 Marangu, fax (55) 52687; hotel has been in exist-

ence since 1889; grand old house in the forest. **Marangu Hotel Kilimanjaro**: Box 40 Moshi, tel. (55) 51307, fax (55) 50639; open, spacious garden with view of Kilimanjaro. *BUDGET: along Marangu-Rongai road:* **Ashanti Lodge**: Box 339 Marangu, tel. 206 Marangu; cabanas with shower and toilet in well-tended garden. **Babylon Lodge**: Box 227 Marangu, tel. 5 Marangu, tel./fax (55) 51315; small hotel in beautiful garden. **Midlands Lodge**: .5 miles/1 km north of Kotela church, signposted; Box 277, tel. 3 Marangu; private house in lush garden, family atmosphere, campsite. *Marangu/Marangu Gate:* **Bismarck Hut Lodge**: 1 mile/1.5 km from Marangu, Box 360 Marangu, tel. 192 Marangu. **Kilimanjaro Peak Hotel**: 3 miles/5.5 km from Marangu, Box 757 Marangu, tel. 238 Marangu.

## THE B1 ROAD (MOSHI-KOROGWE)
### Accommodation

*BUDGET:* Towns with guest houses: **Mwanga**, **Same**, **Mkomazi** (.5 miles/1km off B 1), **Mombo**, **Korogwe**.

## USAMBARA MOUNTAINS
### Accommodation

SONI: *BUDGET:* **Kimalube Hotel**: 9 miles/15 km from Mombo. **New Soni Falls Hotel**: Along Lushoto road west of Soni.
LUSHOTO AND SURROUNDINGS: *BUDGET:* **Lawns Hotel**: On top of hill, at town entrance, Box 33 Lushoto, tel. 5 Lushoto; colonial farm houses. **Mandarin Grand Hotel**: Box 188 Lushoto, tel. 14 Lushoto; prominent view of town, under construction, a few rooms are finished and ready to use. **Stadium Hotel & Lodging**: Next to stadium, Box 41, Lushoto, new, restaurant, bar, popular meeting place. Several more guest houses nearby. *CAMPSITE:* **Bella Vista Viewpoint Campsite**: Next to *Irente Viewpoint*, fantastic views, 3 miles/5 km from Lushoto; walk past Mandarin Hotel. *COLONIAL VILLAS:* **Mueller's Mountain Lodge**, **Grant's Lodge**: 9 miles/14-15 km from Lushoto, near Magamba Forest Reserve with self-guiding hiking paths, tel. Rural Development Associates, Tanga: (53) 42491.
AMANI: Information about Amani Nature Reserve: East Usambara Catchment Forest Project, Box 1449 Tanga, tel. (53) 43453. *BUDGET:* **Amani Rest House**: 22 miles/35 km from Muheza; NIMR (National Institute of Medical Research). **Guest accommodation** of IUCN project: East Usambara Conservation & Agricultural Development, Box 1 Amani, tel. 18 Amani.
MUHEZA: *BUDGET:* **Ambassador**, on the A14 road; and other guest houses.

# ON THE INDIAN OCEAN

**TANGA / PANGANI**

**BAGAMOYO**

**ZANZIBAR / PEMBA**

**DAR ES SALAAM**

**MAFIA / KILWA**

## EAST AFRICA'S GATES TO THE WORLD

The art of building cities was introduced to the East African coastlands by seafaring Persian-Arabian immigrants. Together with the coast dwellers, they have been building harbor towns of durable coral limestone for more than 1,000 years, settlements that prospered as long as circumstances allowed. When the boom was over, they declined, but unlike the mud structures inland, these left sturdy ruins behind them. The oldest harbor towns along the Tanzanian coast were founded by the so-called Shirazi, merchants who were most successful here from the 12th to the 15th centuries. Most outstanding of all these towns is Kilwa, on an island in the south. Most of the smaller and larger islands along this coast can boast stony memorials to this earlier spate of town-building.

The Portuguese arrived in the 16th century, and proved more destructive than constructive. In the 18th and 19th centuries, merchants from Oman resurrected many historical towns (such as Kilwa) or founded new ones (such as Dar

*Preceding pages and left: By bus or by head, local products make their way to the market at Zanzibar.*

es Salaam).After the late 19th century it was the Germans and the British who outfitted the ports according to their ow colonial needs and interests (among them Tanga, Dar es Salaam, Mtwara).

Today, a tourist seeking out East Africa's historic gates to the outer world can find the mysterious decaying remains of once-busy cities, now transformed into sleepy harbors or modern port towns. In the 20th century, Tanzania's coasts on the Indian Ocean have become more attractive. Their white sandy beaches in the shade of coconut palms, as well as the diverse, underwater life of the coral reefs, still intact in places, are factors that have combined to encourage a burgeoning but unobtrusive form of tourism that fortunately demonstrates none of the features of mass tourism.

### TANGA

Once the terminus of the caravans, **Tanga**, in northeast Tanzania, is today a growing regional capital of at least 200,000 inhabitants. Since hydrofoils started making the run Mombasa-Tanga-Pemba-Zanzibar-Dar, a quick, reliable, three-hour passenger service links this port, the third-largest in East Africa, with the largest port, Mombasa. Buses, which run daily, take about four hours to ac-

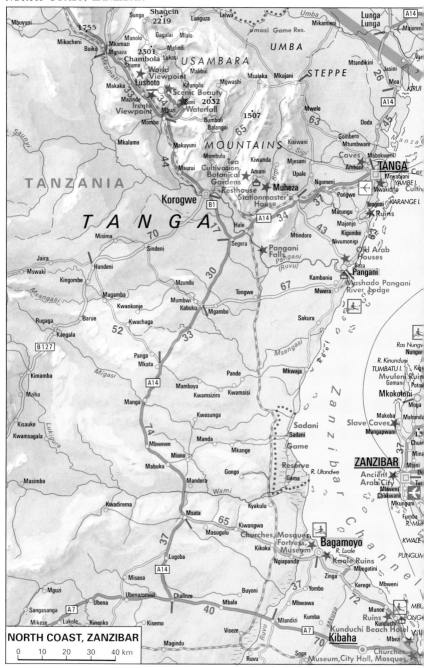

NORTH COAST, ZANZIBAR

0   10   20   30   40 km

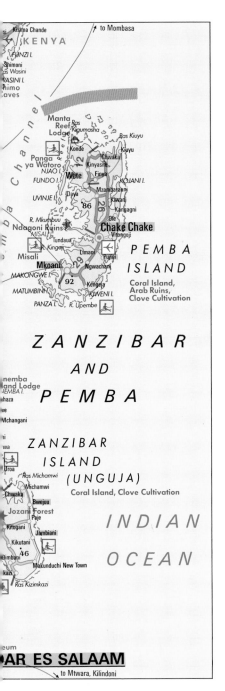

cover the same ground from Tanga to Mombasa (106 miles/170 km, 40 miles/65 km of which are poor sand track up to the Kenyan border), or to travel over perfect asphalt roads to Moshi (219 miles/ 352 km) or to Dar es Salaam (221 miles/ 355 km).

Railway passenger service to Tanga has been discontinued. Yet it was the expanded port and the railway (in 1891 a branch line, no longer extant, to the eastern Usambara Mountains; in 1911 the line to Moshi) which made Tanga a focus of modern development during the German colonial era. In 1893, the Germans began laying out sisal plantations, which still characterize parts of the local landscape.

In its town layout, Tanga still bears the stamp of its colonial heritage. Structures from the German and British eras have continued to hold their own on the three wide main streets in the center of town: **Eckernförde Avenue** (the town of Eckernförde, in northern Germany, is Tanga's sister city), **Market Street** and **Independence Avenue**. A short walk along Independence Avenue is sufficient to expose the kaleidoscope of Tanga's architectural history since the 19th century. The **town hall**, in the west, is a sober building from the early years of Tanzanian independence. The **regional administration**, next door, has its offices in rooms formerly occupied by the Imperial German District Government. This is followed by the **Regional Library**, a neo-Gothic, Moorish-inspired edifice dating from British times, and lovingly maintained. Finally, you reach **Jamhuri Park**, which offers not only benches for the weary under the shade of its trees but also the best view of the harbor and bay. On the left, to the west, you can spy countless little wooden boats in the **fishing harbor**, and to the right, the rest of the **port facilities** with its warehouses and containers as well as its dhows, which skillfully enter and depart the har-

95

bor time and again, bearing heavy cargoes which the dock workers are able to load and unload at remarkable speed. East of the **Clock Tower**, which also dates from the colonial era, you come across the **post office** and shops on a section of Independence Avenue which is quite busy in the daytime, where a modern office building furnishes proof of Tanga's link to the 21st century.

To the east, a green neighborhood of residential villas occupies of the peninsula **Ras Kazone**, a pleasant location for several good hotels, including the **Mkonge Hotel**, situated on the water, which was originally (1951) a house for the Tanganyika Sisal Farmer's Organization.

The railway tracks and station edge the center of town in the south, followed by the densely-built quarter of **Ngamiani** with its checkerboard grid of streets,

*Above: Lateen sails have been the norm on the Indian Ocean for more than 1,000 years. Right: Nets on the beach at Tanga.*

which the colonial regime designed for the city's African population. Here, you can find a busy **bus station** and a large market. Each year, fewer and fewer of the flat-topped houses, roofed with corrugated iron, remain; they are dismantled to make way for new, multi-story buildings, some of them hotels.

**Outings Around Tanga**

Tanga's hotels are a good base from which to explore the tourist attractions of the surrounding area. The Usambara Mountains (see Amani, p. 85) can be reached by way of **Muheza** (A 14 towards Dar, 23 miles/37 km).

In **Amboni** (A 14 towards Mombasa, 5 miles/8 km) you can watch how sisal is processed. Not far away are the sulphur springs of the Greek Galanos, which haven't been in operation for decades and await their revival). Local guides have remarkable stories to tell about the extensive, but untapped network of the limestone **Amboni Caves**, about 1 mile (2

km) away, but most of this information is imparted in Kiswahili. Don't expect either electric lighting or guard-rails along the paths that lead you through this labyrinth of stalagmites and stalactites!

Ocean swimming is an option by the Baobab Hotel, 5 miles/8 km south of Tanga, and the Kingfisher Lodge in **Kigombe** (20 miles/30 km from Tanga or 12 miles/20 km from Pangani). Just 12 miles (20 km) south of Tanga, about half a mile (1 km) off the Pangani road, in **Tongoni** (signposted), is the largest medieval Muslim cemetery on the East African coast, with 40 graves. A mosque and other structures have been dated to the 14th/15th centuries. A local guide is on hand to explain this historic site.

## PANGANI

The **Pangani River** is fed by waterways from Mount Meru and Kilimanjaro as well as from the Pare and Usambara Mountains. On its way through the dry plains south of the mountains, it irrigates fields and supplies electricity. The last energy plants along its course are at Hale and Pangani Falls (37 miles/60 km and 30 miles/50 km from the sea, respectively). While the river flows past forests, bushland and sisal plantations, crocodiles sun themselves nearby, sharing many banks with stands of mangroves. Shortly before it empties into a broad bay of the Indian Ocean, it rushes through a dramatic setting: the right bank becomes a green-grown flank with a narrow strip of beach, on which the mosque and the few houses of **Bweni** crowd together, while **Pangani**, more Arabian in appearance, sprawls over the level ground of the left bank.

Money must have been rolling in from the trade in ivory, rhino-horn and slaves when Mohamed Salim Breki built his palace here in 1810. If he could but see his house today, he would be truly convinced that his macabre superstitions held water: he had live slaves walled into the four corners of the building, in order to ensure its long life. The German colonial administration later had its headquarters here; today, district officials work in this colonnaded, balconied **boma** with its magnificently carved Swahili wooden doors.

By the car ferry, 650 feet (200 m) further on, you reach Jamhuri Street, the promenade along the reinforced bank of the river. Another few steps further on, near the passenger ferry, two very striking buildings lend each other company: the former post office from 1916 with its neo-Gothic portal today houses the **customs** office, while the tall building next door is a slave-dungeon built in the middle of the 19th century. Unruly slaves were flogged on a platform on the second floor; blindfolded slaves were bundled out onto dhows on the river by way of a tunnel in the cellar.

The sand banks at the mouth of the river hinder modern ship traffic; the nearest paved road is 25 miles (40 km) away; the production of sisal has declined: with its **Muhembo Ruins** (2 miles/3 km down the coast, perhaps the fabled *Rhapta* long sought by archaeologists?), and countless Arabian and colonial houses gradually falling into disrepair, Pangani seems to have fallen into a torpor. This is one thing that makes the town so attractive to tourists – together with its river location, pristine ocean coves, several pleasure islands and good fishing. And tourists are well provided for. In addition to diverse lodgings along the river and beaches, there's also a four-star hotel which overlooks the southern bank of the Pangani with unsurpassable views of the town, river and bay.

### South from Pangani

Passing southward through sisal and cashew plantations and lonely coastal lands, 53 miles (85 km) of sand track (no bus transportation) brings you all the way

*Right: Bagamoyo – today a sleepy little town with memories of the glory days of the caravans.*

to **Saadani** (or Sadani), today a fishing village, which saw much more exciting times in its heyday as a 19th century caravan terminus. The town can also be reached from the A14, the Tanga - Dar es Salaam road, via **Miono**, and lies within the boundaries of the **Saadani Game Reserve**. This is famous for its elephants, which come right down to the seashore. The impassable **Wami River** effectively terminates the drive further south.

Even without a four-wheel-drive vehicle, it is possible to travel to **Mabuku** on the A14 during the dry season, continuing south of the Pangani river via **Mwera** through wooded bushland teeming with game. Another 62 miles (100 km) further south along the good asphalt road, a bridge crosses the deep chasm of the Wami valley. **Msata** lies 6 miles (10 km) beyond this bridge.

### BAGAMOYO

Rather than approach **Bagamoyo** via Msata along 40 miles (65 km) of rough mud and sand track, most visitors opt to travel along the 43 miles (70 km) of road from Dar es Salaam, a road which has long been awaiting complete asphalting. The Msata-Bagamoyo track once formed the last leg of the slaves' "trail of suffering" (750 miles/1,200 km), the long hard trek from Lake Tanganyika. "Throw your heart (*moyo*) down," is the way they interpret the town's name, Bagamoyo. How many pitiable figures, but also how many profit-hungry merchants, sensation-seeking travelers and hangers-on did this town see in the 19th century! How many wares were stacked, counted, guarded; how persistently did guides, porters and customers haggle before the caravans finally got underway! And countless dhows sailed past the broad sand beaches of that curving bay.

And where, if at all, can a modern visitor find traces of this tempestuous past in this sleepy district capital? With a good deal

of imagination, he can be transported back to those times of caravans and slaves in the **Caravanserai**, a bit east of the bus stop, which now serves as residential apartments; or, to an even greater degree, with the help of the wealth of documents and artifacts in the **Museum of the Catholic Mission**, founded in 1868. The spacious grounds around its church (from 1872) lie about 1.5 miles (2 km) north of the center of town. The missionaries bought children at the slave market (less often adults, as they were more expensive!), educated them and raised them as Christians. East of the mission, a row of recently-built hotels lines the lovely white sandy beaches, providing different categories of accommodations.

In 1887 the Germans designated Bagamoyo as their capital, but by 1891 they had already moved to Dar es Salaam, where the harbor was more suited to steamships. From the Sultan of Zanzibar they had acquired the privilege of collecting customs duties along the coast. As rulers, they were ruthless. One resistance movement, led by Bushiri, attacked Bagamoyo with, initially, some success. As a reaction, the Germans subsequently erected a number of small fortresses under the guidance of Hermann von Wissmann. One of these has remained, **Dunka Block House** on the road to Msata, and it has been carefully restored. The Germans captured Bushiri in Pangani in 1889, where they hanged him.

Toward the end of the 20th century, many of the town's 19th-century structures were in danger of decaying altogether; recently, however, the responsible authorities have begun to take steps to preseve and restore Bagamoyo's past. Proofs of their interest are the information plaques, renovations and new coats of paint on the caravanserai, the block house, the **fort** (near the BADECO Hotel and the **gallows-tree**), the **boma** and the **customs house**. The town's first **school**, which the merchant Sewa Hadji had built in 1896, is still in use today, open to children of all confessions, as stipulated by the donor. Renovations are underway on more buildings.

On the wide waterfront, lined with mangroves in places, you can watch fishermen, boat-builders and dock-workers at work, the dockers still carrying the heavy burdens from the dhows to shore on their backs, as in centuries gone by. Following the line of the bay southwards, you pass an edifice with a huge *makuti* roof: the **cultural center** (*Chuo ya Sanaa*), where traditional music, dance and theater are preserved and taught. Another 3 miles (5 km) further on, on a spit of land below the village **Kaole**, a caretaker tends the **ruins** of Bagamoyo's predecessor from the Middle Ages: two mosques, a house and graves dating back to the 13th and 15th centuries.

## ZANZIBAR

The city of Zanzibar lies opposite Bagamoyo, hardly 25 miles (40 km) across

*Above: Stonetown and the harbor of Zanzibar. Right: Chatting before a carved doorway in the narrow alleyways of Stonetown.*

the Zanzibar Channel, on a tongue of land on the largest island in East Africa. In ancient writings it was already known as *Unguja*, the "Land of Plenty," and the local population still call it that today. *Zanzibar* was the name of the former island nation that consisted of the islands Unguja (598 square miles/1,554 sq. km), Pemba (348 square miles/906 sq. km) and a few smaller islands, but the name is often used to denote the larger island alone.

The Persian word *zanj*, black, could easily explain the origin of the name, but "Zanzibar" conjures up much more exotic visions: magnificent sultans' palaces; ivory, gold and slaves; the fragrance of tropical spices; dhows full of bold seafarers from India and Arabia; European adventurers, intent on penetrating Africa's unexplored interior...

Zanzibar's legendary fame only grew during the reign of the Omani sultan Seyyid Said (1804-1856), who transferred his seat from Oman to the city of Zanzibar. This was the hub for the sudden increase in slave traffic from the African mainland – at a time when critics had long since condemned the slave trade in Europe and America. Slaves were needed on French-owned plantations in the Indian Ocean and on Pemba and Unguja, after Omani landowners had established the clove plantations which made Zanzibar the world's largest producer of this spice. Clove oil, ivory and copal resin from East Africa were being sold around the world. Indian bankers, American and European consuls, and merchants supported the sultans to serve their own interests. After 1890, the sultanate became a British protectorate.

**A Stroll Through Stonetown**

The fantastic boom in trade, reports of explorers' adventures and unsettling descriptions of the slaves' suffering all influenced the international perception of Zanzibar in the 19th century. Many stone reminders of these times confront the modern traveler in **Stonetown**, the western tip of the peninsula where Zanzibar is situated. For the most impressive first sight of the town, travel by water from the southwest, taking the ships' route from Dar es Salaam. In the lush, tropical green surrounding the city center are nestled such bright colonial edifices as the **hospital**, the former **State House**, or private villas and town houses, all the way to Cape **Ras Shangani**. There, the newly-built hotel **Serena Inn** and, a few steps on, the luxuriously renovated buildings of the **Tembo Hotel**, even mingling with the historic waterfront edifices, hardly spoil the effect. The massive, yellow-gray **fort** from the early 18th century seems subdued by the green expanse of the **Forodhani Gardens**, while it is impossible to overlook the tall, slender tower of **Beit el-Ajaib** (House of Wonders), the palace of the Sultan Seyyid Barghash (1870-1888), an immense white building with colonnades on every

floor. The next palace structure, a rather elongated building, is now a **museum**. The sultan's families lived in the **People's Palace** from 1890 until the sultanate was abolished in 1964; furnished rooms and exhibitions acquaint visitors with their lifestyle. And before you have come so far that the harbor warehouses block your view, there is a crowning finish to this city panorama, the painstakingly restored **Old Dispensary** (*Nasur Nurmohamed Dispensary*), complete with ornate carved wooden ornamentation.

In the narrow confines of Stonetown, the houses are often four or five stories high, not infrequently topped with a roofed observation deck. Towering above this maze of roofs are the slender minarets of several mosques, as well as the single pointed tower of the **Anglican Cathedral**, where the slave market was held until 1873, and the twin towers of the Catholic **St. Joseph's Cathedral**, not far from the fort.

Even closer inspection may not dim one's first impression of a storybook

Oriental city. The intricate network of streets between the high walls of the houses leads to tiny squares of green, past ornately carved doorways, decorative wooden balconies, friendly shops, restaurants and a growing number of hotels and guest-houses in lovingly restored historical buildings. You can get a city map in many souvenir shops or at the Office of Tourism in the northern segment of **Creek Road**, that broad street which separates Stonetown, the upper-class neighborhood, from **Ng'ambo** ("the other side"), where the less privileged live. The island's buses take off from the **bus stand** in Creek Road, a few steps away from the **market**, which is very busy in the mornings and well worth a visit. The **Museum of Natural History** and the **National Museum** are straight on down at the end of the road.

*Above: Colonial buildings are restored with care in Stonetown. Right: The beaches of Zanzibar's east coast aren't just for foreign tourists.*

You can spend hours strolling through and exploring Stonetown's maze of narrow streets; if you're really hungry for knowledge, engage a local guide. On **Hamamni Street** (*hamamu*: public bath) you come upon the **Persian Baths**, which Sultan Barghash (1870-1888) had built and which were in use until 1920. Rarely will you get hopelessly lost, as the heart of town is not overly large: you'll soon stumble across Creek Road or one of the streets which run parallel to the coast – perhaps enabling you to reach the popular terrace of the **Africa House Hotel** just in time for tea, or cocktails. Once a British club, this establishment has seen better days, but its view of the sea at sunset is unsurpassed.

### The Island Unguja – Landscape, Beaches and Ocean

The island presents two different facades. The western half is sheathed in lush green woodland and plantations, with several chains of hills, rivers, fields

of sugar cane and rice: in short, the fertile side of the island, and the only section where you can find clove and other plantations found. On a **spice tour**, a drive round to these spice planatations, you generally get to know a few historic sights and highlights of the island as well as a lot of new information about spices and other useful tropical plants.

The sultans and wealthy landowners can hardly be faulted for laying out their palaces in such a heavenly setting, most with views of the sea. Sultan Barghash not only erected his **Chukwani Palace** (today a ruin) just a few miles south of the city; but he also had a mansion built in **Mbweni**, later called **Kirk House** and inhabited by the British general consul. The **Maruhubi ruins** lie to the north, 2 miles (3 km) outside the center of town, representing the scant remains of Sultan Barghash's harem (he supposedly had 99 wives).

The nearby ruins of the palace of **Mtoni** date back to the 1820s, when the Arab Saleh Bin Haramili introduced the first clove trees to the island. The last sultan's summer palace has been well preserved in **Kibweni**. In 1850 Sultan Seyyid Said had elegant **Persian Baths** built for his Persian wife in **Kidichi**, not by the sea, but rather in the midst of verdant surroundings.

The **Slave Caves of Mangapwani** (12 miles/20 km north of the city of Zanzibar) attest to a completely different chapter of Zanzibar's history. Illicit, undercover slave trade continued long after the slave market was officially closed in 1873 – even into the 20th century. During the daytime, slaves were hidden along the coast in inaccessible limestone caves, thence to be shipped out under cover of night.

In the north of the island, a few miles short of its northern tip (Ras Nungwi), you can find the remains of Portuguese houses in the community of **Mvuleni**, and, further west, the pre-Portuguese **Fukuchani Ruins**. The most extensive fields of ruins of the Shirazi era lie on **Tumbatu**, an offshore island to the west.

103

This was one center of the two realms of Unguja, before Omani rulers made themselves supreme masters in the 18th century. The other center was in **Dunga**, in the middle of the main island, about 12 miles (20 km) east of today's capital. Little remains of the 18th-century palace of the *Mwinyi Mkuu*, the local lord over the Hadimu people. This people suffered greatly under the Omani rulers, who took their fertile land away from them by force and drove many Hadimu east or obliged them to do slave labor on the spice plantations.

Much of the fertile land on the west side of the island was densely wooded before it was converted into plantations. Today only a small nature reserve conveys an impression of the original landscape, **Jozani Forest,** a scant 25 miles (40 km) on good road, southeast of Stonetown. There you can generally

*Above: Kirk's dwarf monkey in the Jozani Forest. Right: Kizimkazi Beach: popular for its dolphins.*

watch the rare endemic variety of red Colobus monkeys romping about in the trees.

The nature trail in **Masingini Forest Reserve**, only 4 miles (7 km) from the capital, gives a general perspective of the range of tropical trees on Zanzibar and their many uses.

And here you come to the other aspect of Unguja: the eastern half is of porous coral limestone, dry bushland brightened up by the occasional baobab tree. Nonetheless, many visitors to the island fondly remember their stay on this eastern half, mainly because of its coast. An unbroken band of coral protects the entire eastern side from the surging waves of the Indian Ocean. Miles of sandy beaches sweep along a coastline subjected to strong tides, with, behind them, a wide belt of coconut palms, and the *makuti*-roofed huts of the fishing villages scattered throughout. Recently, hotels have begun to introduce themselves into this picture, most of them small, offering accommodation in every category between "bud-

get" and "luxury." Bumpy roads lead to the bungalow-hotels in the villages of **Jambiani**, **Bwejuu** and **Pungwe** in the southeast, or to the beaches north of the enchanting **Chwaka Bay**. The reef-islet **Mnemba Island** seems to belong to another world – and boasts a single, fine hotel.

**Ras Nungwi**, the northern tip of Unguja, presents both facets of the island at the same time: the slightly austere, dry east with its wave-cut coral platform, and the lush, verdant growth of the west. Neither low nor high tides noticeably restrict swimming and snorkeling fun; and the budding tourist industry is bringing this village of fishermen and boatbuilders important new employment opportunites in the simple restaurants and hotels.

The few sandy beaches along the west coast seem like precious jewels in their tropical green settings. However, it's beyond these coasts, in the waters of the Indian Ocean, green, turquoise, and all shades of blue, that many visitors become aware of the true wealth of treasure that is Zanzibar: the world of the small islands offshore, before Zanzibar town; the coast, which you can tour by boat; dolphins playing at **Kizimkazi Beach** way south; deep-sea fishing, snorkeling or diving. There are about a dozen well-equipped tour agents operating in the coral gardens all around the island, capable of giving you a professional introduction to this wonderful underwater world.

## PEMBA

Unguja and Pemba are like two sisters, one older and much more glamorous than the other. Most people who hear the name "Zanzibar," which actually applies to both islands, tend to think first of the repute of the larger island, especially its oriental capital with its deep harbors. Is Pemba a wallflower?

There are three small towns on Pemba, all of them ports. However, only **Mkoani** in the southwest has a sufficiently long

landing and deep enough water to accommodate the express ferries that have been in use since 1996. These modern catamarans operate almost daily, taking approximately 2.5 hours to get from Zanzibar to Mkoani (Mkoani-Tanga 1 hour 15 minutes).

The bay of **Chake-Chake**, the capital of Pemba (which was protected by an **Arabian Fort**, and the two canons of its battery between city and harbor, as early as the 18th century), lies at the end of a 3-mile (5-km) long entrance, which very nearly dries up at low tide. The skippers who sail into the small, picturesque port of Wete have to be well-acquainted with the many offshore islands, reefs and sand bars. Travelers who are in a hurry can take one of the daily flights to **Karume Airport,** 3.5 miles/6 km east of Chake-Chake.

*Above: The magical underwater world of Zanzibar's coral reefs. Right: The entertaining, bloodless bullfights of Pemba – a Portuguese legacy.*

The tiny harbors are unsuited to larger developments; nowhere on the banks of Pemba are there deep, wide entries between the shoals. Rather, mangroves cover broad stretches of its shores. Steep inclines make many shores unapproachable. Compared with Unguja, Pemba is only sparingly blessed with sand beaches, the longest, **Panga ya Watoro** in the northwest, is not even 3 miles (5 km) long. And this is exactly why Pemba enthusiasts go into such raptures: one special feature of the island is precisely the fact that its beaches are so short, so rare, and furthermore so difficult to reach (often only accessible by boat).

Given all this, it's small wonder that the tourist facilities on Pemba are so low-key. In 1997, there was only a single tourist hotel open on the island; a second one is planned. Each of the three towns has one hotel (simple quarters, rather for traveling businessmen), as well as modest guest-houses.

The lone tourist hotel lies in splendid isolation on Panga ya Watoro and is an

ideal base for fans of water sports. Its name, **Manta Reef Lodge**, indicates its greatest attraction, which divers encounter here from February to March: giant mantas. Diving season is interrupted by the rainy season from March into June. To compensate for the lack of diving-bases, a 79-foot (24 m) sailing catamaran, the *Inula*, makes 3- to 13-day cruises around Pemba. The best time for deep-sea fishing is from December to March.

The island itself has greater inherent scenic charm than Unguja: it is much greener, a hill country in stark relief with many steep, wooded slopes. A surprising feature are the numerous low-lying valleys, with vegetable plots and irrigated rice-paddies. The plantations are more extensive here than on the neighboring island, with rubber trees, coconuts, and, above all, more than three million clove trees. The fragrance of cloves spices the air of the whole island.

Several considerable settlements date from the Shirazi era. The **Ndagoni Ruins**

east of the tip of **Ras Mkumbuu** peninsula are best reached by boat from Wete or Chake-Chake. Interesting features here include one of the largest Friday mosques of East Africa, houses and tombs dating from the 11th to the 16th centuries. From the 11th to the 14th century, there was a town on the islet of **Mtambwe Mkuu**, which has gained more renown for the hoard of silver coins found there in 1984; the foundations of the town, however, have long since crumbled.

During the 15th century a cruel ruler nicknamed Mkama Ndume ("scrotum milker") reigned over a **fortress,** east of the village of **Pujini** (3.5 miles/6 km south of the airport), complete with ramparts and moat – the only one of its kind on the East African coast. Within the ramparts, remnants of the foundations of several houses are still to be seen, also a well and a subterranean cistern.

Mkama Ndume's son Harouni showed little inclination to live in the compound of his terrible father. He built his own settlement to the east of the village of **Chwaka** (10 minutes' walk from the tarmac road); it seems to have continued to hold its own until the Portuguese finally destroyed it.

Although few traces of the Portuguese occupation of Pemba remain today, the amusing and bloodless bullfights which are held annually in some of the island's villages, before the lesser rains in November, are said to be a Portuguese legacy.

Rather than actually conquering Pemba, the Omani rulers established themselves as rulers by means of a treaty with the local population (1822). The farmers shared in the clove-boom in the 19th century. Few Omani property-owners were actively engaged in plantation cultivation.

The people of Pemba are extremely self-confident and independent, and aren't crazy about interference from their larger sister island. The results of the first multi-party elections in 1996 were characteristic of the contrast: on Pemba, the CUF won nearly all the votes, while on Unguja it was the "established" CCM that triumphed.

## DAR ES SALAAM

Inhabited by more than 2 million people, this largest city on the East African coast is at the same time one of the youngest: **Dar es Salaam** ("haven of peace"). When Seyyid Majid became the Sultan of Zanzibar in 1856, there was a mere fishing village on **Kurasini Creek**, about 47 miles (75 km) from Zanzibar and nearly the same distance from Bagamoyo. On the north bank of a sweeping bend just before the Kurasini estuary, the sultan planned a modern port, suitable for steam ships. His palace, a guest house, a mosque, warehouses and a few houses of commerce were built in 1867. Coconut plantations were put in around the young settlement.

In 1870 Majid died suddenly. His successor, Seyyid Barghash, showed greater ability in building palaces on Unguja than in continuing the city planning of his predecessor. The young port stagnated for two decades, until 1891, when the Germans decided to move their capital here from Bagamoyo, having just purchased from the then-Sultan of Zanzibar, Seyyid Ali, the 10-mile (16-km) strip of coast from the Kenyan border to the Ruvuma river. Thus Dar became the most significant gateway for their import and export trade in East Africa. The Germans even dreamed of penetrating into Africa's interior for the purpose of shipping copper out of Katanga (Congo/Zaire) via Dar es Salaam: it took then nine years,

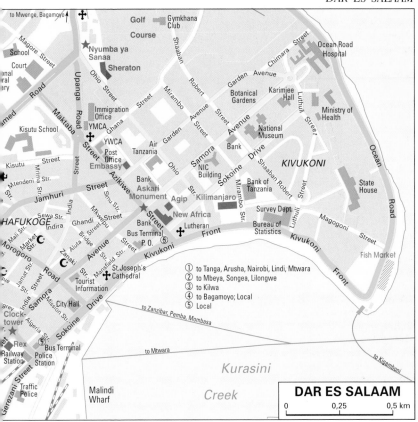

from 1905 to 1914, to build the 777-mile (1,250 km) railway from Dar to Kigoma on Lake Tanganyika. The **Central Line Station** is situated near the harbor.

In Tanzania's more recent history, it was a wise decision to build the 1,162-mile (1,870 km) stretch of railway from Dar to Zambia, with China's help, between 1970 to 1975. The monumental terminus of the **TAZARA Station** lies outside the center of town, about halfway to the **airport**, in the southern part of the city.

### In the Center of Dar

Toward the end of the 20th century, Dar es Salaam is turning into quite a modern city. The original Arabian structures have almost totally disappeared; they were originally concentrated around where today's **ferry landing** and, further west, the warehouses of **Malindi Wharf** are located. **Sokoine Drive** is a busy street along the harbor front, allowing view after view of the surprisingly clear blue water of the harbor and the green shores of the peninsula opposite. The **Old Boma** at the corner of Sokoine and Morogoro Road dates back to 1867, to the times of Sultan Majid. More striking are two churches with their spires, built around 1900: the neo-Gothic, Catholic **St. Joseph's Cathedral**, opposite the ferries, and two blocks further east, the **Lutheran Church**. The latter, with its brown window-frames and brick-red spire, is truly a gem, set off by the modern, functional structure of the **New Africa Hotel**, at the point where the **Kivukoni Front** (*kivuko* = ferry) begins its sweep around the bay to the **Kigamboni ferry**. Walking in the shade of mango and wild almond trees along this street on the harbor side, you pass countless sidewalk vendors, their wares spread out on the pavement before them. On the other side of the street, you can see some colonial-era buildings: the **Hotel Management School** at the corner of **Ohio Street** was once a German, then a British club. Near the driveway to the **Kilimanjaro Hotel** (a functional high-rise building, but with fantastic views from its rooftop restaurant!), you can see a long row of former colonial administrative buildings which now house the **Ministry of Education**, **Department of Statistics**, **Department of Surveying** and **Supreme Court**.

A little further on, just after the Kigamboni ferry, Kurasini Creek flows into the Indian Ocean; from this point of land on, **Ocean Road** follows the coast-line, shaded by casuarina trees. On the offshore side of the road, framed in park-like grounds, stand the magnificent **State House**, a Moorish-style edifice erected in 1922, which served as the governor's seat in British times, and the **Old German Hospital**, a lovingly restored fortress-like construction. The parliament (*Bunge*) holds its assemblies in **Kerimjee Hall**, named for its donor; and the **National Museum** is housed in two buildings, one dating from 1940, decorated with colorful, ornamental tiles, and a simple modern building constructed in 1963. Laid out in 1893, the **Botanical Garden** covers an area equal to several city blocks; further north, the green ex-

panse of a **golf course** can be seen stretching off into the distance.

While these old villas, ministries and important institutions have plenty of room in this quasi-parkland framed by the ocean and the harbor entrance, the picture changes abruptly as soon as you reach **Maktaba Street** and its continuation to the Lutheran Church, **Azikiwe Street**: it's here that the densely built-up business districts – and residentialneighborhoods as well – of the city center begin. As the end of the millenium approaches, more and more austerely functional and post-modern office buildings and hotels are poking up into the skyline, and the streets which were planned in colonial times can hardly handle the volume of today's traffic. There are astounding contrasts in this part of town: in the southern section of busy **Samora Avenue** (south from the **Askari Monument** on Azikiwe Street), tourists can find attractive shops housed in buildings of a whole range of architectural styles from over the last 100 years; **Tourist Information** is located in the modern **UNESCO House**; forking off further south is **Mosque Street**, where there is, as well as mosques, a concentration of residential and business edifices belonging to Muslim Asians, many built during the British era.

The northern part of the city center in **Kisutu Street** has an entirely different flavor: several **Hindu temples**, schools, and recently-built apartment buildings set the tone in this surprisingly quiet inner-city street, which, in the evenings is filled not only with the music and fragrances from the temples, but also with many well-turned out Indian families. It's hard to imagine that, less than 500 feet (100 m) away, traffic is speeding along the ring road which circumnavigates the inner city (**Bibi Titi Mohamed Road**, formerly UWT Road). This street and the broad belt of green called **Mnazi Mmoja** ("a coconut palm") divide the southwest-

*Right: Toward the end of the 20th century, skyscrapers started to crowd out the cozy colonial buildings of Dar es Salaam.*

ern part of the city center from **Kariakoo** (a corruption of the word *carrier corps*), a quarter that was laid out in the colonial period for the African population: today, it's colorful, hectic, loud and not always fragrant, and is new and unfamiliar to many visitors. Right in the middle of all this is a huge covered market, surrounded by throngs of people, with, in the grid of streets around that, bazaars, mosques, apartments and several multi-story, often inexpensive hotels. And although there seems to be hardly any room for anything else, the streets around the market are the last stop for many buses to and from towns in the surrounding area, e.g. Bagamoyo or Kilwa. Make sure to allow yourself sufficient time to find the right bus stop!

### Dar: Culture and Leisure

Dar is a city of many faces: the spacious, modern university on the western outskirts of town; to the north, on a peninsula, the hotels and beaches of the upper-class neighborhoods of **Oyster Bay** and **Msasani**. Any visitor looking for arts and crafts will find quite a variety in the **Nyumba ya Sanaa** (House of Culture) next to the **Sheraton Hotel**, southwest of the golf course; while in the quarter known as **Mwenge**, there are more than 100 Makonde-carvers' workshops, antique shops and souvenir vendors to tempt prospective buyers. On the way there from the center of town, you pass **Kijiji ya Makumbusho** (Museum Village), an instructive facility which presents replicas of the huts of Tanzania's many different tribes; on weekends, traditional dances are performed on the grounds.

Those city-dwellers who can afford to do so generally opt to spend their leisure time in the surrounding countryside, often by the sea. About 12 miles (20 km) north on the good asphalt road, **Kunduchi** has quite a few hotels along the coast and, in addition, several inviting islets nearby, good for picnics and swimming; there are also **ruins** from the 15th-18th

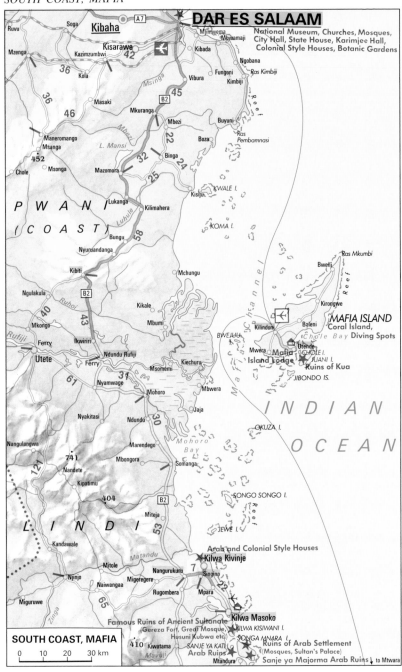

# DAR ES SALAAM

National Museum, Churches, Mosques,
City Hall, State House, Karimjee Hall,
Colonial Style Houses, Botanic Gardens

Ruvu  Soga  **Kibaha**  A7

Mzenga  Kazimzumbwi  42
Kisarawe

36  Kola

Mjimwema  Mbwamaji

Kibada

Ngobana  *Ras Kimbiji*

Masaki  B2  45  Vibura  Fungani  Kimbiji

Mkuranga

Mbezi  Buyuni

Maneromango  32  22  Boza  *Ras Pembamnasi*

Msanga  *L. Mansi*

452  Msonga  Mazomora  Binga  24

Chole  25

Lukanga  Kilimahera  Kisiju  *KWALE I.*

**P W A N I**  58  *KOMA I.*

**( C O A S T )**

Bungu

Nyuruandanga  *Ras Mkumbi*

Bweni

Kibiti  Mchungu  Kirongwe

Ngulakula  B2  *MAFIA ISLAND*

40  43  Kikale  Kilindoni  Baleni  Coral Island,  Diving Spots

Mkongo  Mbumi  *Chole Bay*

Ikwiriri  *BWEJUU*  *CHOLE I.*

*Rufiji*  Ferry  Mwera  Mafia  Utende  *JUANI I.*

**Utete**  61  Ndundu Rufiji  Kiechuru  Island Lodge  **Ruins of Kua**

Ferry  31  Msomeni  *JIBONDO IS.*

Nyamwage  Mohoro  Mbwera

Jaja  **I N D I A N**

Nyakitasi  Ndundu  30  *OKUZA I.*

Nangulangwa  741  Marendego  *Mohoro Bay*  **O C E A N**

121  Nandete  Mbongora  Somanga

Kipatimu

404  B2  *SONGO SONGO I.*

Miteja  53

**L I N D I**  *JEWE I.*

Kandawale  **Arab and Colonial Style Houses**

Mitole  Nangurukuru  7  ★ **Kilwa Kivinje**

Njinjo  Migeregere  Singino

Naiwangaa  Rugombera  Mpara

Miguruwe  65

★ **Kilwa Masoko**

**Famous Ruins of Ancient Sultanate**  *KILWA KISIWANI I.*
(Gereza Fort, Great Mosque,  *SONGA MNARA I.*  **Ruins of Arab Settlement**
Husuni Kubwa etc)  (Mosques, Sultan's Palace)
410  Kiwatama  *SANJE YA KATI*  **Sanje ya Majorma Arab Ruins** ↓ to Mtwara
*Arab Ruins*
Mtandura

## SOUTH COAST, MAFIA

0   10   20   30 km

centuries. The trip to **Ras Kutani** is a bit longer and more strenuous (20 miles/30 km from the Kigamboni ferry), but you're rewarded, when you get there, with a stay in its luxurious hotel, surrounded by a veritable coastal paradise. Bagamoyo is also becoming more and more popular as a destination for weekend vacationers.

## MAFIA

Once a week the former Mediterranean ferry *Canadian Spirit* chugs from Dar to Mtwara and back. On the way it makes a stop at **Mafia Island**. The ship hugs the coast for about four hours and you gaze on white beaches and stands of mangroves, on dhows, dolphins and terns. The ship enters open waters by **Ras Pembamnazi**, passes several coral reefs, then moves into **Mafia Channel**. Count on about eight hours from Dar to Mafia Island; by the time the passengers have reached land with all their luggage, another two hours may have gone by. The port of **Kilindoni**, Mafia's capital, doesn't have a proper landing; so small motorboats and rowboats deal with embarking and disembarking passengers. The tides vary by as much as 11 feet (3.3 m) in the Mafia archipelago: at low tide, no one can avoid the walk through the shallow harbor water to get to shore, since even the flattest-bottomed boats draw too much water to make it in the last 650 feet (200 m).

If you have no time for these amusements, you can take the short, but very lovely flight from the Dar domestic airport to Mafia Island. Small aircraft take only 40 minutes, and there are daily flights, either direct or via Ras Kutani, to Mafia's landing-strip, right next door to the community of Kilindoni. This flight is an attraction in itself: the planes fly over the southern suburbs of Dar, offering a view of the green, sparsely-populated coastlands, then of coral islands, dotted with palms, lying in the clear, blue

Indian Ocean, with, in the distance, the yellow-brown Rufiji fanning out into the sea, its sediments streaking northwards with the coastal current; and, finally, the green cluster of the islands of Mafia, clearly defined by the edges of its reef – all an enlightening perspective on a landscape well known to seafarers for at least 1,200 years.

## Heavenly "Underworld"

The Arab word *morfieyeh* means "group," giving a plausible explanation for the name of the Mafia Archipelago. In addition to Mafia itself, the coral reef, which forms an effective frame to the group of islands and extends far to the south, encircles the inhabited islands of **Chole**, **Juani**, **Jibondo** and, further west, towards the mighty river delta of the Rufiji, **Bwejuu**.

It was probably the Shirazi rulers of Kilwa who seized the Mafia islands and founded the settlement **Kisimani Mafia** on the southwest promontory of the main island, **Ras Kisimani**. Today's visitors can recognize the few 13th-century ruins only at low tide, as the sea has reclaimed this historic spot.

Mafia was still under the rule of the powerful town of Kilwa (a good 60 miles/100 km south) when the Portuguese destroyed it in 1505; they continued to demand taxes from the inhabitants of the islands Juani and Jibondo well into the 17th century. On the northwest side of the island Juani lay **Kua**, a sprawling town of stone houses and mosques. When the Portuguese lost influence in Swahili territories through the fall of Mombasa in 1698, the Mafia islands found themselves no better off: pirate raids caused the inhabitants no end of worry. The cruelest attack occurred during the rule of the Omani sultan Seyyid Said (1804-1856): the Sakalava tribe from Madagascar is said to have landed 80 boats on Juani and killed or made slaves of Kua's inhabitants. The city was given up; you can walk around its ruins, scattered throughout the fields and forests of the area, most of them dating from the 18th century.

On the small island of Chole (only 250 acres/1 sq. km), which you can reach on foot from Juani at low tide, arose the new capital of the archipelago: **Chole Mjini** (Chole in-the-town). Under the rulers of Zanzibar it flourished through trade in coconuts, copal and slaves until 1890, when Mafia fell under German jurisdiction. These colonial lords erected their **boma** right on the small harbor. With the advent of ships with deeper draughts, the Germans moved the capital to its present location in Kilindoni in 1913. Slowly, the stone houses on Chole fell into disrepair and the community dwindled to a mere village. In an unusual project, the villagers have, since 1993, joined the builder of a small hotel in trying to halt the course of decay and maintain and use the old structures. Visitors are provided with information about the town's history, the traditional **shipyard**, the flying foxes (*Pteropus seychellensis comorensis*) resting in the trees during the daytime, as well as guidelines to proper behavior and etiquette with regard to the local population.

The Mafia-Chole crossing takes only a few minutes from **Utende**, where there are two hotels for discriminating guests. Here, in the safety of **Chole Bay**, tourists can not only enjoy the tropical setting, taking in the changing colors of the water and the island, but also, by means of dhows or motorboats, they can take excursions: go fishing, or encounter the unusual colors, shapes and varieties of the flora and fauna in underwater **Mafia Island Marine Park** under the guidance of a diving instructor. While large sections

*Right: Only during the dry season is the mighty Rufiji calm enough for ferries to cross.*

of Tanzania's 500-mile (800-km) long coast suffers increasingly from ecological misdeeds – illegal dynamite fishing, coral mining, and discharge of untreated sewage, among other sins – this park represents an effort to achieve a controlled, conservation-oriented use of this 154-square-mile (400 sq. km) area, which encompasses the southern coast of the main island and the southern and western zones of sea bordering the reefs and the islands.

The 152-square-mile (396-sq. km) Mafia archipelago has to feed around 40,000 inhabitants: they live from fishing and fish processing (there's a factory in Kilindoni); farming with some animal husbandry, mostly on the northern half of the island; or the plantations which dominate in the south, especially coconuts (processd in **Ngombeni**, 2.5 miles/4 km west of Kilindoni). In the dry season, it's no problem to drive the 9-mile (15-km) long road between Kilindoni and Utende; there is no public transportation.

### KILWA

These two extraordinarily attractive tourist destinations of Mafia and Kilwa have one thing in common: they are not easy to reach. During the rainy season, a bus makes the run between Dar and **Kilwa** twice a week. It is a good 190 miles (300 km) and takes 12-13 hours. The slow progress is due mainly to the potholes in the 84-mile (135-km) asphalt road from Dar to **Kibiti**; the wait in **Ndundu** for the Rufiji ferry must also be factored in; nor does the dusty sand track between **Ikwiriri** and **Nangurukuru** allow any speed. Motorists are appeased only by the excellent stretches of asphalt between Kibiti and Ikwiriri as well as Nangurukuru and **Kilwa Masoko**, neither of which are even 18 miles (30 km) in length. Not only are the sand tracks impassable in the rainy season, but the ferry can no longer cross Rufiji's

raging currents at this time of year. Coming from the south, it is only 106 miles (170 km) to Nangurukuru, but this road is in such terrible condition that a bus takes from 6 to 8 hours during the dry season, while no transportation is possible during the rains. Kilwa Masoko has a landing-strip for small planes, but there are no regularly-scheduled flights.

Confusingly, the name Kilwa applies to several of the communities here: Kilwa Masoko is today the capital, complete with district administration. The 19th century slave- and ivory-trade center, **Kilwa Kivinje**, spreads out along the sea 12.5 miles (20 km) to the north. To distinguish it from these two mainland towns, the original Kilwa was designated **Kilwa Kisiwani** ("Kilwa on-the-island"), a fitting name, considering its location.

### Rise and Fall of Kilwa Kisiwani

Despite its historic significance and the irresistible magic of the centuries-old ruins on the islands south of Kilwa Ma-soko, only a few hundred travelers make their way there each year. In order to reach these treasures, the tourist first has to obtain written permission to visit the historical sites; this involves showing his passport at the Department of Antiquities (*mambo ya kale*) in the Cultural Office (*ofisi ya utamaduni*), which is free of charge, and then finding a boat. Dhows make the short crossing to Kilwa Kisi-wani in anywhere between 20 and 45 minutes, depending on the direction of the wind, and it is an unforgettable experience. People have been sailing along the East African coast in quite similar boats for more than 1,000 years, calling at cities very much like the famed Kilwa. Among many others, in 1331, came the "globetrotter" Ibn Battuta, who originally hailed from Morocco.

Whether the legendary Sultan Ali Bin al-Hasan really came from Persian Shiraz is still a matter for conjecture, but he is said to have purchased the island country around the 11th century. The oldest stone structures of Kilwa date back to the 12th century. A 14-day sail further south lay Sofala, where gold from Zimbabwe was brought to the coast; buyers awaited this commodity in Europe, East Asia and the Arab world. African gold, copper, rhino-horn, ambergris and ivory were trans-shipped in Kilwa in exchange for silk, spices, porcelain and other goods from Arabia, India or China. In the 14th and 15th centuries, Kilwa was in its prime, minted its own coinage, and was quite possibly the most important town of its day along the East African coast.

Toward the end of the 15th century, the Portuguese learned of the wealth of East Africa, lusted for the gold from Zimbabwe and saw in the destruction of Kilwa their chance of seizing the trade in gold for themselves. In 1505 they devastated the town, which never again attained its former significance. By the end of the 17th century, Oman had broken Portuguese power with the fall of Mombasa, and this East African coastal region was suddenly infused with new life. Kilwa Kisiwani profited for a time, especially through the slave trade for the French plantations that had been established on Mauritius since 1776. However, by the beginning of the 19th century, a harbor on the mainland proved to be a more desirable terminus for the inland ivory and slave caravan routes. Kilwa "on-the-island" had had its day, and, 16 miles (25 km) farther north, Kilwa Kivinje's star was rising.

### A Walk Around Kilwa Kisiwani

The town lies on the northwest corner of the island. Ships still land in the very same harbor which once formed the northern part of the town center. The eastern half of this historic area is now occupied by a village with clean-swept paths and gardens carefully fenced in as

*Right: The crumbling walls of Gereza still guard the harbor of Kilwa Kisiwani.*

protection from the roving goats, home to families of fishermen and farmers. There is a small shop and a tiny tea-room. The inhabitants draw their water from wells driven many feet deep down into the hard limestone.

The most significant structures stand in open, park-like grounds to the west of the settlement. Rusty railway tracks and an overturned trolley are some of the faint reminders of the archaeological investigations that took place here under the direction of Neville Chittick from 1958-1962. A local guide accompanies visitors to the island, bringing with him an English account of the most important ruins.

An edifice known as the **Gereza** towers over the western end of the harbor, its crenellations visible from afar – although this fortress is no defense against the Indian Ocean, which is wearing down its northern walls. After 1800, Omani troops used guard-post and prison a fort that was built there by the Portuguese, shortly after the destruction of Kilwa in 1505. Until 1513, they kept watch here on the harbor; after that, when there no longer seemed to be any danger of Kilwa's resurrection, they withdrew. In 1857, entering the building through the eastern portal carved in the Swahili manner, Speke, the renowned explorer of Africa, could still decipher its year of construction: 1807.

The **Great Mosque**, 650 feet (200 m) further on, proves to have the longest history. The ground plan reveals two mosques, built one behind the other: in the north, a small one from the 11th or 12th century, today roofless. Its flat roof was presumably supported by wooden columns. To the west, you can make out its place of ritual ablutions. The powerful main edifice continues to the south, its roof of vaults and domes supported by coral-block pillars. Outside the building to the west, delicate octagonal columns lie scattered on the ground. The ground plan and roof of the large building bore

much the same form as they do today as early as the 14th century; in those days, however, these slender pillars supported its roof. In the long run, they proved not to be durable enough, so in the 15th century, in the course of reconstruction, they were replaced by the stronger columns of coral blocks. Another place of ablutions lies immediately to the south, with, behind it, a complicated stone house dating back to Kilwa's heyday in the 15th century, known as the **Great House**.

Further west, you come upon a stone column towering over the **Small Mosque**. Its vaults, domes and *mihrab*, or prayer niche, are decorated with green-glazed ceramic bowls, which enable experts to date the building to the 15th century. More mosques, smaller and less well-preserved, are scattered throughout the town.

In the west, Kilwa had a city district surrounded by its own wall, a *makutani* ("in-the-great-wall"), which probably sheltered the buildings of the sultan and the administration. The most conspicuous building, with towering walls, was the sultan's palace, erected in the 18th century, its massive appearance underlined by the giant baobab trees growing nearby. For many of the structures built in the 18th and 19th centuries, people made use of the coral stones that had originally been used to construct houses in the Middle Ages.

This fate was not shared by the most magnificent structure on the island, as it lies 1.5 miles (2 km) out of town: **Husuni Kubwa**, the Great Palace. Built around 1300, it occupies a commanding position on a spur above the shipping channel between island and mainland. The palace also impressed Ibn Battuta in 1331 with its luxurious chambers, baths and terraces, as well as storerooms, servants' quarters, etc. Steps led down to the strand, where ships could put to shore. Close by, on the other side of a gully, stood a rectangular walled enclosure fitted out with turrets, **Husuni Ndogo**, Small Palace, whose purpose is still a puzzle to archaeologists. Both structures show signs of having been abandoned by

117

the 14th century, although they were still unfinished, and it is thought that the sultans resided in town from then on.

### Songo Mnara

Kilwa's sultans were so powerful in the 14th and 15th centuries that they ruled not only Mafia and other islands, but were even capable of coping with additional town-like settlements nearby. You can reach the largest, **Songo Mnara**, in about an hour and a half by motorboat through the islands scattered west and south of Kilwa. After landing, you pass through a small coconut grove and a quiet mangrove thicket, then the town appears between mighty baobab trees, spreading wide-armed candelabra trees and bushes. Most of the houses line narrow streets; mosques are recognizable from their *mihrabs*, prayer niches, fre-

*Above: When the wind's blowing the wrong way, outboard motor is the best means of propulsion for a dhow to Songo Mnara.*

quently with well-preserved ornamentation. Often, you can find a well-shaft close by, and sometimes graves. One particularly elaborate building in the south of the town is thought to have been a sultan's palace.

The ruins tucked away in the island's jungle aren't the only thing here to entice visitors; there's also the remoteness and solitude of **Songo Mnara Island** with its mangrove forests, sandy inlets, miles of coral reefs, tiny villages and fishing settlements. The natural beauty of the island as well as its mysterious 15th-century structures may well lure many visitors even further south, to the ruins of **Sanje ya Majoma**, or west, to **Sanje ya Kati Island**.

### Kilwa Kivinje

Off the beaten track of the Nanguru-kuru-Kilwa Masoko tarmac road, Kilwa Kivinje lies 2.5 miles (4 km) from **Singino**. In the 19th century, the town was terminus for two caravan routes: one came from the west, from Iringa, crossing the middle of what is today the Selous Game Reserve, to the coast; the other came from the southwest, from the banks of Lake Nyasa.

Kilwa comes across as a poorer, smaller sister of Bagamoyo: the remains of Arab houses, the ruins of a mosque, neglected colonial structures, including a once-stately **boma** from the German period, all mark the middle of town. The adjoining harbor, framed by mangroves, is dry at ebb tide. Kilwa drowses today, the size of its decaying houses a reminder of busier times with its roaring slave trade. Two monuments testify to the bloody uprisings against the German colonial masters: a German one in remembrance of those killed in 1888, and a Tanzanian memorial to the victims of the Maji Maji Rebellion in 1905-1907. The inhabitants hope that the discovery of natural gas on the coast near **Songo-Songo Island** will cause an upswing.

## TANGA
### Accommodation

*MODERATE:* **Mkonge Hotel**: .6 mi/1 km E of center, by the sea; Box 1544 Tanga, tel. (53) 44542, fax (53) 43637. *BUDGET:* **Inn by the Sea**: Near Mkonge H. and Swimming Club, by the sea, Box 2188 Tanga, tel. (53) 44614. *Locations on Cape Ras Kazone, no sea view:* **Raskazone**: Box 5101 Tanga, tel. (53) 43897, fax (53) 42797. **Motel Panori**: Box 672 Tanga, tel. (53) 46044, fax (53) 43295. *City center:* **Hotel Bandarini**: Independence Ave., opposite park, colonial building, needs renovation, cheap, Box 249 Tanga, tel. (53) 46674. **Hotel Centaur**: Taifa Street, near station, Box 5448 Tanga, tel. (53) 43801. **Marine Hotel**: corner Boma/Eckernförde Ave., several A/C rooms, Box 1028, tel. (53) 44362/3, fax (53) 46517. *Hotels near bus stand:* **Asad Hotel**: 10th Street, new, Box 2004 Tanga, tel. (53) 44711/2. **MK Inn**: 10th Street, new, good value, Box 2246, Tanga, tel. 45881. *Out of town: MODERATE:* **Baobab Beach Hotel**: On the beach, 4 mi/ 8 km S of center, turn off E from road to Pangani, disco, water sports, Box 180 Tanga, tel. (53) 40638, fax (53) 40162. *BUDGET:* **Kingfisher Lodge**: at Kigombe, on the beach, 19 mi/30 km S of Tanga towards Pangani.

### Restaurants

**Mkonge Hotel, Baobab Hotel**; plenty of restaurants along Market St.; garden restaurant at corner of Independence St./access road to harbor.

### Transportation

*BUS:* Several departures a day (big, comfortable buses) to Mombasa, Dar es Salaam, Moshi/Arusha; several local buses a day to Pangani, Muheza (change here for Amani), Amboni.
*BOAT:* **MS Sepideh**: To Mombasa: Tu, Sa 3 pm; to Pemba/Zanzibar/Dar: We, Su 11:30 am.
*BICYCLE RENTAL:* Opposite Asad Hotel; others.

## PANGANI
### Accommodation

*LUXURY:* **Mashado Pangani River Lodge**: On promontory, S side of Pangani river, excellent views, boat trips, game fishing, safaris; Box 118 Pangani, tel. 88 Pangani; Mashado Central Reserv.: Box 14823 Arusha, tel. (57) 6585, fax (57) 8020. *MODERATE:* **Tinga Tinga Beach Resort**: On the beach, 3 mi/5 km N of Pangani; Box 129 Pangani, tel. 79 Pangani. *BUDGET:* **New River View Inn**: New, on river promenade, Box 121. **Paradise Inn**: River promenade, Box 4 Pangani, tel. 78 Pangani.

### Transportation

*BUS:* Daily service to Muheza. Several buses a day to Tanga. Irregular service from Bweni (S of Pangani); local buses. *RIVER FERRIES:* Car ferry every hour; passenger ferries on demand, continuous departures. *BICYCLE RENTAL:* Main Road.

### Excursions

Upriver boat trips, crocodile farm "Mamba Ranch" (19 mi/30 km from P.). Maziwe and Mandera Islands 1 hour by motor boat in Ind. Ocean; snorkeling, diving, game fishing; sailing on dhows. 40 mi/63 km south of Pangani: Mkwaja turtle project. 43 mi/70 km: Saadani Game Reserve. Information at hotels and District Cultural Office (next to boma).

## BAGAMOYO
### Accommodation

*1 mi/2 km N of Bagamoyo, on long, sandy beach (several more hotels under construction): LUX-URY:* **Livingstone Club Hotel**: Swimming pool, diving school, many sports facilities; Box 105 Bagamoyo, tel. (811) 324645. *MODERATE:* **Bagamoyo Beach Resort**: near mission; Box 250 Bagamoyo, tel./fax 83 Bagamoyo. *BUDGET:* **Travelers Lodge**: Bungalows and cabanas, good value; Box 275 Bagamoyo, tel. 77 Bagamoyo. *Near center/fort:* **BADECO Hotel**: On the beach, restaurant, bar in extensive hall with sea view; Box 261, tel. 18, 75 Bagamoyo. *6 mi/10 km south of Bagamoyo on Mbegani lagoon* (signposted at Zinga on Dar-Bagamoyo road): **Kasiki Marine Camp**: Former farm by the beach, small; family atmosphere, Box 154 Bagamoyo, tel./fax (51) 324707.

## ZANZIBAR
### Accommodation

ZANZIBAR-STONETOWN: *MODERATE (double rooms above 80 US$):* **Mazsons Hotel**: Comfortable, historic house, Ken-yatta Road, Shangani, Box 3367 Zanzibar, tel. (54) 33694, fax (54) 33695. **Tembo House Hotel**: By the sea, Shangani Street, Box 3974 Zanzibar, tel. (54) 33005, fax (54) 33777. **Zanzibar Serena Inn**: By the sea, Ras Shangani; reserv.: tel. (57) 6304, fax: (57) 4155. *MODERATE (double rooms up to 80 US$):* **Chavda Hotel**: New building, Zanzibar style, Baghani Street; Box 540 Zanzibar, tel./fax (54) 31931. **Dhow Palace Hotel**: Zanzibar style, Ken-yatta Road; Box 3974, Zanzibar, tel. (54) 33012, fax (54) 33008. **Emerson's House**: Historic building, unobtrusive entrance, 1563 Mkunazini Street, Box 4044 Zanzibar, tel. (54) 32153, fax (54) 33135. **Hotel International**: New building, Zanzibar style; Box 3784 Zanzibar, tel. (54) 33182, fax (54) 30052. **House of Spices**: Kiponda, Box 1912 Zanzibar, tel./fax (54) 33520. **Narrow Street Hotel**: Small house in center, rooftop restaurant, Box 374 Zanzibar, tel. (54) 32620, fax (54) 30052. **Shangani Hotel**: Kenyatta Road; Box: 4222, tel./fax (54) 33688. **Stone Town Inn**: Shangani Street; tel./fax (54) 33658. *BUDGET:* **Hotel Kiponda**: Sea view, rooftop restaurant; tel. (54) 33052, fax (54) 33020. **Malindi Guest House**:

Historic house with a lot of atmosphere, Malindi, near harbor, shared showers and toilets; Box 609 Zanzibar, tel. (54 ) 30165, fax (54) 31816. **Pearl Guest House Darajani**: Near market, cheap rooms with shower, toilet; Box 4201 Zanzibar, tel. (54) 32907.

BEACH HOTELS NEAR ZANZIBAR TOWN: *LUXURY:* **Fisherman's Resort**: On beach between airport and Stonetown, large hotel, swimming pool, fitness room, water sports; Box 2586, tel. (54) 30208, fax (54) 30556. **Mbweni Ruins Hotel**: Delightful, small hotel, private atmosphere, in garden setting; Box 2542 Zanzibar, tel. (54) 31832, fax (54) 30536. *MODERATE (double rooms above 80 US$):* **Mawimbini Club Village**: Large hotel, water sports; tel./fax (54) 31163. *(double rooms up to 80 US$):* **Mtoni Marine Center**: Water sports; tel./fax (54) 32540. *BUDGET:* **Bububu G.H.**: tel./fax (811) 324687. **Changuu Island Resort**: On Prison Island; res.: Zanzibar Tourist Corporation, Box 216, tel. (54) 32344, fax (54) 33430. **Paradise Bungalows**, Nungwi, water sports (see Indian Ocean Divers).

UNGUJA, NORTHERN EAST COAST: *LUXURY:* **Mnemba Club Hotel**: Private islet with 10 luxuriously equipped *makuti* huts, surfing, diving, waterskiing, fishing, ferry transfer from Matemwe; res.: ConsCorp. tel. (57) 8078, fax (57) 8268. **Kiwengwa Club Village**: Water sports, tennis, swimming pool; tel. (811) 326205, fax (811) 325304. **Lala Salama**: Ras Nungwi, water sports; Box 1784 Zanzibar, tel. (54) 33767, fax (54) 33098. **Mapenzi Beach Resort**: Pwani Mchangani, water sports; Box 2178 Zanzibar, tel. (811) 325985, fax (811) 325986. *MODERATE:* **Chwaka Bay Hotel**: Tel. (54) 33943. **Club Karibu**, Kiwengwa, tel. (811) 325092. **Matemwe Bungalows**, Zaswi, Box 3275, tel. (54) 33789, fax (54) 31342. **Tamarind Beach Hotel**, Uroa, tel. (54) 33041. **Uroa Bay Hotel**, tel. (54) 32552. *BUDGET:* **Chwaka Beach Bungalows**: Zanzibar Tourist Corporation, tel. (54) 32344. Many small beach hotels between Ras Nungwi und Chwaka.

UNGUJA, SOUTHERN EAST COAST: *LUXURY:* **Karafuu Hotel**, Pingwe; the only large hotel along this part of the coast, diving; Box 71 Pingwe, tel. (811) 325157. *BUDGET:* **Bwejuu, Jambiani** and **Makunduchi Beach Bungalows**: Zanzibar Tourist Corporation, tel. (54) 32344. **Sau Inn Hotel**: Jambiani; tel. (54) 32320. There are plenty of very cheap, small beach hotels between Pingwe and Makunduchi.

PEMBA: *MODERATE:* **Manta Reef Lodge**: Panga ya Watoro, on lonely beach in the NW, for address see under "Diving." *BUDGET:* One **Hotel** each in Mkoani, Chake-Chake and Wete, res. Zanzibar Tourist Corporation, Box 216 Zanzibar, tel. (54)

32344. *Guesthouses:* Chake-Chake: **Star Inn**: Near the stadium, bar, restaurant; tel. 2190. **Nassir Guest House**: Near water tower, tel. 2028. **Venus Lodge**: Mkoroshoni. Wete: **Sharook Guest House**: Near bus stand and harbor, restaurant, organized tours; tel. 4386.

### Main Tourist Transfers to Zanzibar

*HYDROFOIL FERRIES:* Minimum of 12 departures a day on the route Dar-Zanzibar-Dar. Agents: **The African Shipping** (Flying Horse), tel. (54) 330312. **Azam Marine** (Kondor 7), tel. (54) 33046. **Sea Express Services** (four ships), tel. (54) 33013; (51) 114026. **Zanzibar Sea Ferries** (Sepideh, Talieh), tel. Zanzibar (811) 326413, Dar: Easy Travel (51) 23526, 113842; M/S *Sepideh* operates five times weekly Dar/Zanzibar/Pemba and twice a week Tanga/ Mombasa.

*PLANE:* International flights to/from Zanzibar through: **Air Tanzania**, **Kenya Airways**, **Gulf Air**, **Precisionair**. Domestic flights: several planes a day Dar-Zanzibar-Dar; at least one a day Dar-Pemba-Dar. Charter: **Air Zanzibar**, **Coastal Travel Air Charters**, **Island Air Services**, **Zan Air**, **Skyland Safaris and Travel**. Each departure requires airport tax.

### Transportation on the Islands

ZANZIBAR (Unguja): *BUS:* **City buses** depart from Creek Road/or near Gulioni Bridge/or Hospital. **Line number** - terminus: **A** - Amaan Stadium; **B** - Bububu; **M** - Magomeni; **U** - Airport. **Island buses** depart from Creek Road, near the market: **1** - Nungwi; **2** - Mangapwani, Bumbwini; **3** - Kiyanga; **4** - Uzini, Bambi; **5** - Ndagaa; **6** - Chwaka, Uroa; **7** - Fumba; **8** - Unguja Ukuu; **9** - Bwejuu/ Jambiani; **10** - Kizimkazi; **11** - Makunduchi. PEMBA: *BUS:* **1** - Chake-Ole; **3** - Mkoani-Chake; **6** - Wete-Chake (old road); **10** - Chake-Micheweni; **24** - Wete-Konde (old road); **33** - Wete-Shengejuu; **34** - Wete-Chake (new road); **35** - Chake-Konde (new road).

### Tour Operators

On Zanzibar, there are more than 50 tour agencies. **Zanzibar Tourist Corporation**, Government Travel Agency; Tourist Information Center: Creek Road, north of market; main office: Livingstone House, Box 216 Zanzibar, tel. (54) 32344, fax (54) 33430. **Chemah Brothers**, Shangani, Box 1865 Zanzibar, tel. (54) 33385. **Equator Tours & Safaris**: Sokomhogo, Box 2096 Zanzibar, tel. (54) 33799. **Fisherman Tours**: Darajani, Box 3537 Zanzibar, tel. 33060. **Jasfa Tours & Safaris**: Shangani, Box 4203 Zanzibar, tel. (54) 30468. **Maya Tours**: Own buses, Box 3508 Zanzibar, tel. (54) 33108. **Seventy Tours**: Malindi, Box 3268 Zanzibar, tel. (54) 30705. **Stonetown Safaris**: Opposite Anglican Cathedral, Box 2209 Zanzibar, tel. (54) 30423.

## Diving and Fishing

**Cat Diving Club**: 79 ft/24 m *Inula* catamaran makes cruises of 3-13 days to Pemba; Box 3203 Zanzibar, tel. (54) 31040. **Dive Adventures Zanzibar**: Diving base at Matemwe Bungalows; Box 2283 Zanzibar, tel. (54) 31342. **East African Watersports**: Base at Tamarind Beach Hotel, Uroa, tel. (54) 33041. **Indian Ocean Divers**: Stonetown, near harbor; base at Paradise Bungalows, Nungwi; Box 2370 Zanzibar, tel. (54) 33860. **One Ocean**: Shangani, below Africa House Hotel, Box 608 Zanzibar, tel. (811) 323091. **Orca Diving Centre**: Base at Kiwengwa Club Village, Kiwengwa; tel. (811) 326205. **Ras Nungwi Diving**: Base at Ras Nungwi Beach Hotel; Box 1784 Zanzibar, tel. 33767. **Stellina Diving International**: Base at Hotel Karafuu, Pingwe; tel. (811) 325157. **Venta Diving**: Base at Hotel Karibu, Kiwengwa; tel. (811) 325092. PEMBA: **One Earth Safaris & Diving**: Base at Manta Reef Lodge; Box 82234 Mombasa, Kenya; tel. Kenya: 254 (11) 471771, fax 471349.

## Museums

National Museum: Museum of history and **Natural History Museum**: Creek Rd/.Museum Rd., Mo-Th, Sa 9 am-12:30 pm, Fr 9-12 am, Su 10 am -12:30 pm; and daily 3:30-6 pm. **Palace Museum**: Former sultan's palace, Mo-Fr 9 am-6 pm, Sa, Su 9 am-3 pm. **Hamamni**: Public baths, erected under Sultan Barghash, open daily.

## DAR ES SALAAM
### Accommodation

CITY CENTER: *LUXURY:* **New Africa Hotel**: Completely renovated 1997/8; Azikiwe St., Box 9314 DSM, tel. (51) 112495, fax (51) 116731. **Sheraton Dar es Salaam**: Ohio St., Box 791 DSM, tel. (51) 112416, fax (51) 113981. *MODERATE (double rooms 90 US$ and above):* **Kilimanjaro Hotel**: Many services in hotel lobby, rooms need renovating; Kivukoni Front, Box 9574 DSM, tel. (51) 110882-8, fax (51) 113304. *MODERATE (up to 90 US$):* **Hotel Agip**: Corner Sokoine/Pamba St., Box 529 DSM, tel. (51) 110819, fax (51) 117079. **Hotel Embassy**: 24 Garden Avenue, Box 3152 DSM, tel. (51) 111181, fax (51) 112634. **Peacock**: Bibi Titi Mohamed St., Box 70270 DSM, tel. (51) 114071, fax (51) 117962. **Starlight**: Bibi Titi Mohamed St., good value; Box 3199 DSM, tel. (51) 119388. *BUDGET:* "classic" budget accommodations, such as **Luther House** (next to Lutheran church), **YWCA** (next to post office, entrance on Ghana Ave.), **YMCA** (Upanga Rd.) and others, are popular travelers' meeting-points, but rather low quality and often more expensive than such professionally-run hotels as the **Keys Hotel**: Uhuru St., Box 5330 DSM, tel. (51) 182947. **Al Uruba**: Mkunguni St. (Kariakoo, between Livingstone/Sikukuu Sts.), Box 8064 DSM,

tel. (51) 180133/4, fax (51) 180135. **Safari Inn**: Band St., Box 21113 DSM, tel./fax (51) 116550. **T.Y.C.S. Centre**: Kibasira Rd., mansion, family atmosphere; Box 4836 DSM, tel. (51) 152778. OUTSIDE CITY CENTER: *LUXURY:* **Ras Kutani**: On Beach 19 mi/30 km S of Kigamboni ferry; Coastal Travels, Box 3052 DSM, tel. (51) 37479. *MODERATE:* **Bahari Beach**: Kunduchi; Box 9312 DSM, tel. (812) 781771. **Jangwani Seabreeze Lodge**: Kunduchi; Box 934 DSM, tel. (811)325908. **Oysterbay Hotel**: Suburb, on beach; Box 2261 DSM, tel. (51) 668062, fax (51) 668631. **The Haven at Kunduchi**: Kunduchi, on beach; Box 23272 DSM, tel. (811) 323443. **White Sands**: Kunduchi, new; Box 3030 DSM, tel. (51) 113678. *BUDGET:* **Palm Beach**: 1 mi/2 km from center, Ali Hassan Mwinyi Rd., garden bar, popular meeting point; Box 1520 DSM, tel. (811) 327015. **Silver Sands**: Kunduchi, on beach; Box 60097 DSM, tel. (812) 781602.

## Museums, Exhibitions, Markets

**National Museum**: Shaban Robert St. (between Sokoine/Samora St.), open 9:30 am-6 pm. **Kijiji cha Makumbusho**: Reconstructed village houses of Tanzanian tribes, dance performances on weekends; Bagamoyo Rd., 4 mi/6 km from city center; 9:30 am-6 pm. **Nyumba ya Sanaa**: Workshops and sales rooms, next to Sheraton Hotel; Mo-Fr 10 am-5 pm, Sa 10 am-1 pm. **Makonde market at Mwenge**: More than 100 sales rooms and workshops of *Makonde* carvers; 6 mi/9 km from city center, minibuses to Mwenge depart frequently from, Maktaba St. opposite main post office, other stands. **Kariakoo**: Most extensive market.

## Tourist Information

Tanzania Tourist Board: Samora Ave. (UNESCO House), tel. (51) 111244/5

## Mafia
### Accommodation

Utende *MODERATE:* **Kinasi**: Diving; Box 26 Mafia, tel. (51) 31216. **Mafia Island Lodge**: Diving, all rooms A/C; TAHI, Box 96 DSM, tel. (51) 32212, fax (51) 116609. **Kilindoni**: *BUDGET:* **New Lizu Hotel**: Box 162 Mafia, tel. 96 Mafia. **Chole Island**: *BUDGET:* **Chole Hotel**, Information: Emerson's House, Box 4044 Zanzibar, tel. (54) 32153.

## Kilwa Masoko
### Accommodation

*BUDGET:* **Hilton Guest House**: New, clean, near market; Box 55 Kilwa M., tel. 144. **Mjaka**: On main road, next to gas station, restaurant; Box 80 Kilwa M., tel. 89. At **Kilwa Kivinje** several small *gesti*, no accommodation at Kilwa Kisiwani; very simple *gesti* at Nangurukuru.
**District Cultural Office** (*ofisi ya utamaduni*): Main road, opp. post office; Mo-Fr 7:30 am-3:30 pm.

# CENTRAL TANZANIA

## SELOUS GAME RESERVE
## UDZUNGWA / MIKUMI / RUAHA
## MOROGORO / IRINGA
## DODOMA / KONDOA
## SINGIDA / TABORA

## SELOUS GAME RESERVE

**Selous Game Reserve** is one of Tanzania's superlatives. It is the largest nature reserve in Africa and, with its 21,200 square miles (55,000 sq. km) of deserted countryside, it is larger than Tanzania's heavily populated neighbors Rwanda and Burundi. Selous's animal paradise shelters 70% of Tanzania's elephants, about 150,000 wildebeest, 50,000 zebras, almost as many impalas, for Africa a remarkably large number of wild dogs, and more than 350 species of birds. In 1982 the United Nations declared the area a World Natural Heritage Site. The Selous territory, which contains no settlements of any kind, borders on Mikumi National Park and other areas with nature conservation status: an inconceivably large wilderness.

What allows such a vast area of wilderness to remain untouched? Largely infertile soil, a scant yearly rainfall of 30-40 inches (750-1,000 mm), and, moreover, the presence of several different kinds of tse-tse flies all make farming and breeding of livestock a difficult matter. The

*Preceding pages: Morogore before the magnificent backdrop of the Uluguru Mountains. Left: A lioness with her kill in the Selous Wildlife Reserve.*

wilderness thrives nearly undisturbed. Three quarters of the park's land is covered in *miombo* woodlands; in the remaining area, light scrub and grassland dominate. Dense gallery forests line the great rivers, especially in the north, where the rivers join to form the **Rufiji**. The latter meanders through its wide valley, has formed many swamps, lakes and connecting waterways, and fosters a Utopian wealth of habitats for flora and fauna alike. You can get an overview of these on normal safaris in four-wheel-drive vehicles, but you'll have a closer view of them on foot, accompanied by armed park rangers, or on boat tours. During the rainy season, it is difficult to get around, so the best time to visit is during the dry months between June and October. Accomodations are generally closed from February/March until the end of May. Even if, on a map, there seems to be a heavy concentration of camps and lodges in this multi-faceted Rufiji valley, you'll discover that in fact, many miles of untouched territory separate them.

### Overnighting in the Wild

**Near Mtemere**, the eastern entrance of the reserve, on the banks of the great river, lies **Rufiji River Camp** with its

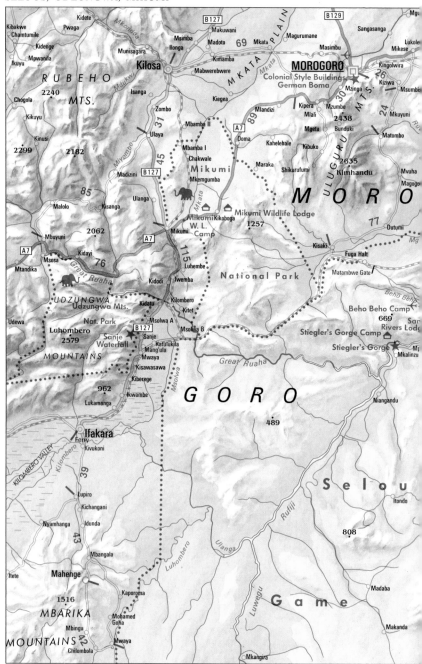

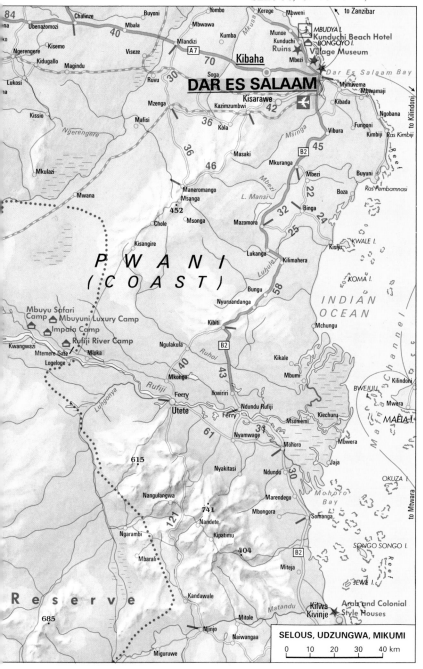

SELOUS, UDZUNGWA, MIKUMI

0    10    20    30    40 km

127

luxurious tents. Its location is ideal for boat trips, for fishing, or for watching game from the water. **Impala Safari Camp**, with well-kept, modest tents, is set up above **Lake Mzizimia**. The **Mbuyuni Luxury Tented Camp** has its tents near an eye-catching baobab tree (*mbuyu*). From **Mbuyu Safari Camp**, on a connecting waterway between **Lake Nzelakela** (also known as Nzerakera) and **Lake Manze**, you can see the animals down at the water, and also arrange boat trips. The **Beho Beho Camp** (formerly Selous Safari Camp) offers magnificent views of **Kipalala Mountain**, where hot springs rise and flow down to feed **Lake Tagalala**, with its wealth of avian life. Here, too, tourists lodge in luxury tents. The campsite is near the **Beho Beho River**, a tributary of the Rufiji. Located not far away is the grave of the leg-

endary British hunter Captain Frederick C. Selous; the game reserve was named in his honor. He died here on January 4, 1917 while pursuing German troops under General Paul von Lettow-Vorbeck. The little lodge **Sand Rivers** has only six single guest-houses, overlooks the Rufiji, has a small swimming pool and offers tours on foot, by car, by boat and by plane. **Stiegler's Gorge Lodge** lies farthest west and began its career as the living quarters of Norwegian prospectors, who planned a hydroelectric power station of gargantuan proportions at this site, although their plans were never realized. Near the houses, the Rufiji plunges 330 feet (100 m) down into impressive **Stiegler's Gorge**, after being mightily swollen with the waters of the **Great Ruaha**. The gorge was named for the German hunter Stiegler, who was killed by an elephant here in 1907.

It is 25 miles (40 km) from the lodge to the northern entrance of the reserve, **Matambwe**. From the north, there are several different ways to reach the reserve: by

*Above: Even on the Selous Reserve, poachers decimate the rhino population. Right: Year-round rivers sustain rice and sugar cultivation in the Kilombero Valley.*

train (TAZARA station **Fuga**) or by car from Morogoro, Mikumi or Kidatu via **Kisaki**. From Matambwe, a 52-mile (83 km) long route traverses the northern part of the Selous area to the post of Mtemere in the east. There are 130 miles (240 km) of bad roads to overcome if you want to travel from Mtemere via **Mloka**, **Mkongo** and **Kibiti** to Dar es Salaam. It is no wonder that most tourists (some 2,000 each year) prefer to fly in, a matter of only an hour. There are landing-strips near the lodgings.

### Big Game is Big Business

While the northern sector of the Selous reserve is set aside for observing nature, the rest of the area puts up parties interested in other activities: nature-conservation staff members, poachers and licensed hunters. The east, west and southern sections of the game reserve are divided into 140 hunting sectors. Each year, a commission decides on the quota of the animals that can be shot, and all the killings are checked and strictly controlled.

Legalized hunting is very expensive and the park authorities hope to earn enough money through this arrangement to enable them to combat poaching of elephants, rhinoceroses and other animals more effectively (the elephant population, about 30,000 at the moment, has fallen from its 1976 count of 110,000; today, there are fewer than 50 rhinoceroses, where in 1976 there were 2,500). There are only 500 employees for the whole Selous area: too few, and often too poorly equipped, to do full justice to their extensive duties in this huge tract of land. Since 1989, inhabitants of the surrounding area have been brought into the struggle. Instead of themselves poaching as they used to, they now take an active part in wildlife protection; at the same time, they are also allowed certain hunting quotas.

### Kilombero Valley

West of the Selous area, between the striking **Mbarika Mountains** (more than

129

5,000 feet/ 1,500 m high) and the steep escarpment of the eastern tract of the East African Rift (TAZARA tracks run along it for a while), unfolds the Kilombero Valley: a green plain, even in the dry period, more than 125 miles (200 km) long and about 30 miles (50 km) wide. Countless arms of the river criss-cross the valley. The central **Kilombero** swells so much in the rainy season that the ferry 4 miles (6 km) south of the district capital **Ifakara** can no longer manage the crossing. The mountain town **Mahenge**, where a fortress remains from the German colonial era, is then isolated from the rest of the country for a period, together with its surrounding villages. To the east, the Kilombero, here called the **Ulanga**, empties into the Rufiji. In places where the course of the river has been brought under control in the plains, especially around Ifakara and in the northern section of the valley, rice and sugar cane are cultivated. Those lands near the river that aren't currently being used for agriculture serve as pasturage for the herds of the Maasai, whose movements into the area are on the rise. The river flats teem with crocodiles, hippopotamuses and a great variety of birds. The few tourists who do visit Ifakara can take advantage of local boat owners' offers of fascinating tours on the river.

## UDZUNGWA MOUNTAINS NATIONAL PARK

After approximately 37 miles (60 km) on the B127, about midway between the towns Mikumi and Ifakara (the 25 miles/40 km from Mikumi to the power-plant town of **Kidatu** on the Great Ruaha are paved), and near **Mang'ula**, lies the entrance to Tanzania's very newest national park: **Udzungwa Mountains**. Op-

*Right: Speeding drivers on the paved road through Mikumi National Park are often brought to their senses for a moment.*

ened in 1992, it covers an area of 730 square miles (1,900 sq. km) at altitudes of between 820 and more than 8,200 feet (250-2,500 m), and consists mainly of forest. In the north, it borders on the **Great Ruaha**, and its eastern boundary is the sharp drop of the escarpment alongside the Kilombero valley. A special attraction of this national park is that it contains no roads of any kind; visitors are forced to proceed on foot through its steep, wooded mountains, accompanied by a park guide. Another reason the park is unique is that its natural forest vegetation, which varies depending on the altitude, has remained almost completely unspoiled over some 6,500 feet (2,000 m) of vertical change, which means, by extension, that the natural habitat of the woodland animals has remained undisturbed. A result of this are a large number of endemic species of flora and fauna, including the Iringa-Uhehe red Colobus monkey, the Sanje crested mangabey, and one species of the servaline genet; several varieties of birds have been discovered only in recent years. The region is one of the three most important bird sanctuaries in East Africa.

However, it isn't only botanists and zoologists who get their money's worth here. The three small camps situated at clear streams in the jungle can attune any nature-lover to the wild. The climb into the mountains can be breathtaking – not just because of the arduous ascent, but also because of the immeasurably broad panoramas out over the Kilombero plains as far as the Selous territory and the Mbarika Mountains. It is impossible to see enough of the overwhelming, green expanse of mountain scenery with its waterfalls, which roar even in the dry seasons – including the splendid **Sanje Waterfall** with a vertical drop of 560 feet (170 m).

The park administration offers a wide choice of walks, from 15-minute rambles to tours lasting several days. Half a mile

(1 km) from the park headquarters, there is a hotel for those who do not care to sleep out in their own tents.

## MIKUMI NATIONAL PARK

One of the many highlights along the excellent asphalt road A7 between Iringa and Morogoro comes just east of **Mikumi**. Here, the main road crosses 30 miles (50 km) of **Mikumi National Park**. The 37-mph (60-km/h) speed limit signs are conspicuous, but in the land of potholes this extraordinarily nice, smooth road surface tempts quite a few drivers to step on the gas. Many of them pay little heed to these road signs until a group of giraffes, whole elephant families, herds of antelopes or other wild animals suddenly appear on the road. It is well worth your while to keep an eye out for game: as a reward, you get a free safari through a Tanzanian national park! Consequently, many people believe it is superfluous to pay much attention to the rest of the 1,242-square mile (3,230 sq. km)

park. But tehose who do so anyway are even more amply rewarded! The variety of animals here is equal to that of the Serengeti.

Town and park take their name from the water-loving *mikumi*, Borassus palms (*Borassus aethiopia*), which grow on the valley plains of the **Mkata** that extend northwards. During the driest time of the year, from August into December, this wet northern part of the park is particularly inviting to many kinds of animals – and to safari vehicles. In this period, they hardly have to struggle at all with the tenacious clay mud, called *mbuga,* tropical black cotton soil. Popular destinations are swamp areas in the process of drying up and river beds east of the Mkata, as well as the watering-holes at **Chamgore** and **Choga Wale** between Mkata and the freight railway line which crosses the park.

When the routes there are just too wet, you may have better luck at the **Hippo Pools** (near the park headquarters and the luxury tents of the **Mikumi Wildlife**

Camp and the **campgrounds**). South of the main road, you can follow **Hill Drive**, a round-trip route through hills covered with *miombo* vegetation, beginning not far from the hotel **Mikumi Wildlife Lodge**.

Mikumi is a popular weekend excursion for Dar es Salaam residents. The 190-mile (300-km) drive takes about 4 hours. A landing-strip near the headquarters ensures even quicker connections by small plane.

## MOROGORO

In 1871 the American journalist Henry Morton Stanley found a fortified stone city, *Simbamwene*, on his way from Bagamoyo to Lake Tanganyika, at almost the same spot where today sprawls the modern regional capital **Morogoro**. Now only the **Kingo Graves**, in a tiny park be-

*Above: Dugout canoes on the Mindu Reservoir. Right: People-friendly: a chameleon from the Uluguru Mountains.*

tween **Station Road** and **Old Dar Road**, remind us of the city's founder. A freed slave, he became a chief who profited, between 1840 and 1865, from the caravans traveling through this town on the important slave and ivory trade-route. The onomatopoetic name "Morogoro" is said to stem from the sound of the river, whose valley cleaves the town in half right down the middle.

Against the dark green backdrop of the sharp inclines of the **Uluguru Mountains**, tempered with a healthy measure of gardens and flowering trees, the town has more than 120,000 inhabitants and, even today, an ideal location from the point of view of transportation: there are paved roads leading to Dar es Salaam and Iringa-Mbeya-Zambia, as well as to Dodoma. In addition, the *Central Line* railway passes through Morogoro, still using the **old German station building**.

The mountains rise up more than 8,500 feet (2,600 m) from the plains (which themselves lie 1,000 feet/300 m above sea level), and provide the town not only

with water, but also with an abundance of fruit, vegetables and wood – something you can see for yourself at the **market**, west of the town center.

**Boma Road** begins at the central bus-stop and, posing for the most part as a shady avenue, passes about 2 miles (3 km) of gardens and fields before reaching the former German **boma** at the foot of the mountains. This castle-like building complex has been carefully restored and now houses several offices of the regional administration. Slightly down the hill, in a deeply cleft, lush green river valley, lies the small, well-tended private park **Rock Garden**, which also has a bar. Further towards the city, there's a spacious **golf course** across from the **Morogoro Hotel**. The town makes a refreshing impression with its flowering shrubs, rows of trees, small parks and flower beds. It has several little hotels, modern and of good quality.

### Hiking in the Uluguru Mountains

In a good two hours you can walk from the boma in Morogoro to the faded eleg-ance of **Villa Morningside**, built in 1912, which lies at the lower edge of the forest of the Uluguru Mountains. During the gradual ascent on a road rarely used by motor vehicles, you enjoy grandiose views of the well-ordered layout of the town, the plains in the northwest with several projecting mountain peaks, the **Mindu reservoir** (the town's water supply) and the incredibly steep mountain slopes, where intensive agriculture is nonetheless practices. Unlike the plains, it is possible, with irrigation, to get two harvests a year here, but only with tremendous effort. That effort is necessary not only in order to till and sow the exposed fields, but also to transport all the necessary goods to the outlying villages and farms, and bring the farm produce back down to the market in the valley. From the tiny village of **Luvuma**, the last half hour of the ascent to Morningside takes you on a footpath between the steep fields, accompanied by the plashing and bubbling of water flowing from pipes or wild mountain streams into

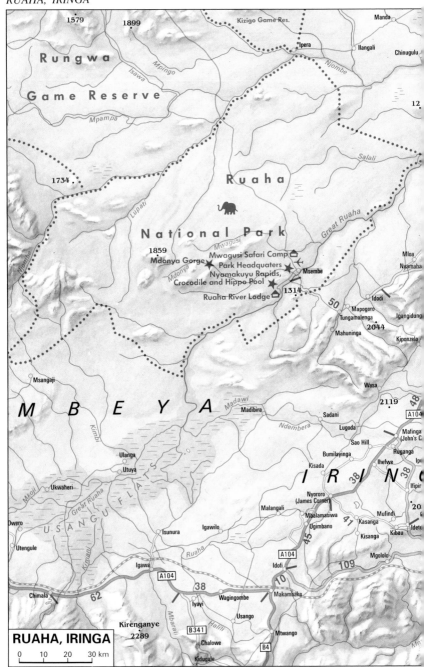

**RUAHA, IRINGA**

0    10    20    30 km

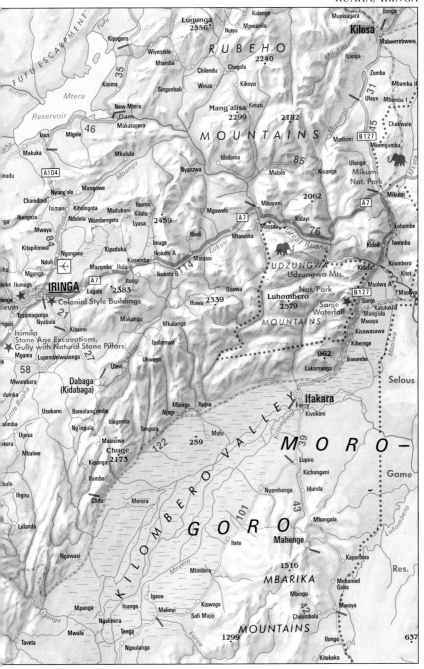

narrow irrigation ditches, even in the dry season. Follow the required etiquette: apply for permission to visit Morningside at the District Office of Culture (*manispaa utamaduni*), opposite the post office in Morogoro.

This outing may arouse your curiosity to get to know other parts of the small but many-faceted Uluguru Mountains. Only about 200 years ago, the Luguru tribe migrated from the Ubena Plains 250 miles (400 km) to the south and settled the rainy, wooded massif of the Ulugurus from the southwestern side, felling more and more unspoilt forest in increasingly higher regions and transforming these areas into arable land. Today this process has been restricted by the designation of two forest reserves in the highest still-extant forest regions of the mountains. As well as conserving the landscape (main-

*Above: Crocodiles don't always confine themselves to lazing in the sun by the waters of the Great Ruaha – here, a Grant's Gazelle met with a bit of bad luck.*

taining the water balance, protecting against erosion), this also serves to protect a number of rare birds, including several endangered and endemic species. However, the enormous increase in population has put a great strain on the region with its growing demand for land, water and wood. It is a good idea to take a guide with you as you roam through the spectacular countryside; the best time for hiking is from June to October. On a clear day you can, for example, climb **Kimhandu**, the highest peak here at 8,645 feet (2,635 m), starting at the village of **Nyandira**, south of **Mgeta** on the west flank of the mountain. It is wise to obtain information first at the Regional Natural Conservation Office (*ofisi ya maliasili*) in Morogoro.

## RUAHA NATIONAL PARK

As a counterbalance to the *Northern Circuit*, where the heavily-frequented national parks of Tanzania's north are concentrated, the Tanzanian tourist industry has coined the concept of the *Southern Circuit*. This is comprised of the clover-leaf of Selous, Mikumi, Udzungwa and a fourth nature reserve, **Ruaha National Park**. Although this park lies almost exactly in the middle of the well-traveled stretch between Dar and the border of Zambia, it receives few visitors: from **Iringa**, you still have to cover 70 miles (113 km) of rather uncomfortable road to reach the park entrance. Because it's so hard to get to, the park has remained a hidden treasure for those in the know. Two landing-strips allow for a faster approach by air: the flight from Dar to Ruaha, for example, takes roughly 2 hours.

Its 4,980 square miles (12,950 sq. km) make Ruaha National Park the country's second-largest national park after Serengeti, but together with the adjacent wildlife reserves of **Rungwa** and **Kizigo**, as well as additional protection and buffer zones, it constitutes an uninterrupted expanse of protected territory as large as Switzerland. Only a fraction of the terrain is set up for wildlife observation: a section in the southeast of the park between the **Great Ruaha River**, which flows through the park and forms part of its eastern border, and a prominent fault of the East African Rift system, which continues outside the park on the **Usangu Flats**. During the dry period between July and December, you can explore this pristine African landscape by car on nearly 250 miles (400 km) of park roads. The animals generally gather at the rivers during this period. While *miombo* woodlands dominate the western sector, especially at higher altitudes in the park, the eastern plains are primarily covered by grasslands and open acacia woodland.

Once you have crossed Ruaha bridge at the park gate and go upstream, the **Ruaha River Drive** leads you across lake-like expanses of broad river with many crocodiles and hippos and the magnificent **Nymakuyu Rapids** to **Ruaha**

**River Lodge**, where the houses are anchored in the landscape, situated on *kopjes* above the riverbed. Downstream from Ruaha bridge, after crossing the **Mdonya Sand River** (which flows only during the rainy season), you come upon the **park headquarters** at **Msembe**. Here, self-caterers can rent *bandas* or put up their tents. Further downriver, Ruaha River Drive passes the **Mwagusi Sand River**; a riverbed that remains dry on the surface, except during the rains. You have a good view of a great variety of East African fauna from the area around the luxury-tented camp **Mwagusi Safari Camp**: besides large buffalo herds and elephants, there are, in particular, roan and sable antelopes, greater and lesser kudus, lions, leopards and cheetahs. To date, 480 different species of birds have been registered.

Near the steep escarpment of the East African Rift, the passage can become rough and difficult in places, but all routes lead to fantastic highlights of a wilderness untouched by man, such as, for example, the ravine of the Mdonya River, **Mdonya Gorge**.

## AROUND IRINGA

In the highlands around Iringa (5,250 feet/1,600 m) dwell the Hehe people; "he-he" was their warriors' battle cry. In the 19th century, their homeland was threatened from many sides. From the south the Ngoni were pushing north-wards, thereby setting the Sangu in motion. The Hehe managed to throw off all these invaders, including the Maasai moving in from the north; under their leader Mkwawa (1855-1898), they even extended their territory so far into the area of the Nyamwezi and Gogo that they were able to secure partial control of the caravan routes from the coast to Lake Tanganyika. Nor were they any more intimidated by the German colonists. In 1891, they inflicted a severe defeat on

German troops near **Lugalo**, 16 miles (25 km) east of Iringa; a German obelisk still stands there today as a memorial. In 1892, they stormed the German fort in **Kilosa** on the eastern rim of the **Rubeho Mountains**. The Germans put a high price on the head of Mkwawa, who held a fortress in **Kalenga**, 7.5 miles (12 km) west of Iringa. After the Germans captured that fort in 1894, Mkwawa waged guerilla warfare against the colonial rulers for four more years. Finding his situation hopeless, he committed suicide shortly before his enemies could seize him; his head was cut off and brought to Germany. In 1919, the Treaty of Versailles stipulated that the Germans return the head, but it did not actually find its way back to Kalenga until June 6, 1954, when it was interred, with formal honors, in the **mausoleum** on the fortress

grounds. The British governor at the time, Edward Twining, had discovered Mkwawa's skull a year earlier in the ethnological museum in Bremen, Germany. The ramparts of the bastion were once 13 feet (4 m) high and 8 miles (13 km) long, but are now virtually leveled; the mausoleum containing the skull of this most famous Hehe chieftain, which is also a small **museum**, stands at the eastern entrance of Kalenga, a mere half-mile north of the Iringa-Ruaha road (signposted).

As contested as the territories around Kalenga were a century ago, today this is a peaceful countryside and an inviting venue for walks and bike tours. A path, 2.5 miles (4 km) long, winds through diverse scenery from Kalenga to **Tosamaganga**, where the multi-storey tile-roofed houses crowd together conspicuously on a hilltop. From a distance, they resemble an Italian mountain village. No wonder. When Italian missionaries reached this locale, they must have felt quite at home among the wooded mountains and dense vegetation of the river

*Above: Flowering jacaranda trees line the streets of Inringa. Right: Carpenter at work in Tanzania's capital, Dodoma.*

valleys; and they built a mission, a hospital and schools.

At the village of **Tanangozi**, 4 miles (6 km) to the south, you hit the A104 from Iringa to Mbeya. If you follow it for 2 miles (3 km) towards Mbeya, you find signs for the **Isimila Stone Age Site** (12.5 miles/20 km from Iringa). The deep **Isimila** river valley lies half a mile (1 km) east of the road. Excavations here in 1958 uncovered thousands of stone tools ranging from rough, rounded hammering stones and sharp axes to fine spearheads, proving that Stone Age cultures lived here 100,000 to 60,000 years ago; bone fragments of antelopes, elephants, hippopotamuses and other animals indicate game-hunting. Two small **exhibitions** in the valley give an overview of the whole spectrum of the finds. From there, it is a ten-minute walk to some impressive **earth pyramids**, created by selective erosion in the river valley.

The regional capital **Iringa** (pop. 90,000) lies high above the green, intensively-cultivated river meadows of the **Little Ruaha River** and its modern industrial complex along the A104, which bypasses the town. The Germans erected a **fort** at a predominant point in 1896, and some of the buildngs from their colonial period still stand today. The busy **market** is especially appealing.

## DODOMA

From Iringa to **Dodoma**, you have a choice between two routes which take approximately the same amount of time: 373 miles (601 km) on an asphalt road via Morogoro, or 165 miles (266 km) on a more direct but rough all-weather road. Both routes are quite delightful. The longer, paved option leads down from the Iringa highlands in a series of breathtaking serpentines to the Lukose and Great Ruaha river valleys in the plains, crosses Mikumi National Park and, after Morogoro, follows the main caravan route from the 19th century. The shorter route, the A104, originally planned by the British as a segment of the Cape to Cairo

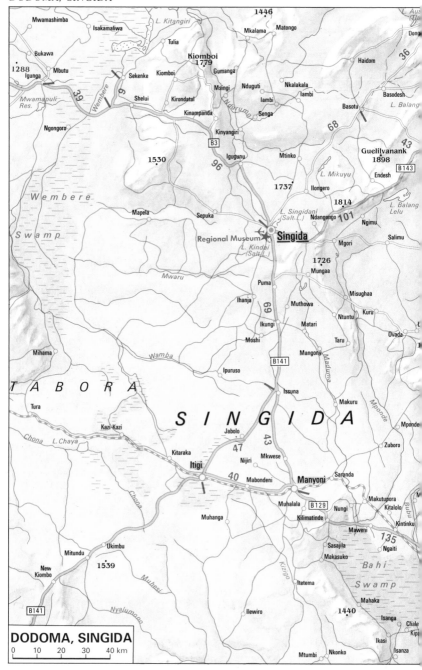

DODOMA, SINGIDA

0   10   20   30   40 km

road, commands broad vistas of the wide basin of the Great Ruaha and the **Mtera Reservoir** which that river feeds. North of this, after you've crossed the low **Fufu Escarpment**, you come to the predominantly dry country of the old caravan routes.

Back in the 19th century, when the trade caravans crossed the territory of the Gogo and the local *ntemi*, or chieftains of individual clans, exacted tribute from the travelers in return for water, food supplies and sleeping facilities, Dodoma did not as yet exist. German colonists found a small settlement bearing this name in 1910, while they were building their railway, the *Central Line*, from the Indian Ocean to Lake Tanganyika, more or less along the historical trade-route, and they planned an important outpost in Dodoma. When the first trains rolled from Dar es Salaam to Kigoma in 1914, the stage was set for this market and administrative town. The commanding boma and the imposing railway station are testimony to those times.

In the mid-1920s, the British supplemented the east-west railway line with a north-south transportion link, conceived as a part of their planned Cape to Cairo road. The A104 links Dodoma with Arusha in the north (260 miles/419 km, most of it in poor condition) and with Iringa in the south (165 miles/266 km). A mere ten years later, Dodoma became an important stop for transcontinental African air transportation: planes had to stop here to refuel, since their range was much shorter then than it is nowadays.

*Ugogo*, that vast, thinly populated land, dry for many months of the year, dotted here and there with towering groups of rocks, where so little grass grows that the inhabitants roof their low, flat huts (called *tembe*) with mud instead, is, because of the chronic lack of rain, frequently plagued by famine. The transportation junction of Dodoma at the center of this region seemed an ideal way of

141

improving the lot of this economically stunted region. One force for change was the young Tanzanian government under Julius Nyerere, who decided to give top priority to implementing their *ujamaa* plans in this area and to declare this city, central to the country in terms of both geography and transportation, the capital of Tanzania in 1973.

A modern **parliament building** (*Bunge*) on the access road from the east, several technical colleges, a few ministries, numerous **churches** and their accompanying facilities, CCM party headquarters and the hotels necessary for the members of parliament, who convene here twice a year, have all greatly helped built up the image of this town of more than 200,000 inhabitants. The **market**

*Above: Collecting water with a calabash from the sand bed of the Kolo River is a laborious process. Right: Rock-paintings of Bushmanoid peoples are a relatively common sight in the Dodoma and Singida Regions.*

142

**center** is well worth a visit, with its streets of amply stocked shops; so, too, are the modern residential areas between the Mlimwa *kopjes* and the airport, as well as the historic buildings south of the railway line, which include the **Boma**, the **train station**, the reception building of the **Railway Hotel** dating from the days of the Germans, and the **Geological Museum** from the country's British past.

The cultivation of grapes, introduced by Italian missionaries in 1958 in **Bihawana Mission**, 11 miles (18 km) south of town, has become widespread throughout the vicinity. Many people find that the sweet, dark dessert grapes, which you can buy at roadside stands and markets, taste far better than the wine which is pressed from the fruit.

## KONDOA

Colossal baobab trees in the center of **Kondoa** remind you how scarce is the rainfall in this district, and yet the **Kondoa River** splashes in its deep valley through the town even during the dry season. Moreover, an **artesian well** (*chemchem ya maji*), set in a modern rounded building, bubbles constantly in the natural conservation area of the town woods and discharges its water onto cultivated vegetable beds. The well is well-guarded, and if you wish to visit it, you need permission from the waterworks office (*idara ya maji*). The district administration has moved into attractive modern headquarters, but some of the buildings around it hearken back to the German colonial era.

Kondoa lies one mile (2 km) off the A104 (Dodoma-Arusha) and can serve as a point of departure for unusual tours to remote areas in northern Tanzania: a bus, for example, runs twice a week through the **Kitwei Plains**, the southern part of the **Maasai Steppe**, to Tanga on the coast, a 300-mile (480-km) route which you should allow two days to cover.

Kondoa is the nearest place that can offer hotel accommodations to visitors to the rock-paintings in the land of the *Rangi.*

### Kolo and the Irangi Rock-Paintings

The village of **Kolo** lies 17 miles (27 km) north of Kondoa (113 miles/182 km from Dodoma; 171 miles/275 km from Arusha) on the northern bank of the river of the same name, which appears only as a broad sand bed during the dry season. From the bridge, you see the village women drawing their daily water supply from holes dug in the ground. The small office of the Antiquities Department is right on the main road, and visitors to the *michoro ya mapangoni*, the **Caves of the Rock-Paintings**, have to register there.

Since Louis and Mary Leakey's research explorations in the 1950s, 186 rock-painting sites have been discovered in Irangi, the home of the Rangi, but also in other parts of the Kondoa district. The Antiquities Department has opened 14

caves for viewing, with Kolo as a starting-point. Three of them are within walking distance, ideal for a half day's tour, the others are as far as 20 miles (30 km) away, and can best be reached in a four-wheel-drive vehicle. Allow three days if you want to see all fourteen. The paintings at **Pahi** (5 miles/8 km from Kolo) and **Cheke** (8 miles/13 km) are particularly fine, but also the pictures in the rocks near Kolo (labeled B1, B2, B3), give excellent insight into the abilities of these early artists. The presence of a local guide from the Antiquities Department is obligatory at all viewings.

The drawings show African wildlife, often, surprisingly enough, immediately and definitely identifiable; human figures, frequently stick-figures; hunting implements; some plants, and other natural phenomena. The Leakeys estimated that they were made between 3,500 and 800 years ago. In an analogy with cave-paintings in southern Africa, these paintings are attributed not to the agricultural Rangi, but rather to Bushman-like

143

peoples, who lived as hunter-gatherers. In all probability, they were fairly extensively distributed in East Africa then, before different peoples from the north and Bantu from the west moved into the area and forced them out. So-called "clicks," a feature of Bushman languages, are also a characteristic of the languages of the Sandawe, an agricultural people based south of Kondoa, and the Hadzabe, who live around Lake Eyasi and still live, in part, as hunter-gatherers. Researchers are of the opinion that a *Bushman* culture was predominant here in the past.

Most of the paintings are found on gneiss surfaces along the eastern slopes of the mountains. On a very clear day, you might just be lucky enough to enjoy the spectacular panorama from there, across the southern part of Tarangire National Park and the Maasai Steppe to Kilimanjaro, 155 miles (250 km) distant.

### Babati

From Kolo, the A104 begins to climb up into the mountainous regions that become more green and wooded the farther you go. Looking west, you may be able to see in the distance the giant volcano **Hanang**, 11,210 feet (3,417 m) high; while to the east, a superb vista over the lowlands of the Maasai Steppe might be in store for you. If you choose to forego the spine-tingling switchbacks of the mountain road, you can experience just as jarring a drive to **Babati** from Kolo via **Masenge** on an almost equally lousy road which follows the eastern flank of the mountain. In the lee of the 7,923-foot (2,4125-m) high local mountain, the volcano **Kwaraha**, vegetables, fruit and brightly-colored flowers thrive even in the tiniest front garden. The country is humid and fertile here at the southern edge of the volcanic plateau, which continues up north as far as Kenya.

Babati serves as a market town, being a traffic hub for north-south transportation and just as important for connections to the west. There, along the B143 to Singida, surprisingly vast expanses of wheat dominate the scenery, but corn and other vegetables also flourish in the fertile fields around the projecting Hanang near **Katesh**.

### SINGIDA

In the plains south of the volcanic highlands, the luxuriant green fades away. In its place, unusual humpbacked granite hills rear up from the savannah. Such boulders emerge abruptly between the houses of the regional capital **Singida**. In addition to these local hallmarks, this town, verdant with trees and flowering bushes, is also adorned with two nondraining lakes, the smaller **Kindai** and the larger **Singidani**. Standing in these are groups of rounded rocks, encrusted with white salt deposits; for these are soda lakes. In some years, thousands of migrating flamingoes feel quite at home here and make a long stopover between September and November.

In a little stand of trees near the shore of Lake Singidani, this town of about 90,000 inhabitants offers an excellent **Regional Museum** which presents an detailed introduction to the peoples of the Singida Region and describes their individual characteristics. A folklore display includes different handcrafts and articles of daily use, as well as musical instruments.

#### Singida Region

Singida region is larger than Denmark and has just under a million inhabitants. The southern part of the region is made up almost entirely of game reserves (Rungwa, Kizigo, Muhesi). You can observe the middle from the window of a *Central Line* train, if you don't feel the urge to acquaint yourself with the course of the historic caravan route along the road via **Kilimatinde**, **Manyoni** and **Itigi**

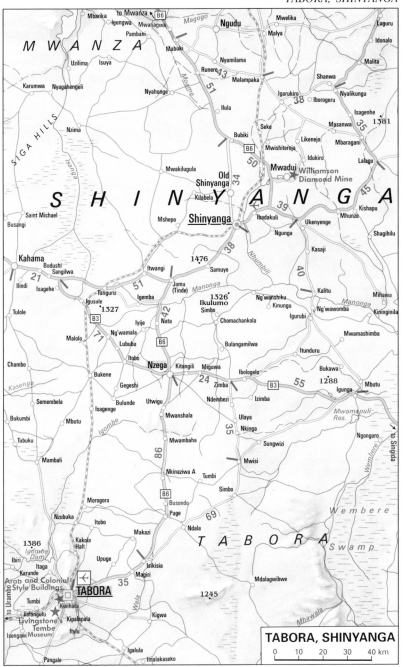

**TABORA, SHINYANGA**

0    10    20    30    40 km

or even, as in the 19th century, on the footpaths that are still used today by the local population.

Traffic to the west is seriously impeded by a swampy basin of the East African Rift; the **Wembere Swamp** is the most extensive swamp area. A track, plagued by floods, crosses it arduously 60 miles (100 km) northwest of Singida, beyond the escarpment of the **Iramba Mountains**, leading into the neighboring province Tabora. The **Wembere River** forms the border.

### Tabora Region

With an area larger than all of Ireland, and only slightly more than one million inhabitants, **Tabora Region** is one of the most sparsely-populated provinces of Tanzania. At least since the 18th century, its inhabitants have been known as Nyamwezi; they had a name as wandering

*Above: Watching Mommy at work, with considerable interest. Right: African beehives hang from the trees.*

traders in East Africa. Their wares included salt from Uvinza, iron hoes from the land of the *Fipa*, copper from Katanga and ivory. The Arab traders on the coast of the Indian Ocean used the knowledge and abilities of the Nyamwezi people when they themselves fitted out caravans in the 19th century, the men of the Nyamwezi functioning as bearers. The trade routes led right through the middle of this people's homeland, and branched off in its center into a northerly route to Lake Victoria and a westerly route to Lake Tanganyika. Standing up against the increasingly powerful influence of the Arabs in Unyamwezi, the *ntemi* Mirambo took military action, subjugating large portions of the country that had originally been split up into numerous small clans and blocking off the central caravan route for a time. In 1871, Henry Morton Stanley was forced to make a great detour to the south to avoid Mirambo and his feared *ruga-ruga* (bandits) in order to get to Ujiji to meet Livingstone.

More than a third of the Tabora region is covered with forest. Its wealth of blossoms makes Tabora a main supplier of honey and beeswax in Tanzania. The beekeepers usually hang the elongated beehives, made of hollowed-out tree stumps, in the branches of the striking *mgua*, the large-leaved star chestnut (*Sterculia quinqueloba*); the smooth bark of the tree hinders climbing honey badgers (*Mellivora capensis*). The land around **Urambo** on the *Central Line* is very productive tobacco country.

You're thrown on the mercies of the railway if you want to continue on to the west, to Uvinza, Kigoma and Mpanda, as there no roads which are passable all year round. A train runs to Mwanza on Lake Victoria, as does the B6, which passes through the important traffic junction **Nzega**. The northern parts of the country are given over to the cotton plantations of **Shinyanga Region**.

## TABORA

The regional capital **Tabora** (pop. 100,000) is the successor of *Unyanyembe*, an important 19th-century trading-post for the Arabs, who left their mark there. A few Arabian houses are still to be found in the middle of town, and several mosques still exhibit the cultural stamp of the past. After 1880, Christian missionary work started to set the tone, something visible in the many churches, but also in the schools. As in Dodoma, the secular buildings still in use are the **railway station**, the tastefully renovated **Tabora Railway Hotel** nearby and the impressive, castle-like **boma**. For centuries, Tabora has maintained its function as a traffic junction. In addition to road and rail connections, there are flights to Kigoma and Dar es Salaam several times a week.

### Livingstone's Tembe in Kwihara

Not far from the market in Tabora, Sikonge Road courses south. About 4 miles (6 km) further down this road, a signpost directs you to **Livingstone's Tembe** to the west. A reconstructed caravanserai lies 1 mile (2 km) further westward in **Kwihara**; it was here that Stanley stayed for three months in 1871 and, together with Livingstone, for an additional month in the following year. The building itself is a spacious, rectangular structure with an open inner courtyard, planted with trees. In no way does it resemble the *tembe*, the low, flat mud huts of the dwellers of the central provinces, especially with regard to size. Kitchen and pantries surround the inner courtyard, with stalls in the modest rear quarters; the guard rooms of the *askaris* and the living-quarters of the caravan guides are in the more public front part of the building. A small informative **museum** has been put in here, with maps and documents outlining the extent of Livingstone's explorations, and copies of the *New York Herald* evoking anew the suspense that Stanley's articles imparted to his readers back in 1872.

147

## SELOUS GAME RESERVE
### Accommodation
*LUXURY-TENTED CAMPS, LODGES:* **Beho Beho Camp**, **Impala Safari Camp**, **Mbuyu Safari Camp**, **Mbuyuni Luxury Tented Camp**, **Rufiji River Camp**, **Sand Rivers**: 150-360 US$ per day and person for overnighting, full board, park fees, transfers from/to airstrip or station; game drives, boat trips and walking safaris usually included; additional payments for flights, drives into game reserve. Ask for special rates for all-inclusive offers during certain periods. Agents/tour operators at DSM: **Coastal Travels**: Upanga Rd., Box 3052 DSM, tel. (51) 37479, fax (51) 46045. **Easy Travel**: Kilimanjaro Hotel lobby, Box 1428 DSM, tel. (51) 23526, fax (51) 113482. **Oysterbay Hotel**: Box 2261 DSM, tel. (51) 668062, fax (51) 668631. **Southern Tanganyika Game Safaris & Tours**: Box 2341 DSM, tel. (811) 781971, fax (51) 116431.

### Transportation
*PLANE:* **Coastal Travels** flies daily DSM-Selous-DSM, three times a week Selous-Ruaha-Selous, two times a week Selous-Zanzibar. *TRAIN:* **TAZARA** local trains stop at Fuga station, near Matambwe Gate; have someone from your camp pick you up at the station. *CAR:* Bad roads; use the Mtemere entrance coming from DSM; use the Matambwe gate from Morogoro or from the Mikumi park via Kisaki.

## UDZUNGWA MOUNTAINS NATIONAL PARK
### Accommodation
*BUDGET:* **Twiga Hotel**: Outside the park, .5 mi/1 km from park entrance, restaurant, bar, in well-tended garden; Box 30 Mang'ula, tel. 38, 39. Three *CAMPSITES* in forest along two rivers near park HQ.

### Transportation
*BUS:* Mang'ula is situated 37 mi/60 km from Mikumi or 31 mi/50 km from Ifakara. Several buses a day between Mikumi and Ifakara; ask driver to stop at park gate. *TRAIN:* Mang'ula **TAZARA** station is 2 mi/3 km from park entrance.

### Shopping
**Mang'ula's** center has a small market and simple restaurants, 1.5 mi/2 km from park entrance.

## MIKUMI NATIONAL PARK
### Accommodation
*MODERATE:* **Mikumi Wildlife Lodge**: 2 mi/3 km S of main road (A7), signposted; reservations recommended, especially on weekends: **TTB**. *BUDGET:* **Mikumi Wildlife Camp**: near park entrance, bandas, restaurant; res.: **Oysterbay Hotel**, Box 2261 DSM, tel. (51) 668062, fax (51) 668631. Three *CAMPSITES* (no water) near park entrance. In Mikumi (town), outside the western

park boundaries, several *gesti* and private campsites, as well as reasonable restaurants along the main road where many long-distance buses stop for meals.

## MOROGORO
### Accommodation
*MODERATE:* **Kola Hill Hotel**: Old Dar Rd., 2 mi/3 km E of city center, new, quiet, well-tended premises, nice rooms, very good value; Box 1755 Morogoro, tel. (56) 3707, fax 4394. **Morogoro Hotel**: spectacular building before backdrop of the Uluguru Mountains, rooms need renovation; Box 1144 Morogoro, tel. (56) 3270-2 or res.: Bushtrekker Hotels, Box 5350 DSM, tel. (51) 117373. *BUDGET:* **Hilux Hotel**: Old Dar Rd., near city center, several A/C rooms, new; Box 763 Morogoro, tel. (56) 3946. **Mama Pierina**: Station Rd., new, small rooms, in garden behind restaurant; **Masuka Village Hotel**: Boma St., less than 1 mi/1 km from bus stand, green surroundings; Box 930 Morogoro, tel. (56) 4774. **Mount Uluguru Hotel**: City hotel, several stories high, new, good value, restaurant, near bus stand; Box 1557 Morogoro, tel. (56) 4093. Many cheap *gesti* along University Ave., W of market, and some on Boma St., near Masuka Village Hotel. Cheap, modern accommodation at the **Tushikamane Vocational Training Centre**, off Old Dar Rd. (turn S at sign for Kilakala Secondary School); Box 765 Morogoro, tel. (56) 2438, fax (56) 3526.

### Transportation
*BUS:* Fast, frequent service to all places along Tanzania's major paved roads: Arusha, Dodoma, Iringa/Mbeya, Tanga, frequent departures for DSM; at least one departure daily to Ifakara (past Udzungwa NP). Bus stand at beginning of Boma Rd., local minibuses depart from market. *TRAIN:* Four departures a week in each direction of Central Line. *BICYCLE RENTAL:* Many stands along University Ave.

### Hiking
**Morningside**: Ask permission from the *District Cultural Officer* at municipal cultural office (*Manispaa Utamaduni*) opposite post office, Mo-Fr 9 am-3:30 pm. Hiking suggestions, **Guides** provided: Lameck and Maria Noah, Box 1668 Morogoro, tel. (56) 2279.

## RUAHA NATIONAL PARK
### Accommodation
*LUXURY-TENTED CAMP:* **Mwagusi Safari Camp**: Small, comfortable camp, 5 mi/8 km from park HQ; Chris Fox, Box 84, Mufindi, or Coastal Travels, Box 3052 DSM, tel. (51) 37480, fax (51) 46045. **Ruaha Tented Camp**: Res.: Flycatcher Safaris & Hotels, Box 591 Arusha, tel. (57) 6963, fax (57) 8261. *MODERATE:* **Ruaha River Lodge**: Bandas around centrally-located restaurant atop hill up from Great Ruaha river; Box 10270 Dar es Sa-

laam, tel. (811) 327706. *BUDGET:* Bandas and campsites can be booked through park authority.

## IRINGA
### Accommodation
*MODERATE:* **Huruma Baptist Conference Center**: 1.5 mi/2.5 km from bus stand, signposted, modern self-catering apartments and rooms, extensive garden premises, meals by order, good value; Box 632 Iringa, tel. (64) 2579. **Motel Mount View**: Dodoma Rd. between airport and town center; Box 658 Iringa, tel. (64) 2503. **M.R. Hotel**: New, downtown hotel, good value, 120 yds/100 m from bus stand, restaurant; Box 431 Iringa, tel. (64) 2006, fax (64) 2661. *BUDGET:* Several older hotels and *gesti* along and off Dodoma road; **Lutheran Center**: Cheap, clean, but strict regulations; Box 484 Iringa, tel. (64) 2286.

### Transportation
**Note:** not all long-distance buses stop at Iringa city center (2 mi/3km from A7), but bypass Iringa on the A7. From Iringa there are many buses daily to Dar es Salaam, Mbeya; one a day to Dodoma via Mtera.

### Excursions
**M.R. Hotel** (see above) and **Iringa Safari Tours**: Dodoma Road, Box 107 Iringa, tel. 2718, organize tours and provide rented cars in Ruaha NP, Iringa area etc. *BICYCLE RENTAL* from stand near market or through hotels. You can cycle to **Isimila**, 15 mi/25 km on mostly paved road (turnoff signposted on A104); **Kalenga**, museum/memorial of Chief Mkwawa, 8 mi/13 km, solid sand road (toward Ruaha NP).

## DODOMA
### Accommodation
*S of railway line: MODERATE:* **Dodoma Hotel** (Railway Hotel): Opposite railway station, modern rooms around inner courtyard with nice garden, restaurant; Box 239 Dodoma, tel. (61) 24042, fax (61) 24911. *BUDGET:* **Jamboree Hotel**: SW of Boma, in garden, rooms need renovation; Box 2692 Dodoma, tel. (61) 24395. **Kilimanjaro Villa**: Private house with family atmosphere, in well-tended garden, near station, signposted at S end of Boma Street; Box 894 Dodoma, tel. (61) 20258. *City center: BUDGET:* **Christian Council of Tanzania**: N of railway line, next to Anglican church, professional service, clean, good value, cafeteria, kiosk; Box 372 Dodoma, tel. (61) 21682, fax (61) 24445. Cheap *gesti* near market. *N of airport: MODERATE:* **Nam Hotel**: on Arusha road, new; Box 868 Dodoma, tel. (61) 22255. *BUDGET:* **Capital Lodge**: In green upper-class residential neighborhood; Box 1763, tel. (61) 24861.

### Transportation
*TRAIN:* Both the *up train* (towardTabora, Kigoma) and the *down train* (toward Morogoro, Dar es Sa-

laam run four times a week). *BUS:* Bus stand for long-distance buses .25 mi/300 m from market, several buses a day to Morogoro/Dar es Salaam; daily service to Kondoa/Arusha, once a day to Iringa on direct route (A104); once a week directly to Singida (via Kwa Mtoro or Manyoni).

### Museum
**Museum of Mineralogy** (*Nyumba ya Naonyesho ya Madini*), behind Dodoma Hotel, opposite Ministry of Geology and Mines, Mon-Fri 7:30 am-3:30 pm.

## KONDOA, KOLO, BABATI
### Accommodation
**Kondoa**: *BUDGET:* **New Splendid Hotel**: .25 mi/300 m from bus stand, new, clean; Box 454 Kondoa, tel. 41. **Savana Inn**: Near bus stand, rooms with shower, toilet; Box 67 Kondoa, tel. 169. In **Kolo** there's a simple *CAMPSITE*, and you can sometimes find private accommodation; bring your own gear. **Babati**: Several *gesti* near bus stand and along main road.

### Transportation
*BUS:* **Kondoa**: Long-distance buses to Singida, Dodoma; (during dry season:) Tanga; all buses to Babati/Arusha stop at **Kolo** (14 mi/22 km).

### Sighseeing
KONDOA: **Chemchem ya Maji**, artesian well, permission from *Idara ya maji*, Waterworks Department. KOLO: **Rock paintings:** 500 TSh, guide obligatory.

## SINGIDA
### Accommodation
*BUDGET:* **Legho Singida Motel**: in well-tended garden, signposted on main road; Box 141 Singida, tel. (606) 2426. **Stanley Motel Singida**: Near bus stand, restaurant; Box 450 Singida, tel. (606) 2351. Many *gesti* near bus stand.

### Museum
Regional Museum: 200 yards/150 m from main road on Lake Singidani, Mon-Sat 9 am-6 pm.

## TABORA, NZEGA
### Accommodation
TABORA: *BUDGET:* **Tabora Hotel**: Stylish colonial building in garden; Box 810 Tabora, tel. 4566. Lots of *gesti* near P.O., market. NZEGA: *BUDGET:* **Four Ways Executive Hotel**: Box 75 Nzega, tel. 2577.

### Transportation
*PLANE:* Air Tanzania flies Dar es Salaam-Tabora(-Kigoma)-Dar es Salaam on Mo, We, Fr. *TRAIN:* Service to Kigoma, Dar and Mwanza 4 times a week, 3 times to Mpanda. *BUS:* Daily to Singida; 3 times a week to Shinyanga, twice a week Kitunda-Mbeya. *BICYCLE RENTAL:* **Hadji Mzanzibar**, near market.

### Sightseeing
**Livingstone's Tembe**: Kwihara, from market, 4 mi/7 km on Sikonge road, 1.2 mi/2 km from sign.

# THE SOUTH: LAND OF CONTRASTS

### THE ISOLATED SOUTHEAST
### LINDI / MTWARA
### SONGEA / LAKE NYASA (WEST)
### MBEYA CENTER
### TUKUYU / LAKE NYASA (NORTH)

## THE ISOLATED SOUTHEAST

The Rufiji River, lengthened and reinforced by its most important tributaries, Luwegu and Great Ruaha, surges along even during the dry season, and its load of yellow-brown sediment fans far out into the Indian Ocean, more or less off Mafia island. To date, this river remains a significant obstacle to any road connections between Dar es Salaam and the southeastern part of Tanzania, which comprises mainly the Lindi and Mtwara regions.

A series of low mountain ranges extends for some distance along the coast. Sometimes nearer, sometimes farther away from their eastern slopes runs the B2, the road that represents the main traffic artery from Dar es Salaam into the southeast of the country. The poor condition of this road, combined with the fact that there are no bridges over the Rufiji, are the main reasons that the southeastern regions are cut off from the rest of Tanzania. Motorists should expect to proceed at an average speed of 12-20 mph (20-30 km/h). The road is only passable during the dry season in any case; after heavy

*Preceding pages: The ebony carvings of the Makonde carvers are world renowned. Left: A satisfied smile in Lindi.*

downpours it becomes a veritable mud-pit. A few larger rivers which are only really significant during the rainy season, such as the Matandu or the Mbwemkuru rise in the eastern Selous area and flow into the Indian Ocean. The bridges over them are laid out with loose wooden timbers and require some very careful driving.

The road connections with the western parts of Tanzania's southeast area are no better. There is a good asphalt road from the north only to Songea, the capital of Ruvuma Region, but after that, there's no more asphalt – for a stretch of more than 280 miles (450 km) of bad road to Masasi in Mtwara Region. Tanzania's southeast is veritably trapped during the rainy season. The ferry *Canadian Spirit*, which is primarily a cargo rather than a passenger ship, commutes between Dar and Mtwara once a week; and there are scheduled flights to Mtwara. Only these lifelines keep the channels of communication open during the rains.

If you're not put off by the prospect of difficult transportation and don't expect to find a well-developed tourist infrastructure, Tanzania's southeast will reward you with everything that its nature and culture have to offer – in a pure form, moreover, that hasn't yet been processed to make it salable on the tourist market.

153

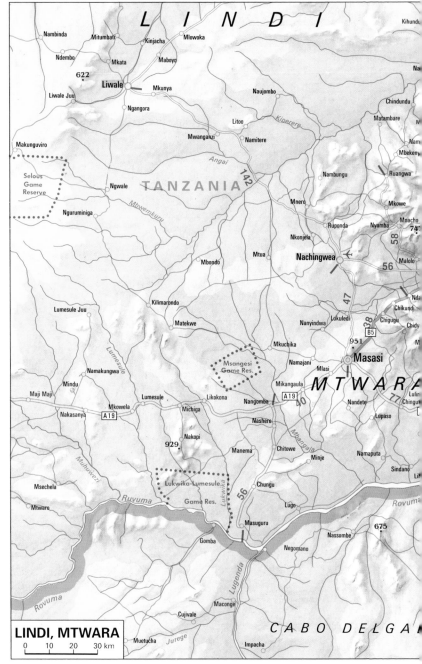

**LINDI, MTWARA**

0    10    20    30 km

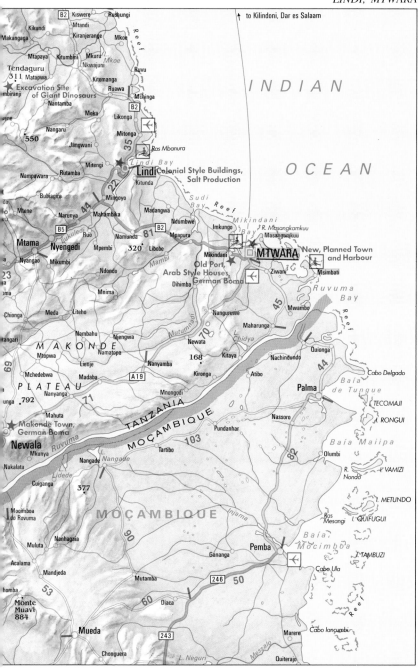

to Kilindoni, Dar es Salaam

INDIAN

OCEAN

B2 Kiswere  Rushungi
Kikundi
Mtandi
Makangaga          Kiranjerange  Mkoe
Mtapaya  Kitumbmi  Mkuru
Nkwajuni
Tendaguru        Kitomanga       Ruvu
311 Matapwa
Excavation Site    Ruawa
of Giant Dinosaurs          Mchinga
mbiranji      Nantamba           B2
vene        Moka      Likonga
Nangaru            Mitonga
550         Jangwani
35
Ras Mbanura
22
Mitengi   *Lindi Bay*
Nampawara  Rutamba      **Lindi** Colonial Style Buildings,
44       Kitunda      Salt Production
Bubiagire  Mingoyo
do    Mtene  Narunya   Mahambika   *Sudi*   Madangwa
u           *Bay*  *Reef*
B5  Ruo  Namunda  81  B2  Ndumbwe   *Mikindani*
**Mtama** **Nyengedi**      Imkungo   R. Masangkamkuu
Nyangao  Mikumbi  Mpembi  **320**  Libobe  Mpapura  Masangamkuu
23                Mikindani  **MTWARA**  New, Planned Town
oma        Ndondo       Old Port,  Ziwani  and Harbour
Chionga  Meda  Liteho   Dihimba  German Boma  Msimbati
Mnima    Arab Style Houses  *Ruvuma*
angari            Nangurwe  *Bay*
Nambahu  Njengwa
M A K O N D E  *Mutumndi*  Maharunga
Mtopwa  Namatopa  Newata  *Chidya*
69           Lienje  Nanyamba  **168**  Kitaya  Nachindundo  Quionga  Cabo Delgado
Mchedebwa  Madaba  A19  Kironga  Atibo  44
P L A T E A U     Mnongodi  *Baía*
unga  792  Nanyanga  71  **Palma**  *de Tungue*
Mahuta  I. TECOMAJI
Makonde Town,  *T A N Z A N I A*  Nassoro  I. RONGUI
German Boma  *M O Ç A M B I Q U E*  Pundanhar  *Baía Maiipa*
**Newala**  103  Olumbi  82
Mkunya  Nangade  *Nangade*  Tartibo  R. I. VAMIZI
Nakalata  *Lidede*  Nondo
Cuiganga  377  I. METUNDO
Ras  I. QUIFUGUI
Mocimboa  Mesangi
do Rovuma  M O Ç A M B I Q U E  *Injama*  *Baía*
Muluta  Nanhagaia  90  *Mocimboa*
Acalama  **Pemba**  I. TAMBUZI
Mandjeda  Gananga
homba  53  Mutamba  246  50  Cabo Ula
Monte  60  Diaca
Muavi  884  Cabo Iancumbi
**Mueda**  243
Chongueta  *L. Neguri*  Marere  *Messalo*  Quiterajo

155

## LINDI

**Lindi** is the capital of the region of the same name, an area of 25,400 square miles (66,000 sq. km), slightly smaller than the state of New York (or the Republic of Ireland), yet populated by only 760,000 people. A third of the land surface is taken up by the Selous Game Reserve, and the most populous areas are the coastal lowlands and the mountain country in the south.

With about 40,000 inhabitants, the town extends along the western bank of the **Lukuledi**, shortly before the river flows into the Indian Ocean at one of the few openings in the reef barrier. Its protected location on the broad estuary was the decisive factor in the decision to choose this site for the port and city when, in the 18th and 19th centuries,

*Above: In the harbor of Lindi, passengers board a ferry to Lukuledi. Right: When the tide is low, a narrow path leads through the mangrove thickets.*

ocean-going ships had lower draughts and the slave and ivory trade from the interior flourished. A caravan route from Lake Nyasa ended here. The sultan of Zanzibar ruled this part of the coast.

Compared to Kilwa Kivinje, where another caravan route had its terminus, modern Lindi has almost no historical monuments from its Arabian past. Still visible, although long since romantically overgrown with fig trees, is an **Arabian Tower** near the middle of town, northeast of the football stadium, almost fully integrated into a garage; nothing about it indicates any sense of coherence with the rest of the present townscape. Characteristic of that townscape is a grid network of streets with blocks of buildings, rarely as tall as two storeys, which only become really concentrated in the area around the harbor. Here are grouped the post office, police and offices of the local administration, near the remains of a German **boma**. As kind of counterpart to this are the picturesque remains of a **German warehouse** which stand nearby, south of the port facilities (which are closed to the public). The building appears to be constructed on stilts: each of its iron pilings is fitted out with a plate-shaped sleeves that could be filled with oil to hinder vermin from invading the house.

### On the Lukuledi

Lindi's downtown streets are not particularly enticing, so a visitor is more likely to be drawn to the beach of the Lukuledi. Its clear water, slightly salty due to the proximity of the ocean, winds around the town in an S-curve, forming a broad, sandy bay beside the northern residential areas. From ther market, it is about 3 miles (5 km) north on the B2 to the half-mile long (1 km), perfectly white sands of **Mitema Beach**. The beaches south of the harbor are not as wide, but they are hives of activity: the ferries for Kitunda peninsula on the other side of the river depart from here. A few steps farther along the beach and you come to the **fish market**.

Additional pockets of beauty on this arm of the Lukuledi estuary can be explored by boat: about 7 miles (12 km) upstream you can see crocodiles; downstream, you come to the ocean and the coral reefs, or you can undertake an excursion to *kisiwa cha popo*, the **island of the bats**, to visit a colony of fruit bats who rest in the trees by day. Traveling on the river is itself a pleasure: luxuriantly green mangroves line the edge of the startling blue water, and bizarre, dark rock ledges of coral limestone rising up out of the sea are interspersed with white, sandy beaches.

South of Lindi's city limits, there are huge basins for salt extraction on the west bank of the river.

### Kitunda Peninsula

The Kitunda Peninsula lies alluringly on the eastern bank of the Lukuledi, opposite the town of Lindi. In the morning,

at the ferry dock, you can see many inhabitants crossing over from there to Lindi carrying on their heads woven baskets of fresh vegetables and delicious fruit to be sold at the market and in the streets of Lindi. The lush green profusion of vegetation is especially astounding during the dry season.

Cross over on one of the roomy wooden boats, packed to the gunwales with bags, baskets of vegetables, chickens, bikes and people. There's a lot to see on the short trip, from scenery to the entertaining spectacle of the loading and unloading process. The ferries with outboard motors don't bother to use the dilapidated landing: you just wade barefoot a little way out into the warm water and climb on board.

If you turn north on the coastal path at the **Kitunda** ferry landing, you will soon discover the secret of the superb vegetables grown here: groves of bananas create a pleasantly cool atmosphere, tall trees shade the intensively irrigated plots of vegetables, and, although salt water murmurs between the mangroves on the Lukuledi side, on land the water plashing through the little canals is clear and fresh. Kitunda peninsula is so blessed with fresh water that it can afford to pipe drinking water across the broad river to Lindi.

As it leads towards the estuary, this scenically varied route sometimes takes you up onto high, steep platforms of coral limestone or along enchanting, sandy beaches, at other times through tiny fishing harbors or mangrove thickets. If you would prefer a panorama of the Lukuledi, take the steep path up into the village from the ferry landing. The main path is lined with fields and sparse stands of trees and bushes, and if you wander along it you will come upon neglected sisal plantations, processing and transport facilities left to wind and weather. They are overgrown and populated by swarms of birds.

The various paths on the peninsula allow hours of excursions, and you can always find a guide among the friendly villagers if you wish to go exploring.

### Rondo Plateau

North and south of the broad, branching course of the Lukuledi, high tablelands rise up out of the hinterland behind the coast. The most extensive of these is the Makonde Plateau in Mtwara Region; the tallest is the **Rondo Plateau**. To reach it, take the asphalted road B5 to Masasi and turn north at **Nyengedi,** about 40 miles (60 km) from Lindi. There are several villages scattered on the plateau at elevations of between 2,300 and 3,000 feet (700-900 m). However, many mountainsides are so steep that they cannot be farmed, and so they still boast their natural plant cover. Since the Rondo Plateau towers above its surroundings, its slopes

*Right: Fossilized dinosaur bone, found on Tendaguru Hill.*

trap more precipitation than the rest of the area, making it a splash of green in an otherwise comparatively dry environment. Reforestation with pine trees has been successful here. The woods and the verdant slopes, abundant with endemic plant life, are an open invitation to adventurous hikers. A local guide is strongly recommended, and a four-wheel-drive vehicle is almost imperative, since public transportation services only thetowns along the B5.

### Giant Dinosaurs on Tendaguru Mountain

Since the Jurassic Period (about 200-145 million years ago), the sea has often flooded East Africa's coastal region and its hinterland, an area of mountains running almost parallel to the coast, but the area was always subsequently elevated and transformed back into mainland once again. Dinosaurs were the dominant life form during the Jurassic and Cretaceous Periods. Between 1909 and 1913, during their scientific expedition around the hill **Tendaguru**, about 60 miles (100 km) northwest of Lindi, German paleontologists were able to establish that many dinosaurs had fallen victim to three periods of flood catastrophes here: they were embedded in loose sediment, their bones petrified. The scientists were fascinated by their gigantic size. Over a period of almost five years, the explorers and their local helpers, sometimes numbering as many as 500, recovered and dispatched 250 tons of carefully packed material, which was sent to the Museum of Natural History in Berlin. After decades of preparation the most magnificent dinosaur skeletons were exhibited there, the largest of them belonging to the *Brachiosaurus brancai* – 75 feet (23 m) long and 39 feet (12 m) tall. This colossus was, the evidence indicates, of a peaceful nature: its teeth show that it was a vegetarian. It consumed an estimated 1 ton of greenery every day.

Mainly covered in *miombo* forest, this area was robbed of its most glorious dinosaur fossils during the German colonial period. Later, other scientific investigations took place; you can still see the excavation trenches which different expeditions left behind. There are still fossils around on the site, but they may be removed only with special permission. Today as then, the hike to the site is itself an experience, albeit very arduous. Only during the dry season, and with a four-wheel drive vehicle, is it possible to penetrate as far as one of the villages near the mountains. The month of October is especially well suited, when the tall grass has been burnt off, providing a better overview of the direction of the road and the general lie of the land. The village **Namapuia** lies closest to Tendaguru; from there, accompanied by one of the locals, you can inspect the grounds. One thing you have to do in advance is get advice and permission from the regional administration in Lindi (office of culture and office of natural conservation); in light of the difficulty of accessing the area, this is not only a duty, but a great help.

## MTWARA

Coming upon **Mtwara** for the first time, whether to the market or to the busy bus station, you might wonder at the strangely roundabout route that the paved main street takes through the town. It leads you through extremely diverse, widely separated districts of town: past the modern buildings of the regional administration and post office, then past a densely built-up business and banking complex, dating for the most part from the 1950s and 1960s; next, you see a large park area with trees, simple row huts, and, finally, the market and the bus station. And you haven't even yet touched the exclusive residential quarters, nor the port and the industrial area, which are kept well separated from the rest of the town by fields and open ground.

159

The town Mtwara is only a half century old. It has not yet fulfilled the dreams of the urban planners who designed it in the middle of the 20th century: it was to grow into a big city of 200,000 inhabitants and become the most important transportation and trade center of the southeast. Those plans took into account the fact that in this process the traditional center, Lindi, would lose some of its importance.

In 1946, the British administration determined that Tanzania should become an important supplier of vegetable fat. This ambitious British project envisioned clearing wide swaths of *miombo* forest in the district of Nachingwea, about 90 miles (150 km) west of Lindi, and transforming the area into fields of peanuts. At that time, the nearest port for shipping the peanuts was Lindi, which could be used

*Above: In a kitchen near the coast. Right: The slave market in Mikindani once marked the end of the caravan routes and the beginning of untold new sufferings.*

only by ships with a shallow draught; and the road to Lindi was unpaved and therefore only really navigable during the dry season. These factors led not only to the erection of a deep-water port in the bay of the former fishing village Mtwara, thereby advancing it to the status of regional capital of the southeast, but also to the construction of the Mtwara-Masasi railroad line.

By 1950, it was already more or less clear that the mammoth peanut project had failed. Still, the port has remained a blessing for the southeast of Tanzania. The train line proved to be unprofitable and was abandoned in 1962; its planned function has since been taken over by an excellent asphalt road between Mtwara and Masasi.

Today, the southeast is divided into two administrative regions: the large, sparsely-settled Lindi Region, with its attractively situated, but economically marginal capital, and the comparatively small, densely-populated Mtwara Region (6,540 square miles/17,000 sq. km; one

million inhabitants), its capital equipped with a better infrastructure, even if its merits are somewhat dubious from the standpoint of urban planning.

### Mikindani

Mtwara's most important sight lies 7 miles (11 km) west of the regional capital: mangroves line the symmetrical, rounded bay of **Mikindani**, which is protected by coral reefs. The name of the town was most probably derived from *msikiti ndani* (in-the-mosque) and reveals its Arabian origins. Like Lindi, 60 miles (100 km) distant, Mikindani was once the terminus of a caravan route from the southern part of Lake Nyasa, which brought slaves and ivory through the Ruvuma valley. Like Lindi, the town was under the influence of the Sultan of Zanzibar in the 19th century. Back in those days, the houses of the Arabian traders must have looked splendid with their carved doors and wooden balconies; today, they are deteriorating. You can't miss the wide front of the German **boma**. Now that it no longer serves as a police station, it, too, has been abandoned to ruin.

David Livingstone disembarked from a dhow at this port, when he began his last Africa journey in 1866. The picturesque bay with its wooden boats and the busy market make Mikindani a town worth visiting, especially since there is a pleasant new hotel in **Mitengo**, a little way out of town.

### Beaches and Shores Around Mtwara

Do not expect any seaside hotels in Mtwara. There are a number of better lodgings in the upper-class residential area **Shangani** on a peninsula between the bays of Mikindani and Mtwara. More inviting are the beaches on the peninsula **Masangamkuu** opposite, which embraces the bay of Mtwara; a ferry there operates just south of Shangani. On the peninsula you have a choice: you can either entrust yourself to the rough west-

ern side, to the open sea, or to the eastern side with its sheltering bay.

Those inhabitants of Mtwara with access to a car like to go on outings to the virtually endless beach of **Msimbati**, 25 miles (40 km) to the southeast, about an hour's drive on passable roads. The port of this town is used when crossing to Mozambique, which begins on the other side of the Ruvuma estuary.

Another outing takes you on an hour and a half drive from Mtwara near **Kitaya** to the **Ruvuma**, languid during the dry season (June-October) and torrential during the rainy one (November-May). Here you can watch crocodiles, hippos, waterbuck and reedbuck, among other animals.

### Makonde Plateau

The Makonde represent a large number of the approximately 100,000 inhabi-

*Above: Heavyweight hippos prefer fresh water swamps and ponds. Right: Ebony figure executed by a Makonde carver.*

tants of Mtwara, and some of them actually do occupy themselves with the activities which some naive tourists may exclusively expect of them: they carve ebony sculptures. Particularly because of this, the tribe has become well-known in the latter half of the 20th century. However, the Makonde are primarily farmers, and did not originally settle the coastal area. They originated in the mountainous country south of the Ruvuma, in today's Mozambique; and some of them still live there. As far as anyone can tell, a wave of migration began as early as the middle of the 18th century, sparsely settling the fertile Ruvuma valley, which is in constant danger of seasonal flooding, and spreading out along the coast. In the first quarter of the 19th century, there was another wave, out of the flood-endangered valley flats to the steep highland plateau which juts up like an island to the north of the river. The ground here is dry, sandy and drains off water, but the Makonde preferred these elevated plains, at altitudes of 1,600-2,300 feet (500-700 m), to the valley: through this move they escaped flooding and famine, and on the heights malaria mosquitoes, wild animals, and therefore also tse-tse flies, were less of a nuisance to the settlers. The caravan route of the slave traders may have given them an additional reason for going. In the late 19th century, the population on the **Makonde Plateau** continued to grow: famine in Mozambique and the aggressive Ngoni striving northwards out of South Africa forced more and more Makonde up to these heights. To this day, it has remained the main area of settlement for this tribe, one of the numerically largest in Tanzania. In Mozambique, Makonde continue to settle the high country between the Ruvuma and Messalo rivers.

Two principal reasons led to the Makonde taking up residence in other parts of Tanzania or even in Kenya. The heavy pressure of overpopulation on the plateau and the expulsion during the civil war in Mozambique led many Makonde take on types of work to which members of other tribes would not have been so quick to subject themselves. Employment possibilities on the sisal plantations in the northeast of Tanzania led many Makonde to move there, and many have settled, usually in close-knit groups. Another reason for leaving their original homes was, and still is, the chance to earn money with their ebony carvings, which can best be sold where the demand for them is greatest: in Dar es Salaam, Nairobi or other places in East Africa frequented by tourists. These extraordinary works of art, articles of trade which have found wide currency since the 1950s, initially through the activities of the Indian merchant Mohamed Peera, have blessed the Makonde with a public which they did not have before. In fact, they inhabited such remote areas of Mozambique and Tanzania that even the colonial powers could not reach them easily. This is how they managed to maintain many of their

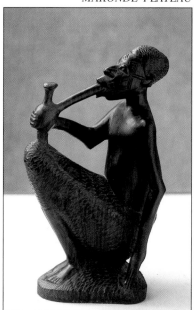

traditions so much better than other tribes did elsewhere. Besides their music and their famous acrobatic stilt-dancing, the best-known of these traditions is the custom the women have of piercing their upper lip with an ebony peg, which they wear as a form of personal adornment. In Tanzania, you sometimes still encounter this in villages with Makonde immigrants from Mozambique. However, filed front teeth seem to have gone out of fashion as a mark of beauty.

### Newala

The sand track A 19 passes the airport of Mtwara, and is a fairly good road for driving. Well-tended cashew plantations prevail on the Makonde Plateau. Sizable villages emerged here during the Tanzanian socialist era. At junctures where larger rivers slice into the plateau, especially west of **Nanyamba**, sharp precipices interrupt the sedate landscape. After a ride of about four hours, you reach the district capital of **Newala**, 90

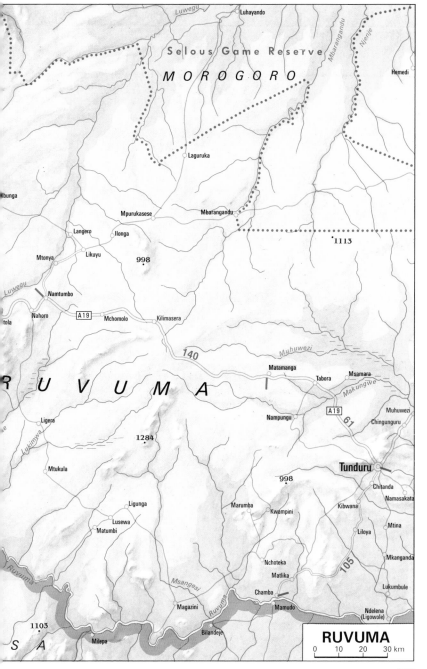

Luwegu

Luhayando

Selous Game Reserve

*MOROGORO*

Mbarangandu

Njenje

Hemedi

Laguruka

Mbunga

Mpurukasese    Mbarangandu

•1113

Langero    Ilonga

Mtonya    Likuyu

998

Luwegu

Namtumbo

Nahoro    A19    Mchomolo    Kilimasera

tola

140

Muhuwezi

Matamanga

Tabora    Msamara

*RUVUMA*    I    Makungwe

Muhuwezi

Ligera    Nampungu    A19    61    Chingunguru

1284

Mtukula

**Tunduru**

998    Chitanda

Ligunga    Marumba    Kwampini    Kibwana    Namasakata

Lusewa    Mtina

Matumbi    Liloya

Nchoteka    Mkanganda

Matlika    105

Ruvuma    Msangesi    Chamba    Lukumbule

Magazini    Ruvuma    Mamudo

Ndelena    (Ligowole)

1103

Milepa    Bilandeje

S    A

**RUVUMA**

0    10    20    30 km

Lukimwa

165

miles (140 km) distant. An extensive **market** makes up the middle of the town. Most of the administrative offices lie further west, directly on the sharp edge of the plateau. Immense mango trees line the sandy roads to the **boma**. From there a steep, serpentine path leads down the slope. The Germans built this fortress, which resembles an enchanted castle more than anything else; the district administration offices are located here. The view from up here makes the commanding position of the boma clear: you can view the forested breadth of the **Ruvuma Valley** for a long way south and west. Beyond that, the mountains of Mozambique rear up, where Makonde also make their homes. There is no bridge over the river. A suitable spot for one would be 25 miles (40 km) southwest of Newala.

## Masasi

The district town **Masasi** can strike you a bit like a Wild West frontier town: the paved eastern road from Lindi and Mtwara ends here, and a sand track turns off to Newala which makes fairly good traveling, passing through one vista after another, between the plain dotted with hummocks of gneiss and the plateau. A poor trail leads north via **Nachingwea** into the solitude of the extremely thinly-settled Lindi district to **Liwale**. You can reach Selous Game Reserve from there, but only with a four-wheel-drive vehicle and accompanied by a gamekeeper.

To the west, a predominantly rough dirt track ambles over 280 miles (450 km) to Songea; by bus, you can generally cover this distance in two days – but only during the dry season. Before undertaking this long, bumpy "seated tour," you can climb the legally protected rocks of the **Masasi Hills** (3,120 feet/951 m), and delight in the lovely view, but beware of

*Right: Young girls from the district of Tunduru.*

snakes. There is no lack of simple hotels. Masasi can also serve as a point of departure for visitors to the game reserves of **Lukwika-Lumesule**, on the border of the neighboring Ruvuma Region and the Ruvuma River, and **Msangesi**, west of Masasi, on the border of Lindi district.

## Tunduru – Between Selous and Ruvuma

The road conditions of the A19 from Masasi to the west may hold little appeal, but the traveler is instead captivated by the scenic countryside: endless plains of few trees and shrubs, with huge, rounded gneiss boulders jutting out bizarrely. Tall termite hills stand between flat-topped umbrella trees. The villages lie near the river-meadows, often sheltered by grandiose, free-standing stone cliffs. The rivers all drain towards the Ruvuma; that river's sandy valley courses 30 miles (50 km) south of the road through the almost deserted landscape, without a single bridge along the more than 560 miles (900 km) of its course along which it forms the Kenyan border. It has its source west of Songea and runs for the most part through very old rock strata, which often enough contain precious stones – garnets, for example. For this reason, **Tunduru** is, along with Masasi, an important starting-point for prospectors wishing to scour the river valleys of the Ruvuma and its tributaries for worthwhile mineral finds. In addition, it is these rivers which virtually predestine the area around Tunduru for farming, though sales are made difficult by poor traffic connections in all directions.

Tunduru also marks the center of the land of the Yao. They were known, among other things, for their iron-forging, trade and use of European weapons; their traders traveled throughout the country, between Lake Nyasa and Kilwa, and south to Zambezi. Through their contact with the coastal dwellers

they converted to Islam. They traded in ivory and were notorious slave-hunters, acquired firearms early on, and managed to drive the German colonial rulers out of the southeastern coastal area for a time. Not until the end of the 19th century did the Germans subdue their chief Machemba, who fled to Mozambique, where Yao also make their home.

When you leave Tunduru northwest on the A19, you stay for a while in the flats, which are marshy in places and can be difficult to drive on, even during the dry season. A bridge crosses the great **Makungwe River**. On its banks, 12 miles (20 km) upstream in **Nampungu**, there once lay the seat of the legendary chief Mataka I, who led the Yao in the middle of the 19th century, at a time when their territory was larger than ever before – or since. **Matamanga** is the last major community you pass before you travel along the divide between the Ruvuma and Rufiji systems, continuing almost 60 miles (100 km) through endless, but never monotonous *miombo* forest.

## SONGEA

Two important rivers rise in the mountains, more than 5,000 feet (1,500 m) high, where the town **Songea** sprawls over the northern slopes with its almost 100,000 inhabitants: the **Luwegu**, which becomes the Rufiji in the Selous area, and the 680-mile (1,100 km) long Ruvuma.

In 1897, the Germans erected a wooden fort on one of the foothills. Shortly before that, they had taken pains to convey the impression that their intentions were peaceful when meeting with the Ngoni chieftains, one of whom was also the *nduna* (regional chief) Songea Mbano (for whom the town was later named). At their next meeting, which took place in the fortress, the Germans were rather more direct, arresting the dignitaries instead and shooting five of them dead.

The following years were scarcely happier. The Maji Maji War, which began in the Matumbi Hills, 125 miles

(200 km) south of Dar es Salaam in 1905, spread out over most of the then-German colony and raged longest right there in Ngoni territory. This tribe did not migrate to this area from South Africa until 1840, but they had soon asserted themselves as hardheaded rulers. The Germans managed to break this position of power after cruel executions in 1906 and managing, with difficulty, to resist the Ngoni's guerilla warfare tactics, which lasted until 1908.

What an unhappy beginning for a town! Against this background, however, the town's present aspect is all the more pleasant: at an elevation of 3,800 feet (1,600 m), it boasts agreeable temperatures. The area receives comparatively high precipitation, which is why the town is so green, with lots of shade trees, blossoming front gardens, and a small, lovingly tended public **park** in the center of town. The most important central streets are paved.

*Above: A women's group marches confidently to a wedding in Songea.*

The main road, **Sokoine Road**, ascends the hill on which the boma once stood, now dominated by state-owned administration buildings and modern office blocks, all framed by tall trees, and a pleasant spot for casual walks. A few steps east of the summit (on Njombe Street, *mtaa wa Njombe*) a sign at the edge of a grove of trees announces that this was the **execution grounds** for 40 Ngoni on February 27, 1906.

Turning south on the next asphalt street (Mahenge Street, *mtaa wa Mahenge*), a five-minute walk takes you to the **Maji Maji Memorial**. Larger-than-life sculptures remind us of 12 great chieftains of this area; the 81 rebels executed in the Maji Maji War rest under shading trees in a common grave, while the *nduna* Songea Mbano was laid to rest in an extra grave. A two-story **museum** takes a look back on historical events of the last 150 years in pictures and documents; folk artifacts reveal much about different local crafts and trades, including the forging of iron; and there are photos of traditional ceremonies and festivals, as well as weapons of hunting and warfare.

## TO THE WEST BANK OF
## LAKE NYASA

The paved road which enters Songea from the north continues on to the west for only 12 more miles (20 km) before branching off to **Peramiho**. In 1898, German Benedictine monks founded a mission here, which was discontinued for a while during the Maji Maji War. Later, the Benedictines returned, founding a monastery, abbey, seminary, schools, trade schools, an important printing works and a sizable hospital. This community, which bears a marked European stamp, also has very agreeable lodgings to offer visitors.

The unpaved main road then takes off into mountainous country of *miombo* forest. In the marshy flats there are farming localities with little plots of land, where the locals grow, among other things, cassava and, near the river, sugarcane. However, you will find huge areas of corn fields on a former British farm around **Kitai**.

Farther west along the road to **Mbinga** you will notice a dramatic change in the land use: small, almost rectangular patches of land creep up to the very tops of the rounded hills. In the 19th century, the Ngoni penetrated into the area east of Lake Nyasa. Forced by necessity to get by with less land, the pressured Matengo people turned this into a virtue by carefully adapting their methods of farming to achieve a continuous use of their remaining fields. The secret lies in planting crops on a series of right-angled, intersecting dams. The hollows between the dams collect water and take on the compost from the rest of the cultivated plants and the weeds. To "rotate" the soil, the dams and hollows are regularly restructured; furthermore, the farmers maintain a well-balanced crop-rotation.

The densely wooded mountain country around Mbinga is ideal for the cultivation of coffee. Once a year, in October, coffee buyers come from the capital to this remote area. In order to provide them with suitable accommodation, the *Cultivators Union* built them a hotel with many amenities. Other travelers should not pass up the chance to stay here, if they are here at any time other than October!

### Mbamba Bay

The 42-mile (67 km) section of unpaved road between Mbinga and **Mbamba Bay** on Lake Nyasa forces its way through the eastern mountain chain which edges the lake. The highest peaks are more than 6,600 feet (2,000 m) high; the route is varied, its attraction augmented by the suspense of finally catching sight of the lake. The open, blue arc of the bay and the horizon merging with the surface of the lake give you the impression that you have arrived at a vast, placid ocean. However, *Mbamba Bay* means "Thunder Bay." The contrast between the 6,600-foot (2,000 m) high mountains and the water level of this giant lake, which fluctuates by as much as 1,550 feet/472 m (the lake itself is 37 miles/60 km wide and 348 miles/560 km long north to south), occasionally provokes mighty thunderstorms.

The long landing dock waits for the one ship a week from **Nkhata Bay**, Malawi, and for the Tanzanian ship *M.V. Songea*, based in Itungi Port on the northern edge of the lake, a ship which services the little communities on the lake's eastern shore. This is an essential service, since transportation connections into the eastern hinterlands are either lacking or, at best, difficult. A speciality in Mbamba Bay are the flat, little, smoked *tilapia*, which, thanks to the road, can also be transported from here into the hinterland.

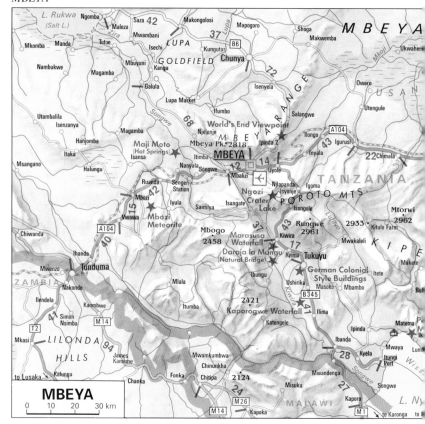

MBEYA
0   10   20   30 km

The lush, green countryside and the backdrop of high mountains are a veritable invitation to hike along the coastal road, rarely used by cars, but oft-trodden by the local inhabitants, which winds along from village to village through the foothills. It is easy, for example, to take a day trip from Mbamba Bay to **Chinula**, a village 4 miles (7 km) to the north. With a four-wheel-drive vehicle, you can navigate the coastal strip as far as **Liuli**, even, under favorable conditions, as far as **Lituhi** on the **Ruhuhu River**. The ferry crosses only during the dry season, which, at these times, makes it possible to continue the journey into the adjacent **Ludewa District** and on to Njombe on the B4. The water in Lake Nyasa is quite clear here and suitable for boating, fishing, swimming and diving.

### From Songea to Makambako

The excellent asphalt road B4 between Songea and the traffic junction **Makambako** is almost 200 miles (300 km) long. However, it is not only the good road which delights travelers; there is also the pleasure of the wide-open landscapes, a magnificent panorama gliding past speedy motorists. The 37 miles (60 km) from Songea to the **Rutukila** bridge (or Rutukira) lead through fairly flat farmland north of the river; the road at first cuts straight through the undulating *miombo* landscape, then has to climb up

(2,000 m) and is an important point of departure for roads to those mountain villages that are so difficult to reach in the **Kipengere Range**, such as **Kitulo**, or in the **Livingstone Mountains**, such as **Ludewa**. In **Makambako**, the B4 links up with the main traffic artery, the road that runs between Dar es Salaam and Zambia.

## MBEYA

Hardly any other town in Tanzania is so well linked with inland and abroad as this fast-growing regional capital, **Mbeya**. There are good asphalt roads: the B 345 to Malawi and the A 104 to Zambia in one direction, and the road to Iringa-Morogoro-Dar es Salaam in the other direction. TAZARA supplies five comfortable train connections a week to Dar es Salaam or Zambia. Yet this young town was born of a feverish passion that began towards the end of the 1920s, on the other side of the mountain chain of the **Mbeya Rang**e, and continues today, to an insignificant degree, during the rainy season in April and May: the exploitation of the gold deposits in the **Lupa Goldfield** in the district of **Chunya**. The unpaved road which snakes up many curves to 8,660 feet (2,640 km), bears the distinction of being the highest main road in the country. During the dry season, buses tackle the route several times a week, and continue on through sparsely settled country via Itigi to Singida.

Not only do traffic routes meet here in Mbeya, but different landscapes also intersect. The spiny, barren peaks of the 9,200 feet (2,800 m) high Mbeya Range, north of the town, form a gusset-seam of steep cliffs running south and east between the systems of the Central and East African Rifts. From the northwest, the long, drawn-out, non-draining **Lake Rukwa** valley points its southern tip towards Mbeya. The **Usangu Flats**, where

into the hills, revealing wide vistas out over the northern plains of Ruvuma. The heights near **Magingo** are partially planted with huge fields of millet. Climbing higher still, the road gains the land of the Bena, who, by utilizing hillside terracing, make optimal use of their farmland in these windswept mountains, plagued by heavy rainfalls. Travelers like to take **Lilondo** as a good excuse for a break; there is coffee planted all around, grevilleas often serve as shade trees. The road winds its way farther and farther upward to treeless tableland, overgrown with grass and ferns. In the **Njombe** area, there are tea and wattle plantations and more and more pine forests. The town of Njombe lies at an altitude of 6,560 feet

171

the Great Ruaha flows, stretch out into the area northeast of Mbeya. Both lowland areas lie more than 3,300 feet (1,000 m) lower than the Mbeya Range. **World's End Viewpoint** is what they call the lookout near **Ipinda 2** (a good 1.5 miles/2 km off the road to Chunya), and it affords breathtaking views of Ruaha Valley and its surroundings.

The Great Ruaha and some of its tributaries from the south have their sources in the **Poroto** and the **Kipengere Mountains**. Important east-west road and rail (TAZARA) connections to Mbeya run along the northern foothills of these two ranges. The little volcanic cones dotting the slopes south of the road cannot be overlooked. From here to the northern end of Lake Nyasa is all volcanic mountain country, that was active well into the 18th century, with the **Rungwe** volcano

*Above: There are no taboos surrounding the subject of condoms – signpost by the entrance to Mbeya. Right: It's a heavenly feeling to ride the Mbozi meteorite.*

forming its highest point at 9,715 feet (2,961 m). It connects both rift systems, which together, now as a single line, continue toward the south in the form of Lake Nyasa.

### The Town of Mbeya

Not only do both of the roads from Mbeya prove to be broad and in good condition, but so do both of the streets accessing the middle of town. Local buses roll briskly mainly along the eastern approach, **Karume Avenue**, while long-distance buses head up and down the western approach, **Mbalizi Road**, to the busy central bus stop. The town center, with banks, a market, shops, restaurants and administrative offices, continues north right on up the hill.

At an elevation of about 5,600 feet (1,700 m), the town nestles into the southern slope of the Mbeya Range, a slope divided over and over with canyons. Shaded avenues, little groves of trees, gardens and fields provide pleasant

contrasts in this area, settled by nearly 200,000 inhabitants. On clear days, you feel you can almost touch the mountain peaks. A walk to the nearest mountain, **Loleza Peak**, is a recommended half-day's outing in clear, dry weather. A fence obstructs the climb to the top, which reaches an altitude of 8,713 feet (2,656 m), but even at this lower point, you have a fantastic view of the town and the Poroto Mountains.

### Day Trips from Mbeya

A four-wheel-drive vehicle is almost a must for day-trips from Mbeya. As enticing as the barren, pointed summit may appear from town, **Mbeya Peak** with its 9,245 feet (2,818 m) is no picnic to manage on foot from town in only one day. It is better to drive about 8 miles (13 km) up the Chunya road, and then continue straight on along a track in **Kawetire Forest Reserve**, while the road to Chunya makes a curve to the right. The route takes you northeast for about 1.3 miles (2

km) and then west for 8 miles (13 km). From there, you continue on foot for another hour and a half to reach the top. You should only try this outing in dry weather with good visibility; make sure to take a guide along, and don't forget to bring warm clothing and plenty of drinking water.

One of the best-known sights of Mbeya Region is the **Mbozi Meteorite**. About 34 miles (54 km) south of Mbeya (2 miles/3 km northeast of **Mbozi**), on the A104 is a sign stating *Meteorite 13 km*. Take this Mbozi ring road (it returns to the 104 in the town Vwawa), following it to **Marengi Hill**, an elevation south of the village of **Isela**. There, about 660 feet (200 m) east of the road, lies the iron-nickle meteorite, about 10 feet (3 m) long, its estimated weight 12 tons. An attendant is always present to hand round the visitors' book and tender detailed descriptions to anyone thirsting for knowledge.

Also convenient to the A104, are the **hot springs** (*maji moto*) near the scenic

173

valley of the **Songwe** river, which flows into Lake Rukwa. Drive past the town of **Songwe**, 16 miles (26 km) west of Mbeya; the tall smokestacks of its cement plant are a landmark. The A104 crosses the deep, steep-sided valley of the Songwe 1.2 miles (2 km) further on. After crossing the bridge and before the road goes up the southern side and back to the plateau, take the sand track west for about 1,000 feet (300 m), behind a ford, follow the track up the slope. Some 6 miles (9 km) further on, at the camp of the limestone quarry, ask for a guide. It is an hour's walk through open bushland and along the southern bank, high above the Songwe. After magnificent prospects of the river's horseshoe bends and of secluded farmholds, you reach the colorful hot springs, which hot enough to boil eggs. The *pango la popo* or **bats' caves** near the quarry are an addition attraction that beckons visitors.

### Ngozi Crater Lake

Lush green scenery awaits travelers in the mountains south of Mbeya. It isn't only the volcanic soil that makes this area so fertile; its heights also receive considerably more precipitation than do the sterile plateaus east and west of Mbeya, which are crossed by the A104 and the TAZARA. If there is not enough time to undertake more intensive tours of this volcanic region, you should at least try to get a first impression of its beauty by scheduling a day trip to **Ngozi Crater Lake**, in the caldera of the **Ngozi** volcano. If you are in good enough shape to hike, you can dispense with a car and get on one of the many buses from Mbeya towards Tukuyu, Kyela or Malawi, getting off about 22 miles (35 km) from Mbeya on the B 345 at the crossing, about 1.2 miles (2 km) south of the village of **Ison-**

*Right: The basalt bridge "Daraja la Mungu," God's bridge.*

**gole**, where a sign greets you with the words *Welcome Lake Ngozi 4 km*. This welcome on the rusty sign is as inviting as it is misleading: after hiking 2.5 miles (4 km) through flat fields west towards the volcano, what you reach is a small farm. Northwest of that, you enter the wooded region of the **Itunza Forest Reserve**, which goes on up to the top in the **Poroto Ridge Forest Reserve**. For the first 1.5 miles (2-3 km), there is a poor motor track through the tall, dense woods; if you are on foot, you see more of its ample vegetation and bird life. For the last 40 minutes, to the southeastern edge of the crater, you have to make do with a narrow footpath, steep in places, slippery in the least bit of damp weather, but always in the shade. Your efforts are amply rewarded by the sight of the diversity of luxuriant vegetation along the way: you pass gigantic forest bananas, groves of delicate bamboo, countless blossoming trees, and mighty clinging vines. Occasionally, you catch a glimpse of the classic proportions of the giant Rungwe volcano, southeast of Ngozi. The lookout point on the cliff lies at an altitude of about 7,200 feet (2,200 m), and although the calm surface of the elongated crater lake may tempt some to attempt the 660 feet (200 m) descent, the climb back up to the crater's rim is a struggle because of the loose scree that covers the slope.

### TUKUYU

43 miles (70 km) from Mbeya, the road to Malawi, the B345, passes through **Tukuyu**. In 1901 the Germans erected a **boma** on the 5,250-foot (1,600 m) volcano peak here. The town which evolved below this, named Neu-Langenburg by the Germans, became the capital of the district of Rungwe. From the fortress, there is a commanding view toward Lake Nyasa and, in the opposite direction, northward, a view of the **Rungwe** vol-

cano, 9,715 feet (2,961 m) high. Seemingly barren, its summit thrusts up out of a thick belt of trees. It is possible to start the climb from any of the villages lying southwest of its lower extremity (from the B345 you can reach them west of **Kiwira** or north of **Kyimo**, respectively). A local guide, warm clothing and field rations are necessary. Birdwatchers, don't forget your binoculars.

Tukuyu is the heart of the surrounding area, an area intensively farmed by the Nyakyusa. There are many lovely natural phenomena in this volcanic landscape, which you can easily explore with a four-wheel-drive vehicle on the roads of the surrounding villages during the dry season; your efforts will be amply rewarded.

### On the Kiwira

The river **Kiwira** has its source on the north flank of the Rungwe volcano; it turns south, and crosses the B345 near the village Kiwira. Its water and that of

its tributaries has eaten deeply into the soft volcanic stone, and where, occasionally, the rock base is harder, rapids, waterfalls and natural stone bridges occur. The **Marasusa Waterfall** is one of these, 3 miles (5 km) south of the village of Kiwira, where the river of the same name plunges into the depths. A poor road accompanies this picturesque river valley downstream, providing a wonderful trail for hikers. Beyond a stand of bananas, 6 miles (10 km) further on, the road comes upon a narrow bend in the river, where the water has to force its way through harder rock. The water roils and boils so noisily in the basalt hollows that this spot is called **Kijungu**, cooking-pot. South of this, the road passes through the grounds of a training institute for prison security personel. Here, you can apply for permission to cross the area and visit the basalt bridge **Daraja La Mungo** (God's Bridge), which arches over the Kiwira 2 miles (3 km) south of Kijungu. From there, it is only 5 miles (8 km) on a fairly good sand track to a

175

the other side of the deep canyon which the Kiwira has formed. Another tributary flows into the Kiwira gorge, 3.5 miles (6 km) further north, and feeds the **Mosiya Waterfall**, actually several individual falls, another 1.3 miles (2 km) further east of that (2.5 miles/4 km west of Lutengano).

## ON THE NORTHERN SHORE OF LAKE NYASA

There are two ways to get from Tukuyu to Lake Nyasa: one, recommended only during the dry season, is to take a secondary road through intensively farmed countryside, past the volcano **Masoko** (with a crater lake) to **Ipinda**, and on to **Matema** on the lake shore. The more comfortable route is the asphalt road B345, from which the road to **Kyela** branches off some 4 miles (7 km) before the Malawi border. From this district capital, it's approximately 7.5 miles (12 km) to **Itungi Port**, the modest pontoon landing stage for the small ship which leaves here once a week to call at the tiny Tanzanian ports on the east side of Lake Nyasa, all the way down to Mbamba Bay.

From Kyela, there is also a road to Ipinda, and from there, it is about 14 miles (23 km) to Matema. The lake's surface lies at an altitude of a good 1,550 feet (470 m), and from this tiny village, you can get a close-up look at the long chain of bizarre pinnacles of the **Livingstone Mountains**, more than 6,600 feet (2,000 m) high, forested still at unusual heights. The flatland at the northern rim of the lake is wet and fertile, ideal for growing rice. Crocodiles live in the rivers. Scores of Nyakyusa villages dot the countryside, rampantly green: oil palms, bamboo, teak, banana and cocoa groves afford shade for intensively farmed plots of vegetables. Huts made of bamboo poles and mud join rounded storage receptacles made of woven bamboo,

simple camping ground belonging to the Pentecostal Holiness Association, or another 6 miles (10 km) to Kyimo on the B 345.

South of Tukuyu, there are two charming waterfalls on tributaries of the Kiwira. To reach the first, you turn, 2.5 miles (4 km) further west on the B345, onto a sand track signposted *Lutengano Moravian Centre* (camping and overnighting), a facility you reach after 4 miles (7 km). From here, it is another 4-mile (7-km) walk to the **Kaporogwe Waterfall** (spelt also Kapologwe); the route is a bit less direct by car. The clear water of the little river here plummets over a stone platform of monumental proportions. The soft layers of sediment below have been so worn away that you can walk behind the veil of water in comfort and marvel at the vista of the cliffs on

*Above: How to carve a dugout canoe, by Lake Nyasa. Right: Pots from Ikombe are renowned for their quality throughout the country.*

with cone-shaped grass roofs, in a picturesque ensemble.

There has been a branch of the Evangelical Lutheran Berlin Mission in Matema for more than 100 years. Beside a hospital and a church, there is the **Matema Conference and Retreat Centre** with ample accommodation and community facilities. You can undertake a range of marvelous hikes and boat trips from this heavenly starting point right on the lake. The Livingstone range beckons with waterfalls and steep footpaths through the green mountains to such destinations as **Bulongwa**, to the lookout over the endless lake or the volcano peaks in the north. The lake itself invites you to go swimming, diving, or to engage in other water sports. A walk along the eastern lake shore, now sandy, now rocky, or a boat trip will bring you to the peninsula of **Ikombe**, the pottery village whose products are traded every Saturday at the market on the lake, half an hour's walk east of Matema. Every morning, the fishermen of Matema sell their catch right on the shore and all day long you can watch boatbuilders working on dugout canoes.

### Tunduma

The Mbeya Region actually has common borders with two countries: Malawi and Zambia. **Tunduma** is the border crossing for the international route A104 as well as for the TAZARA railway line. Even travelers who only have a visa for a single entry into Tanzania here have a chance to take a quick step over the border onto Zambian territory and immediately return: Tunduma is a divided town. Entering the market place, you pass, unchecked, several thigh-high concrete pylons, which represent the frontier. The merchants sell products from both countries, and payment is accepted in both currencies. In its role as a border- and market town, Tunduma is quite a hectic center for the wide-open, rural countryside and has several guest-houses and restaurants.

177

## LINDI
### Accommodation
*BUDGET:* **South Honour Guest House**, Amani St., one block SE of bus stand; some 10 *gesti* located around the town, none by Lukuledi river.
### Restaurant
**Biashara Club**: Market Ave., next to stadium.
### Transportation
*BUS:* Daily service from/to Dar es Salaam (c. 18 hrs) (in Dar: bus stand Morogoro/Libya St.), as long as B2 is passable (discontinued during rainy season), or the Rufiji ferry is in operation. Frequent buses to Mtwara, they pass *Mnazi Mmoja* (Mingoyo) intersection, 14 mi/22 km (about 1 hour) south of Lindi, from here, good asphalt road: some 50 mi/80 km to Mtwara or 78 mi/125 km to Masasi.
*FERRY* to Kitunda peninsula: at Lukuledi river bank, S of port; frequent service, according to demand.

## MTWARA, MIKINDANI
### Accommodation
MTWARA: *BUDGET:* The better hotels are on the Shangani peninsula, about 1 mi/2 km from market/bus stand: **Finn Club**: Guest apartments, sports, restaurant; Box 113 Mtwara, tel. (59) 3020. **Tingatinga Inn**: in beautiful garden; Box 378 Mtwara, tel. (59) 3146. **Shangani Club**: By the sea; Box 84 Mtwara. *MODERATE:* **Mtwara Oceanic Hotel**, near the Masangamkuu ferry, Box 544 Mtwara (still under construction in 1997). **Chilindima Guest House**: Simple, clean, near the bus stand. Many more *gesti* around town. Near the town entrance is the **Lutheran Centre** guest accommodation. MIKINDANI: **Litingi Hotel**: in suburban Mitengo, new, pleasant, with disco; Box 569 Mtwara, tel. (59) 3635.
### Transportation
*PLANE:* **Air Tanzania**, three flights a week to/from Dar es Salaam.
*BOAT:* **F.S. Candian Spirit**: Wed 9 am from Malindi Wharf, Dar es Salaam; the trip takes about 24 hours, depending on number of stops. Returns to Dar Fri 2:30 pm. Ticket kiosk at bus stand Mtwara.
*BUS:* Several buses a day to Lindi, Newala, Masasi; daily service to Dar es Salaam, as long as road conditions and operation of Rufiji ferry permit.
### Makonde Carvers
Several stands along the main roads. For more contacts inquire Father Ildefons, St. Paul's church community, a few hundred yards/meters from bus stand.

## NEWALA
### Accommodation
*BUDGET:* **Mang'ambe Inn**: Near bank, post office: new, very clean rooms with shower & toilet; Box 388 Newala. More *gesti* along main roads near market.
### Transportation
*BUS:* daily to Mtwara, Masasi, Lindi.

## MASASI
### Accommodation
*BUDGET:* **Masasi Hotel**: On main road, restaurant, bar, some rooms have shower and toilet; Box 51 Masasi, Tel 174. **Hidden Bar & Guesthouse**: Near bus stand, toward district offices. Masasi has plenty of bars, restaurants and *gesti*, especially, along the main road.
### Transportation
*BUS:* Daily service to Dar es Salaam, Tunduru/Songea, Newala, Nachingwea, road conditions permitting.

## TUNDURU
### Accommodation
*BUDGET:* **Hunters Guest House**: Best hotel in town, slightly east of center; good restaurant opposite the hotel. **Hunters Annex**: Next to market/ bus stand, rooms with shower, toilet; Box 289 Tunduru, tel. 148. More *gesti* near market & along main street.
### Transportation
*BUS:* In the dry season daily service to Masasi and Songea, as long as road conditions permit; each leg takes approx. 9-10 hours, very dusty roads.

## SONGEA
### Accommodation
*BUDGET:* **Angoni Arms Hotel**: Lindi Rd., .25 mi/300 m from regional offices, pleasant site in garden, under construction 1997; Box 204 Songea, tel. 2279. **OK Hotel**: One block south from market; Box 232 Songea, tel. 2640. **Yapender Holiday Lodge**: in the block south of the market, pleasant garden; Box 575 Songea, tel. 675; **Yapender Annex Lodge**: A little S of Holiday Lodge, corner Makita Rd., new, very well-tended; Box 575 Songea, tel. 2855. Many *gesti* around main road (Sokoine Rd.), three *gesti* by bus stand. **Peramiho Mission**: Guest accommodation, 15 mi/25 km from Songea.
### Restaurant
Inside **Songea De Luxe Hotel & Guest House**: Sokoine Rd. opposite market, entrance from side street. **Malindi Inn**: Opposite western side of market, modern style.
### Transportation
*BUS:* Several buses a day to Mbeya, Dar es Salaam; frequent service to Peramiho. Several buses a day to Mbinga, and at least one a day to Mbamba Bay. Daily to Tunduru-Masasi (dry season only).
### Sightseeing
Maji Maji Memorial: Mahenge Street. **Museum** on the premises, open 7:30 am-6:30 pm.

## MBINGA
### Accommodation
*MODERATE:* **MBICU Hotel**: restaurant, spacious rooms with bath & toilet, each with terrace, in well-tended garden, very good value; Box 562 Mbinga, tel. 168. *BUDGET:* **Pacific Bar & Guest House**: At bus stand, new, very clean, courteous service; Box 86 Mbinga. More *gesti* around bus stand.

### Restaurant

MBICU Hotel; **Stand Hotel** next to bus stand.

### Transportation

*BUS:* Several departures daily to Songea (takes 3-4 hours); one or two a day to Mbamba Bay (2-3 hours); difficult road during rainy season (December-March).

## MBAMBA BAY
### Accommodation

*BUDGET:* **Nyasa View Lodge**: At northern end of Mbamba Bay, less than 1 mi/1 km from landing, restaurant, several rooms with shower/toilet, boat trips; Box 15 Mbamba Bay, tel. 15. Rather poor *gesti* near market/bus stand/ landing.

### Transportation

*BOAT:* **M.V. Ilara** Tue (2 pm) from/to Nkhata, Malawi. TRC (Tanzania Railway Corporation) has a small motor vessel, **M.V. Songea**, which runs from Itungi Port to the eastern ports of Lake Nyasa, thence to Mbamba Bay-Nkhata and back to Itungi Port, if not discontinued due to repairs.

*BUS:* Daily departures to Songea, if road conditions permit. No buses to Liuli.

## NJOMBE, MAKAMBAKO
### Accommodation

NJOMBE: *BUDGET:* **Milimani Motel**: On main road, modern, rooms with shower/toilet, restaurant, bar, good value; Box 176 Njombe, tel. 2408. Several *gesti* near bus. MAKAMBAKO: Hotels along main rd.

### Transportation

*BUS:* **Njombe:** Songea, Mbeya: every 1-2 hours; Dar es Salaam: several departures daily; daily departures to Ikonda, Makete, Bulongwa and other towns in the mountains. **Makambako:** Important transportation hub, with the *TRAIN* station **TAZARA .**

## MBEYA
### Accommodation

*MODERATE:* **Mbeya Peak Hotel**: Acacia St., E of market, centrally located, quiet, renovated, restaurant, garden bar, good value; Box 822 Mbeya, tel. (65) 3473. **Mount Livingstone Hotel**: in thriving garden, restaurant, bar, slow service; Box 1401 Mbeya, tel. (65) 3331-4. **Rift Valley Hotel**: near stadium, restaurant, bar; Box 1631 Mbeya, tel. (65) 3756. *BUDGET:* **Newtons Hotel**: Near city center, at turn-off of Chunya road, next to European Development Fund; new, clean apartments in beautiful garden; Box 536 Mbeya, tel. (65) 2170. **Karibuni Centre** (church community center): 1.5 mi/2.5 km from city center, or, from main road A104: from bus stop next to Caltex gas station, walk 5 min. N on sandy road; well-organized guest service, several rooms with shower/toilet; Box 144 Mbeya, Tel (65) 3035. **Moravian Youth Centre Hostel**: Near bus stand, on top of hill next to radio mast, popular with backpackers, cheap; Box 1119 Mbeya, tel. (65) 3263. Many *gesti* near bus stand and along main roads.

### Restaurant

**Mbeya Peak Hotel**: Good food, meals served in lovely garden, if desired. **Babu Kubwa Bakery**: Lupa Way, across from market, bread and cakes, snacks on upper floor.

### Transportation

*TRAIN:* **TAZARA** 5 departures weekly to Dar es Salaam, 2 express trains (takes 19 hrs. 45 mins.) and 3 local trains (23 hrs. 30 mins.); terminus is at Kapiri Mposhi (Zambia). Mbeya station lies 4 mi/7 km SW of city center on B104, local bus connection to city.

*BUS:* Excellent connections to all destinations along the paved main roads: frequent departures to Dar es Salaam, Songea, Malawi (also Tukuyu, Kyela), Zambia; once daily to Arusha via Chalinze; daily to Sumbawanga; twice a week to Singida, Tabora. Long-distance bus stand at Mbalizi Rd., below city center. Local buses operate mostly along Karume Rd. (eastern approach road to center). More departures and important transfer point: intersection B 104/ Karume St./turnoff to airport.

## TUKUYU AND ENVIRONS
### Accommodation

TUKUYU: *BUDGET:* **Kamalos Hostel**: At bus stand; Box 54, tel. 2101. **Langiboss Hotel**: Box 597 Tukuyu, tel. 80. Many more *gesti*. LUTENGANO: **Lutengano Moravian Centre**: Rooms and campsites, lush garden, canteen; apply in writing: Box 36, Tukuyu. MATEMA: **Matema Conference and Retreat Centre**: Lovely location directly on beach, bandas with shower and toilet, group accommodation, campsite, restaurant; ELCT Konde Diocese, Box 445 Tukuyu, tel. 2006.

### Transportation

*BUS:* Frequent service to Mbeya; buses several times a day to Kyela, and at least once a day to Ipinda/Matema.

## KYELA, ITUNGI PORT
### Accommodation

*BUDGET:* **Pattaya Centre**: At market, rooms with shower, toilet. **Kimwaga's Guest House**: At market. **Vatican City Lodge & Bar**: On Itungi road, near school and TRC ticket office, surrounded by gardens. There's no accommodation at Itungi Port.

### Restaurant

**New Steak Inn**: Opposite market; modern, professional, friendly.

### Transportation

*BOAT:* **M.V. Songea** Wed from Itungi Port (about 8 mi/13 km S of Kyela); the TRC office (ticket sales, waiting room) lies at the southern outskirts of Kyela. Bus- and *daladala* transfers to Itungi Port.

*BUS:* Frequent service to Tukuyu/Mbeya; several times daily to Ipinda (from there, change to *daladala* for Matema).

# ON LAKE TANGANYIKA

### RUKWA REGION
### KATAVI N.P. / MPANDA
### MAHALE N.P.
### GOMBE STREAM N.P.
### KIGOMA / UJIJI

## ON LAKE TANGANYIKA

Four countries share the longest and deepest lake in Africa, Lake Tanganyika. Tanzania owns 41% of the 12,646-square mile (32,880-sq. km) body of water, Zambia 6%, Congo (Zaire) 45 % and Burundi 8%. The lake is 420 miles (676 km) long and at most 43 miles (70 km), on an average 20-30 miles (30-40 km) wide. A first look at the map makes it appear like a dramatic cut between East and Central Africa, but for the people on its shores and in its hinterland it serves more as a link: between boat traffic and the trade in its wealth of fish resources, it provides the lake dwellers with markets hundreds of miles inland.

The air is not often clear enough that you can see the mountainous western shore of Lake Tanganyika from the Tanzanian side: the horizon seems to go on forever, the immense expanse of water seems more like an ocean. The lake lies 2,536 feet (773 m) above sea level, and you would never suspect how far down reach the sides of this oldest lake in the East African Rift system. The deepest

*Preceding pages: A suspenseful process: loading and unloading "Mwongozo" on Lake Tanganyika. Left: Chimpanzee baby in Gomba National Park.*

point is 4,711 feet (1,436 m) below the surface of the lake: in other words, 2,175 feet (663 m) below sea level. This chasm has developed over the last 20 million years. Before it formed, the landscapes of East and Central Africa were joined and the Malagarasi on the Tanzanian side, today the most important of the lake's tributaries, flowed on, uninterrupted, in a river bed that now belongs to the Lukuga in Congo (Zaire), forcing its way westwards through the mountains near Kalemie. The Lukuga, in turn, flows via the Lualaba into the mighty Congo River. All the rivers which flow into Lake Tanganyika follow this course before finally emptying into the Atlantic Ocean.

### Ornamental Fish and Dried Fish

The lake is very old and has no exchange with any other larger body of water. Over a period of time, a totally unique fauna has developed here. Most of its 250 species of fish are found only here and nowhere else in the world. A majority of these cichlids, of which the lake houses about 200 varieties. Particularly colorful cichlids are exported from Lake Tanganyika and found in home aquariums the world over.

Far more important to lake dwellers is the *dagaa (Stolothrissa tanganyikae)*, al-

though he makes a rather inconspicuous impression on first acquaintance. No more than four inches (10 cm) long, slim and glittering like silver, this fish feeds on plankton and often appears near the surface in extremely large schools. It is generally fished for in the dark, by night; attracted by the light of the kerosene lanterns which the fishermen attach to the prows of their wooden boats, it is then caught in the traditional nets or, more recently, in large trawling nets. The following morning the fishermen spread their catch out onto specially prepared, even stretches of particularly large-grain gravel. Thus, the fish is dried in the sun and can be turned over without any sand sticking to it. *Dagaa* fishing is one of the most lucrative occupations for the local residents.

*Above: Dagaa from Lake Tanganyika – an albumin-rich product for residents of the interior. Right: Loading and unloading boats in Kigoma can take hours.*

## Whims of Vegetation

The highest mountains surrounding the lake, especially on its western shore, are 6,500 feet (2,000 m) high; in the lake's northern section, which is no longer a part of Tanzania, there are even 10,000-footers (3,000 m). These help to catch enough rain to prevent the countryside from drying out, even during the cool, dry period from June to October. *Montane rain forests* grow here, while further westwards in the gigantic Congo basin *evergreen tropical rain forests* extend all the way to the Atlantic, where it is constantly wet. *Miombo forest* dominates the eastern (Tanzanian) shore, where many trees shed their leaves during the dry months.

At first glance, the long stretch of the lake appears to separate the humid western vegetation zone from the dry eastern zone like a tear in nature's fabric. The lake shore certainly forms a sharp boundary, but not, however, for either its vegetation nor its animal population. On the

eastern side of Lake Tanganyika, two "pockets" of the plant cover natural to the western regions have held their own, existing side by side with the vegetation that's typical of East Africa. The government of Tanzania has put these valuable remnants under protection, going so far as to resettle people who had already established themselves in these areas, in order to enable nature to unfold itself undisturbed: they are located in the Gombe Stream and in the Mahale Mountains National Parks.

### Lake Cruise On a "Sunken" Ship

People can tell them apart by their chugging, even before they've come into view: the motor vessels *Liemba* and *Mwongozo*. Without these two, countless sacks of dried fish could not be transported from the many roadless villages on the lake, let alone legion other goods, and not to mention all the lakeside dwellers who want to go shopping or visiting somewhere else. And sturdy and versatile

ships they are too, with cabins for first- and second-class passengers, benches for those in third class, and lots of space for the large amounts of cargo loaded and unloaded on the way from Kigoma to Zambian Mpulungu.

Slightly smaller than the *MV Mwongozo*, the 1,300-ton *MV Liemba* has an amazing history. It was built at the Meyer shipyard in Papenburg, Germany in 1913, disassebled and shipped to Dar es Salaam. Upon arrival, the pieces had to lie in storage for a time until the Dar-Kigoma railway was completed in 1914. Only then could it all be loaded onto the train and at last be reassembled in Kigoma. But the steamer, under its original name of *Graf von Götzen*, crossed the lake for a short time only. In 1916, during World War I, the tracks of the *Central Line* fell into British hands, and the Germans, loath to surrender their ship to them as well, simply sank it. After the end of the war, the Belgians intially controlled the area around Lake Tanganyika, and it was they who organized the first

**LAKE TANGANYIKA (SOUTH)**

0    10    20    30    40    50 km

efforts to raise the ship. But they were out of luck: they had just managed to tow it to Kigoma when it again sank. The British were finally successful in raising and restoring the steamer and they put it back into service under the name *Liemba* (the local designation for Lake Tanganyika). Since then, it has been running tirelessly – especially after the addition, in the 1970s, of a diesel motor.

The only real landing docks are found at the ports of Kigoma and Kasanga on the Tanzanian side and at the end of the line at Mpulungu in Zambia. At the other stops, goods and passengers are ferried by boat between ship and shore. You might like to watch things being shifted between the swaying wooden boats and the motorship: hundredweight bags of *dagaa*, long wooden building timbers, furnishings for an entire house, freight sewn into bags. Spectators can also enjoy the adventurous ways the colorfully-dressed passengers embark and disembark, how daring fellow travellers curry attention by diving head first into the crystal-blue water (at least from the middle deck, but sometimes even from the top deck!). All of this helps make a cruise on Lake Tanganyika a superb experience. Back out on the lake you can delight in the shore scenery, sometimes from close up and sometimes from farther away; in conversations with the most varied lot of passengers; in the lights of the fishing boats on the lake at night. On paper, the journey between Kigoma and Mpulungu takes 40 hours.

## RUKWA REGION

The southern part of Lake Tanganyika belongs, administratively speaking, to the **Rukwa Region**, a huge area (roughly the size of Lake Victoria) with fewer than 1

*Right: Siesta – at least until the next customer arrives with a heavy load to be transported.*

million inhabitants – one of the most thinly-populated parts of the country. The most important connecting road comes up from the south, from the Zambian-Tanzanian border town of Tunduma: a new, well-built gravel road, it enables buses to run daily between Mbeya and the capital, **Sumbawanga**, all year round. The route crosses the home of the Fipa, a tribe famous for its traditional production of iron. The hoes and spears of the Fipa were trade items much in demand in East Africa in the days before cheaper imports flooded the market in the 19th century.

Even if plows, tractors and chemical fertilizers have brought forth good corn harvests in recent times, they do detract from more conventional methods of farming and fertilization, which are, however, still in use. A kind of compost heap of plant-refuse and earth is piled onto the field and later distributed over the ground to improve the soil. These manmade earthen mounds are a common sight on trips through the rolling highlands.

187

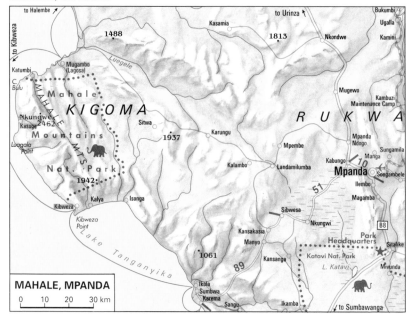

**MAHALE, MPANDA**

0   10   20   30 km

The region takes its name from the non-draining **Lake Rukwa**, which extends more than 100 miles (160 km) from northwest to southeast, almost in the same direction as the more southerly Lake Tanganyika, except that it's 60 miles (100 km) farther east. Narrow mountain ranges of altitudes of more than 6,500 feet (2,000 m) run parallel to Lake Rukwa, dividing up the country between the two lakes into broad, long depressions. Lake Rukwa is itself just such a flat hollow, its expanse and its water-level greatly dependent on the rainfalls. If you would like to have a look at the lake from the ranges of the **Mbizi Mountains**, take a bus from Sumbawanga to the village of **Mawenzusi**, just 12 miles (20 km) distant; the condition of the roads makes a four-wheel-drive vehicle a necessity.

### From Sumbawanga to Lake Tanganyika

No matter how modest the capital town **Sumbawanga** may appear, it is of utmost importance for all transportation in this thinly-populated region. All the roads are gravel-paved and rocky, wherever they cross the mountain chains. You can find trucks and pick-ups (and even a few buses) to various destinations along the main road at the filling-stations and places of business opposite the market-places.

For a boat tour on Lake Tanganyika, there are several different possible points of embarkation. If you would like to cruise from the southern end of the lake, take the road to **Mpulungu**, crossing the Zambian border via Mbala. The next port that the ferries put into, the Tanzanian town of **Kasanga** (in the German era it was called "Bismarckburg") has had a landing dock since 1996 and has therefore seen increased cargo traffic; pick-ups travel there on a daily basis.

The boundary river **Kalambo** runs between the two ports, its source being near Sumbawanga. Shortly before flowing into the lake, it plunges more than 690 feet (210 m) at the **Kalambo Falls**, which can be reached by boat (more easily from the Zambian side) and then a hike over green, dripping pathways.

Buses run every day northwards from Sumbawanga to the district town **Namanyere**, and from there on through the *miombo* forests of the mountains surrounding the lake, via **Katongoro** to **Kirando**, a harbor town with guest-houses. There is a sand track – with no public transportation – to the pleasant little inlet of the fishing village **Kipili** (4 miles/ 6 km from Katongoro), where the ferries also call.

Proceeding north from Sumbawanga (towards Mpanda), you can turn off 4 miles (6 km) past **Paramawe**, near **Liazumbi**, where a road limited to vehicles of less than 5 tons takes you to the port of **Kabwe**.

## KATAVI NATIONAL PARK

The bus between Sumbawanga and Mpanda runs only three times a week. The road is little-used past Paramawe, there are next to no settlements here (the last filling-station before Mpanda lies 10 miles/15 km off the main road in Namanyere). A rough, rocky stretch of road leads you through extensive *miombo* forest across the mountains onto the plains which becomes **Katavi National Park**. The track in the park is frequently very sandy. The depression in which the park lies is an extension of a row of basins 60 miles (100 km) north of Lake Rukwa.

As in Mikumi Park, the motorist can enjoy approximately 30 miles (50 km) of free safari when driving through the park on the main road. While passing through, you might suddenly have sable and roan antelopes bound onto your path. The dominant impression is of woodland, and you never really get an overview of the various landscapes that frame the central bodies of water, the life's blood of the park: **Lake Katavi**, surrounded by marshland and short-grass plains in the north, and palm-fringed **Lake Chada** in the southeastern tip of the park. Elephants, buffalo, hippos, leopards, lions and many different species of antelope, as well as a wealth of avifauna, are the attractions here. Accompanied by a gamekeeper, you can even go on a walking safari; in addition, the area is crossed by a number of tracks. Because of its remote location, the park is only rarely visited – which is a very good reason for going there! This is possible even if you don't have a vehicle of your own: for a fee, you can use one of the cars of the park administration. There are simple accommodations and a campsite near Lake Katavi. Bring your own rations and equipment.

The rainy season lasts from March to May; the best time to visit is from July to October. Park headquarters lie near the northern boundary of the park; about half a mile (a few hundred meters) further on, the road crosses a deeply clefted river valley. There are simple shops on the other side, in the village **Sitalike**.

## MPANDA

The 22 miles (35 km) from Katavi Park to **Mpanda** can be easily managed in half an hour, so that this district town is a convenient place to stay overnight if you want to visit the park. Hunting parties headed for the game reserves between **Ugalla Game Reserve** and Lake Rukwa like to use Mpanda as their point of departure. The town has an airport for small planes and is the terminus for a branch line of the railway, which connects with the *Central Line* to Tabora (via Kaliua).

Mpanda is an important center of road transportation in this remote area, but the poor road to Uvinza (on the *Central Line*), the 87-mile (140-km) long connection from Kabungo (6 miles/10 km west of Mpanda) to Karema or Ikola on Lake

Tanganyika, as well as the track eastward past Inyonga are, like the road to Sumbawanga, nothing for the faint-hearted or the novice driver.

It can happen that poor connections force you to remain in Mpanda for a few days, but a stay in this outlying province town can lead to interesting encounters. The district Cultural Office (*ofisi ya utamaduni*) arranges visits with, for example, the folklore group *Maji Moto Sanaa*, which is known nationwide.

Mpanda's dusty, broad streets have little appeal, but the **market**, widely important for the surrounding area, displays many conventional articles which have disappeared from markets in other parts of Tanzania: for example, clay water jars, long replaced elsewhere by the ubiquitous plastic bucket.

If you have found a ride to **Karema**, you experience not only the wide bay on the blue lake (with the option of boarding one of the ferries), but you also chance upon a reminder of the colonial past. In 1878, the Belgian King Leopold II had a fort built here, although he later concentrated his campaigns of conquest in the area west of the lake. Catholic missionaries have been using the historic building ever since.

## MAHALE MOUNTAINS NATIONAL PARK

Doubtlessly the most magnificent landscape on the cruise between Mpulungu and Kigoma lies on the peninsula formed by the **Mahale Mountains** chain. You meet up with it between the ports of **Kibwesa** in the south and **Mugambo** (or Lagosa) in the northeast of this bizarre and jagged range. These extremely steep mountains, verdant even in the higher altitudes, reach their highest point in **Nkungwe**, which measures 8,077 feet

*Right: A fisherman in Kirando, on Lake Tanganyika, sorts his catch.*

(2,462 m). The ferry does not normally stop off at **Kasoge**, on the coast beneath the highest summits, the location of the **Mahale Mountains National Park** headquarters, which have existed since 1985.

None of the Tanzanian national parks is as remote as this one, even though it's almost in reach of the ferry routes. To get to the ranger station **Kasiha**, where overnight huts and campsites are located, you disembark from the ship at Mugambo and charter a local boat, which takes two to three hours to reach the headquarters. Or take a charter boat from Kigoma, which takes 10-16 hours, depending on its speed. There is a landing-strip for small planes on the grounds; but the park is not accessible overland.

A safari is possible only on foot and only in the company of a gamekeeper. What you decide to do depends on your own personal physical condition. Nkungwe can be climbed in a 2 or 3 day tour; it is just as possible to find enjoyment on the beach, or in snorkeling and swimming in the lake.

The 6,000 foot (2,000 m) peaks and the lake shore mark only the two extremes of the large range of topography you can encounter in the 650-square mile (1,613-sq km) park. Three-fourths of its surface is covered by the *miombo* forest so common in Tanzania, but the unusual element is in the remaining quarter, particularly on the lake side of the mountains: lush green lowland forests cover the slopes as high up as 4,300 feet (1,300 m); tropical montane forest and bamboo underbrush grow in the upper regions; grasslands cloak the summits above 7,500 feet (2,300 m).

The wet forests are rife with many different species of fauna, and here the woods seem to have more in common with the vegetation of the country west of Lake Tanganyika than with that of East Africa. In keeping with the plant life, the animals you find here are more common

in Central Africa. First and foremost among these are the chimpanzees, of which there are about 700 in the park. In 1961, long before the national park was created, Japanese researchers began to observe the behavior of the animals; today, in their station **Kansyana**, east of park headquarters, they continue with their studies.

No one can guarantee that you will catch sight of any chimpanzees (*Pan troglodytes schweinfurthii*) during your visit. Accustomed to the wild, they avoid contact with humans. Only two of the 15 groups living in the park are familiar with the researchers, and they will be easier to observe. What really distinguishes this park is the chance to encounter nature in this unrivalled, diverse landscape.

It's important to know that it not only takes a long time to reach the park by ship, but many visitors also find the fee for a 24-hour stay in the park a bit high (US $50). A luxury-tented camp is open only during the dry season from May to October.

There are also chimpanzees outside the woodlands along the lake shore: these have been observed more than 60 miles (100 km) inland, in swampy forest and even in the wooded savannahs, especially in the forest reserve west of the **Ugalla River**. Here, the primates' habitat is wet only in the rainy season, but comparatively dry during the remaining six months of the year. For this reason, they can only live widely scattered and are extremely rarely seen.

### GOMBE STREAM NATIONAL PARK

Even prior to Tanzania's independence, the 10-mile (16 km) long, less than 2.5-mile (4 km) narrow woodland strip of today's **Gombe Stream National Park** was a nature reserve. It lies barely 12 miles (20 km) north of Kigoma between the shore of Lake Tanganyika (2,536 feet/773 m in altitude) and the 5,000-foot (1,500 m) high mountain crest to the east. People knew even then that

191

chimpanzees lived there, and also that these apes were normally indigenous much farther west. Other than that, little was known about them, as they are rather timid woods dwellers.

Interest in primate research did not come from biologists, as might have been expected, but rather from the anthropologist and paleontologist Louis Leakey. He and his wife Mary had just made some sensational discoveries in the Olduvai Gorge at the edge of the Serengeti, discoveries which confronted them with the world of early man. What was more natural than that they should attempt to come to terms with his nearest modern-day relations?

In 1960 Leakey sent his secretary and assistant, Jane Goodall, off on this very mission. What was then planned as an expedition of several months' duration has grown into four decades of research, a project known the world over, thanks to Goodall's tireless initiative.

### Jane Goodall and the Chimpanzees

After some months of frustration in the early stages of her research, when the young scientist was fortunate just to catch sight of any of the agile, cautious apes, she gradually became so familiar with them (and the apes with her), that she could carry on meticulous observations of their behavior. And she made astonishing discoveries: chimpanzees are not exclusively vegetarians; they use tools (such as a blade of grass, with which they fish termites out of their mound); and they display a whole range of emotions and distinctly individual behavior.

Jane Goodall's findings on the living habits of the chimpanzees, which so closely resemble those of humans in so many ways, have led to her becoming an advocate for the humane treatment necessary for the survival of every species, a cause she furthers through pub-

lications (including *In the Shadow of Man*, 1971; *Through a Window*, 1990), lectures, and fund-raising.

### Gombe Park – No Bargain

The Gombe Stream Nature Reserve was declared a national park in 1968. Nearly 300 people visit it each year. A park which has attracted so much public interest worldwide, which lies so near a larger city, in which so many endearing creatures make their home – should not such a park be overrun? The park administration did well to take measures to avoid this.

The hefty US $100 entrance fee (for a 24-hour stay) is intended to encourage only truly motivated visitors and deter the superficial, as well as support the park and help improve its hitherto fairly simple accomodations for visitors and researchers.

There is no way to reach the park by car or by plane: boats are the only possible means of transport. You can charter a motorboat (about US $120 from Kigoma) or take an inexpensive water-taxi, along with the many lakeshore inhabitants and their luggage, from **Kalalangabo**, a village in the northern sector of the Kigoma inlet (a 2-mile/3-km walk or a few minutes' ride by taxi or mini-bus from the train station in Kigoma). Since the taxi-boat stops for passengers at numerous lakeside settlements, there is a lot to see. The open boats afford no protection from the sun and it can get quite hot in them; if the boats are well-laden, you can be grateful to be able to sit or lean anywhere at all. A trip to the park headquarters at **Kasakela** takes 2-3 hours.

The park provides very simple lodging, huts with twin-bed rooms (US $10 per person); bring your own rations and store them in the hut well away from the baboons – barred windows keep their busy fingers out.

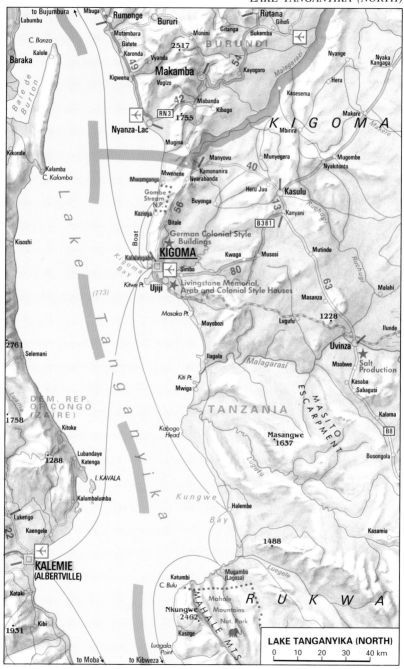

to Bujumbura
Lubumbu
Mbuga
Rumonge
Bururi
Rutana
Gihofi
C. Banza
Kalole
Mutambara
Munini
Gitanga
Bukemba
BURUNDI
Baraka
Gatete
Karonda
Vyanda
2517
Kigwena
Makamba
Kayogoro
Baie de Burton
Vugizo
Kasesema
Nyange
Nyaka Kangaga
42
Mabanda
Makere
Kikonde
Kalamba
C. Kalamba
RN3
1755
Kibago
K I G O M A
Nyanza-Lac
Mbirira
Mugina
Manyovu
Munyegera
Mugombe
Nyakitonto
Kisoshi
Mwamgongo
Mwenene
Kamonanira
40
Nyarabanda
Gombe
Stream
N.P.
56
Buyonga
Heru Juu
Kasulu
Kazinga
Bitale
German Colonial Style
Buildings
KIGOMA
Kwaga
Musosi
B 381
Kanyani
Mutinde
Kalalangabo
Simbo
80
Boat
Kigoma
Bay
63
Malahi
Kitwe Pt.
Ujiji
Livingstone Memorial,
Arab and Colonial Style Houses
Masanza
(773)
Masaka Pt.
Mayobozi
Lugufu
1228
Ilunde
2761
Selemani
Ilagala
Malagarasi
Uvinza
Msobwe
Salt
Production
Kiti Pt.
Kasaba
Sabagusi
Mwiga
T A N Z A N I A
Kaloma
DEM. REP.
OF CONGO
(ZAIRE)
Kabogo
Head
B8
1758
Kitoke
Masangwe
1637
Busongola
1288
Lubandaye
Katenga
I. KAVALA
Kalumbalumba
Kungwe
Halembe
Kasamia
Lukengo
Kaengele
Bay
1488
22
Luegele
KALEMIE
(ALBERTVILLE)
Katumbi
Mugambo
(Lagosa)
R U K W A
C. Bulu
Kataki
Mahale
Mountains
Nat. Park
Nkungwe
2462
Kibi
Kasoge
1951
Luagala
Point
to Moba
to Kibweza

**LAKE TANGANYIKA (NORTH)**

0    10    20    30    40 km

193

Tenting is also possible, but you'll have to pay US $120 for the armed night watchman; most of the threat is posed by belligerent baboons.

Hiking in the park is allowed only accompanied by a guide (US $10), the size of the group may not exceed 6 persons (counting the guide).

### Visiting "Relatives"

For hours, the boat slips quietly past steep banks and homely sandy inlets of fishing villages with the shadows of their dark mango trees and oil palms. The arable land on the mountain slopes extends right up to the very top of the rounded peaks. The blue lake water is so clear and fresh that the locals among the passengers do not hesitate to drink it during the trip.

*Above: Chimpanzees sometimes take a dip in the Kakombe waterfall. Right: Three friends in Gombe National Park check out a visitor.*

**Kazinga** is the last village before the park boundaries. Immediately past it, thick forests scale the steep slopes as far as the grass-grown mountain crest, furrowed by dark green river valleys, with, on the banks, the odd lean-to and drying-space, which the *dagaa*-fishers use only during fishing season.

Here you find the mere 20-square mile (52-sq. km) realm of roughly 150 chimpanzees, which has become, in Jane Goodall's own words, "a pitifully small stronghold, almost imprisoned through encroaching land exploitation right up to the park boundaries. Then you reach Kasakela's long pebbled beach, clamber over the sides of the boat and wade onto dry land – whereupon you step into paradise.

When hiking, you are in the knowledgeable hands of the park guides, who introduce visitors to the necessary etiquette of the wilderness: no flash, take no food along, keep your distance in the presence of wild animals, eye-contact is taken as a threatening gesture, etc.

You get off to a random start, at first on narrow forest paths, often unrecognizable as such, using narrow chimpanzee "roads" on the slopes, usually in the shade of the forest. In the higher regions it is more open: and you have views of the lake and neighboring valleys. It is quite thrilling, since there is no way of knowing whether you will see any sign of the shy chimpanzees.

And then you gasp: there are black-haired "relations," surprisingly casual, walking along the same path as the visitors; grooming each other; picking fruit, breaking it up, eating with obvious gusto; building sleeping-nests; swinging in whole groups through the tree-tops, screeching all the while at the top of their lungs...

On your hike you pass the little research station where observers can take notes. **Kakombe Waterfall** and the small rivers are not only cool, idyllic resting places for humans, they also beckon the chimpanzees to quench their thirst there. The guide knows many of their names, although not all of them. Only the chimpanzee group in the middle of the park has been intensively studied and is quite used to humans. Both of the other populations (which number about 50 members each) in the northern and southern sectors of the park tend to hide from intrusive eyes.

If you stay overnight in the park, you can experience the moods of an entire day and night, you have time to go swimming, diving or snorkeling in the clear lake (bring your own equipment) or to watch birds, insects and other animals in the park. You will certainly see baboons, and must be on the alert for their advances. There are other primates living in the park: red Colobus monkeys, blue monkeys, vervet monkeys and redtail monkeys.

Plans have been made to replace the simple offices and lodgings in Kasakela with new buildings in **Mitumba**, 2 miles (3 km) north. When ferry service is eventually resumed between Kigoma and Bujumbura in Burundi (the border was

closed in 1997), the **Mwamgongo** station on the northern boundary of the park would be only a good 1.5 miles (2 km) from the location of the new headquarters.

## KIGOMA

The largest Tanzanian town on Lake Tanganyika is a young one: **Kigoma** owes its origins to railway construction in the German colonial period. The first train to roll along the 775 miles (1,248 km) of *Central Line* track arrived at the new double-bay port-town in 1914. The ships *Liemba* and *Mwongozo* set sail regularly from the landing dock only a few hundred yards' walk from the majestic train station that was built when Germany still had an emperor (now operated by the TRC, *Tanzania Railway Corporation*). No matter what the political situ-

*Above: A farewell on the platform at Kigoma's train station. Right: Snorkelers can observe the cichlids in Lake Tanganyika at very close range.*

ation, these trains continue to make the runs to Burundi (port **Bujumbura**) and to the Democratic Republic of Congo/Zaire (port **Kalemie**), always servicing the Tanzanian ports along the eastern lake shores as far as Zambian Mpulungu. The connection with Tanzania is so important for the eastern part of the Congo that Congolese ships also make the Kalemie-Kigoma run on a regular basis.

If you approach **Kigoma Bay** from the south by ship, the town unfolds before your eyes, its houses tucked into the shade of the dark mango trees, and one imposing edifice jutting out halfway up the slope: the *Regional Commissioner's* residence, another German colonial building, once planned as a hunting lodge for the German emperor. More conspicuous is a slightly homogeneous row of tile-roofed cottages on the platform of the steep precipice which terminates the southern end of the bay: the modern four-star hotel **Hilltop** overlooks the lake and leads the way into Kigoma's touristic future.

Less obvious, but with a direct path to the lake shore (for boat tours only; so near to town, the water is not good for swimming), more hotels line the bay, one of which is recommended to aquarium fans and diving enthusiasts, **Aqua Lodge**. Here, you are in the very best hands of expert tropical fish traders, who have dealt with every and all matters pertaining to the cichlids of this lake for the past two decades.

The visibility in the extraordinarily clear lake water is still good at 70 feet (22 m) down, and conditions are ideal for diving with water temperatures hovering around 77-82°F (25-28°C). Most of these colorful cichlids can be observed merely with the aid of a diver's mask and snorkel.

If you are interested in fish and the scientific research of the lake, you'll find some like-minded individuals at TAFIRI (*Tanzania Fisheries Research Institute*); the abbreviation MMWRC (next to Aqua Lodge) stands for Mahale Mountains National Park Research Center.

## UJIJI

From Kigoma, the paved and heavily-trafficked main road, shaded by large mango trees, runs between the train station and the market (with a bus stop) and continues uphill to its sister-town Ujiji, 5 miles (8 km) away. Small buses frequently run between the two towns, passing in the middle through **Mwangu**, an expanding suburb with many guest-houses. There is a large **market** at the turnoff for the important road to **Kasulu**; a bit further on, you also pass Kigoma **airport** with scheduled flights to Dar and Tabora.

It becomes a little calmer on the next segment of the road to Ujiji. This town once saw livelier times, before the railway came to Kigoma. Caravans through the middle of East Africa began or ended in Ujiji; its counterpart was Bagamoyo on the Indian Ocean. Not content to stop on this side of the lake, Arab merchants were active much further west, well into the Congo region.

### "Dr. Livingstone, I presume?"

Even before you reach the center of town, a great, huge Coca-Cola sign marks the wide side road south to Ujiji's best-known sight: the **Livingstone Memorial**. A ten-minute walk brings you to fenced, well-tended gardens with lovely flowering shrubs. Several mango trees cast inviting shade next to a stone **monument** which stands as a reminder of the missionary and Africa explorer David Livingstone and his encounter with the American journalist Henry Morton Stanley: here, under the ancestors of these very mango trees, on November 10, 1871, the *New York Herald* correspondent greeted the man whom many people believed to have been lost without a trace, who had ended up here, sick, impoverished, and at the end of his strength. At that time, there were no other whites in the area: he could be none other than Dr. Livingstone himself. The 30-year old reporter had carried out to the letter the instructions given him two years earlier by the newspaper publisher James Gordon Bennett: "Find Livingstone!" Stanley, himself exhausted by his adventurous 236-day march from Bagamoyo to this spot, could think of nothing else to say at this historic moment but the words: "Dr. Livingstone, I presume?" – thereby equalling the talents of Livingstone's compatriots for genteel understatement.

As a handshake leaves no lasting impression, the visitor is grateful to the custodian of the site, for he is able to recount something of the life stories of these two famous men. A little **museum**, furthermore, contains paintings by Andrew Alhamisi, in which he has portrayed significant events from Livingstone's and Stanley's lives. The famous handshake scene

*Right: Banner headlines in 1871: the journalist Henry Morton Stanley finds the African explorer David Livingstone, who had been presumed dead.*

is even reproduced in painted papermaché.

### Facts and Fiction about the Lake

The custodian can tell you still more. Back behind the mango trees the ground falls off a bit, and there he has planted some vegetables; of more interest is the fact that Lake Tanganyika came all the way up to that spot behind the trees in Livingstone's time.

Today, Livingstone's house is no more; however, it once stood quite near the embankment. If you take a look around, there is no sign of any water. The first Europeans ever to sight Lake Tanganyika in 1858, the two Africa explorers Richard Burton and John Hanning Speke, reported that the town Ujiji lay on an island. That was most likely a very accurate observation: the water level of the lake has since fallen several feet due to altered drainage conditions.

Both Burton and Livingstone were convinced that Lake Tanganyika was the source of the Nile. Livingstone was acquainted with the Lualaba on the west side of the lake and believed that this river turned northwards, then flowed into the Nile. Only during his second expedition to Africa (1874-1877) was Henry Morton Stanley able to produce evidence to the contrary. Under adventurous and difficultn conditions he managed to cross Africa from east to west: from Bagamoyo across Lake Victoria and the Congo River to the Atlantic. He recognized that the Lualaba had to be a tributary of the Congo River, thus putting an end to the many theories and assertions as to the source of the Nile.

### At the Port of Ujiji

It is roughly a half-mile (600-m) walk from the memorial to the wide, sandy beach. Here, crowds of people, often accompanied by ample luggage, wait for

water taxis to other points on the lake shore. Along the public beach there are a number of **boatyards** for wooden boats; 30-foot (10 m) craft are not an uncommon sight. The gigantic skeletal frames of as-yet unfinished boats lie about; men nail planks one beside the other with millimeter-exact precision; nowhere are there any technical drawings or highly-calibrated measuring instruments, but in the end it all fits. Men sit next to the planked boats, carefully caulking small openings and cracks with cotton fibers soaked in palm oil.

While things are very lively down by the ship terminal, the town itself rather dozes peaceably on its low hill. The large number of mosques and some of the Swahili houses remind you of the influence of the Arab caravan traders. The **post office** in the center of town is a remnant of the German colonial period.

### From Kigoma into the Interior

The road connections from Kigoma into the hinterland are not very appealing.

A bus runs once a week to Bukoba on Lake Victoria. The rather poor road to Mpanda first makes a loop to the north, almost as far as Kasulu, then turns back and passes through **Uvinza** on its way into the Rukwa Region andpoints southeast.

The 19th-century caravans used the direct route east and met up with the Vinza people near the confluence of the **Ruchugi** and **Malagarasi** rivers. This people was widely known for its seasonal production of high-quality salt. Nowadays, salt water is pumped from underground watertable and boiled out over wood fires or left in large, flat pans to evaporate in the sun.

Four times a week there is a train to Dar es Salaam (it's wise to book a few days in advance for first and for second class!), a trip which involves spending two nights on the train.

In general, flights to Dar are still more likely to be booked out than the train; short-notice reservations are rarely possible.

## TUNDUMA
### Accommodation
*BUDGET:* **White House**: Near market, on main road to Sumbawanga. Several simple *gesti*.
### Restaurant
Bush Baby Restaurant: On main road to Sumbawanga, near market entrance; clean; tasty food.
### Verkehrsverbindungen
*TRAIN:* TAZARA station 15 min. walk from center.
*BUS:* Frequent service to Mbeya and points east. Several buses a day to Sumbawanga and Zambia.

## SUMBAWANGA
### Accommodation
*BUDGET:* **Upendo View Inn**: Kiwelu St. (turn off from main road at Agip gas station), biggest hotel in town, restaurant, bar, well-equipped rooms with shower and toilet; Box 336 Sumbawanga, tel. 2242. **Gloria Visitors Lodge**: centrally located, renovated, several rooms with bath and toilet; Box 785 Sumbawanga, tel. 2298. **Rukwa by Night Hotel**: Mission Rd., next to bus stand, restaurant, bar, several rooms with bath and toilet, hot showers, safe parking lot; Box 346 Sumbawanga, tel. 2243. Several very simple *gesti* near Total- und Esso gas stations (W of market): **Mpanda Guest House**: Box 3 Sumbawanga, tel. 2056. **Mambwe Nyumba ya Kulala**: Box 430 Sumbawanga. **Dawood Guest House**: Box 478 Sumbawanga, tel. 2054. More guest houses S of market: **Sodo Guest House**: Box 3 Sumbawanga, tel. 2056.
### Restaurant
**Upendo View Inn**, **Rukwa by Night**, restaurant at Total gas station (**"Mbwilo"**) N of main road.
### Transportation
*BUS:* Daily service to Tunduma, Mbeya, Namanyere (Nkansi) and other places in surrounding area. Three buses a week to Mpanda. If you want to go to Lake Tanganyika, there's a daily bus to Kirando (via Namanyere).
*TRUCK, DALADALA, ETC.:* For Lake Tanganyika: trucks or *daladalas* to Kasanga leave daily from "Mbwilo"/Total gas station at main road, opposite the market, c. 9-11 am. For lifts to Mpanda, ask at "Tawakali"/ Esso gas station, W of the market.

## ZAMBIA: MPULUNGU
Tip for drivers who want to avoid the bad roads between Sumbawanga and Kigoma: it's about 60 mi/100 km from Sumbawanga to the Zambian border; from there, via Mbala, another 40 mi/60 km to **Mpulungu** on Lake Tanganyika. Here, you can board the ships *Mwongozo* and *Liemba*; each departs once a week for Kigoma (*Liemba* Fri, *Mwongozo* Wed, both at 6 pm, arriving at Kigoma two days later at 10 am). Mpulungu harbor is equipped with a landing (as is Kasanga, see below), so your car can be taken on board as cargo.
### Excursions
From Mpulungu, you can take a boat (about 2 hours) to the start of the hiking trail to Kalambo Falls.

## KASANGA
Since 1996, the small Tanzanian port of Kasanga (about 80 mi/130 km from Sumbawanga) has had a landing, so that drivers can also load cars on board here, to avoid the road to Kigoma.

## PORTS BETWEEN KASANGA AND KIGOMA
A wide, sandy beach with many houses; a bay, overgrown with reeds; a few huts before a backdrop of sheer cliffs: these small "ports" along the shores of Lake Tanganyika have little to do with port cities in the usual sense. The boats *Liemba* and *Mwongozo* maintain a safe distance from shallow waters or other obstacles near the shores, so cargo and people have to disembark onto smaller, wooden boats which bear them to shore – a procedure that can take hours. Unfavorable wind and choppy water can make it extremely difficult to load or unload between the small wooden boats and the large ship; as a result there is no exact schedule. Passengers have to have a certain degree of agility to scramble from boat to ship or vice versa: there are no ladders or gangways, so you have to clamber on board as best you can, with your luggage, to boot.

You have to pay an **embarkation fee** to the boatman.

On land, the police generally give information about when the next ship is arriving, and give audible signals familiar to everyone in town – these are especially important if you're trying to leave at night.

You can only find **accommodation** in the larger shore communities, generally in villages which have regular road and bus connections, such as Kasanga, Kirando or Karema. If you find youself somewhere where you're a complete stranger, etiquette requires that you pay a visit to the local village headman.

## MPANDA
### Accommodation
*BUDGET:* **Super City & Light Hotel**: on the road to Sumbawanga, near the railway line, best hotel in town, new, several rooms with shower and toilet, restaurant, bar; Box 336 Mpanda, tel. 160. **Rukwa View Guest House**: Near "Super City & Light Hotel," at roundabout, cheap, appealing; Box 257 Mpanda. Mpana's town center is .5 mi/1 km further north. There are several *gesti* W of the market area: **Garden Guest House**, **Magandula's Guest House**, **Tamarin Guest House**. Mo-

ravian Hostel: near the other guest houses, S of district offices, simple, clean, restaurant; Box 42 Mpanda, tel. 187. **Mpadeco Guest House**: Near CCM building; Box 10 Mpanda, tel. 183.

### Restaurant

Super Light & City Hotel: Popular outdoor grill. **New Babylon Restaurant**: Downtown, near the CCM building.

### Transportation

*PLANE:* No major airlines fly here, but the airport is frequented by many small aircraft.
*TRAIN:* Three trains a week to Tabora: Tue, Thu, Sat. The station is more than a mile/2 km S of center.
*BUS:* Three buses a week to Mpanda (same days as train); buses to Uvinza/Kigoma, as well as Tabora (via Inyonga) only run during the dry season.

## KATAVI NATIONAL PARK

There's an extensive network of tracks for four-wheel-drive vehicles; you can also take walking safaris, but only with an armed gamekeeper.

### Accommodation

*BUDGET:* **Rest House**: 9 m/15 km from park gate; bring your equipment, food and water. *CAMPING:* like the Rest House, has to be booked in advance with park authorities. *TENTED CAMP:* **Greystoke Safaris**: Box 1658 Dar es Salaam.
You can also stay in Mpanda (about a 45-min. drive).

### Transportation

It's best to bring your own four-wheel drive vehicle; you can also rent a car from the park authorities.
*BUS:* There are three buses a week to Mpanda/Sumbawanga.

## MAHALE MOUNTAINS NATIONAL PARK

Walking and mountain safaris, fishing (permit US$ 50), swimming, snorkeling.

### Accommodation

*BUDGET:* Simple hut, and *CAMPSITE* bookings at park headquarters at Kasoge; bring your own equipment and food. *TENTED CAMP:* (May to October only) **Greystoke Safaris**: Box 1658 Dar es Salaam. **Ngare Sero Mountain Lodge**: Box 425 Arusha, tel. (57) 3629, fax (57) 8690.

### Transportation

*PLANE:* **Kalolwa**: There's a runway for small planes outside the boundaries of the park; boat transfers available.
*BOAT:* Take the *Liemba* or *Mwongozo* as far as **Mugambo** (Mgambo/Lagosa), from there, charter a boat to **Kasoge** (about 2 hours).

### Information

MMWRC Mahale Mountains Wildlife Research Centre: next to Aqua Lodge, Kigoma. Box 1053 Kigoma.

## GOMBE STREAM NATIONAL PARK

Walking safaris, accompanied by guide; fishing (permit US$ 50), swimming.

### Accommodation

*BUDGET:* **Visitor Hostel**: At park headquarters in Kasakela; bring your own food. *CAMPSITE:* near hostel, has to be guarded at night by an armed gamekeeper (US$ 120).

### Transportation

*BOAT:* Can be chartered through **Aqua Lodge**: Box 34 Kigoma, tel. (695) 2588, fax (695) 3707 (US$ 120, good for 20 people). Taxi boats depart from Kalalangabo (Tsh 2000 per person), 2 mi/3 km N of Kigoma (a few minutes by taxi or minibus from Kigoma station).

## KIGOMA
### Accommodation

*LUXURY:* **Kigoma Hilltop Hotel**: On top of a promontory, overlooking Kigoma bay, new; Box 1160 Kigoma, tel. (695) 4435-6, fax (695) 4434. *MODERATE:* **Aqua Lodge**: On the lake, with access to beach, well-tended garden, restaurant, boat trips, diving; Box 34 Kigoma, tel. (695) 2586, fax (695) 3707. *BUDGET:* **Lake Tanganyika Beach Hotel** (formerly: Railway Hotel): On the lake, near to harbor, restaurant, reasonable rooms with shower and toilet; *CAMPING* on the hotel premises; Box 9 Kigoma, tel. (695) 2694. **Kigoma Hotel**: In the town center, on Lumumba Rd. near the Air Tanzania office; popular meeting place with restaurant; Box 18 Kigoma. Many more *gesti* along the road to Ujiji; also in suburban Mwanga (halfway to Ujiji).

### Transportation

*PLANE:* Air Tanzania has two weekly flights from/to Tabora and Dar es Salaam (Mon, Fri). Precision Air plans regular flights to Arusha.
*TRAIN:* Four times weekly to Dar es Salaam: Tue, Thu, Sat, Sun (departure 5 pm, arrival at Dar es Salaam 8:50 am on the day after next).
*BUS:* To Ujiji, frequent departures from the market, to Kasulu several times a day, Biharamulo once a week, Mpanda only during dry season.

## UJIJI
### Accommodation

*BUDGET:* Several *gesti* in center.

### Transportation

*BUS:* from/to Kigoma: freqent departures. Bus stop for Livingstone Memorial: **Bakwata Bus** Stop (.3 miles/500 m from the town center).

### Excursions

**Livingstone Memorial**: Half a mile/1 km from Bakwata bus stop, signposted. The **port** is located a few hundred yards (or meters) from the Livingstone Memorial.

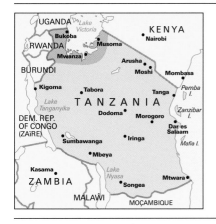

# ON LAKE VICTORIA

**BUKOBA**

**RUBONDO ISLAND**

**MWANZA**

**UKEREWE**

**MUSOMA**

## LAKE VICTORIA

Lake Victoria lies at an elevation of 3,720 feet (1,134 m), and its vast expanse of water ensures that the area nearest the lake and the neighboring mountain ranges all receive sufficient precipitation.

While the lake has only one outlet in the north, the Victoria-Nile, water flows into it from all directions. The river bringing in the most water comes from the southwest, from the mountains along the lake system of the Western Rift Valley, the **Kagera**. It joins the lake in Uganda, a few miles north of the Tanzanian border. Before that, it winds its way through more than 90 miles (150 km) of northern Tanzania. Further on upstream, almost as far as its source, the Kagera is a border river, forming, for a stretch, the border between Uganda and Tanzania, then the entire length of the Rwanda-Tanzania border, and then that of Rwanda and Burundi. One of the Kagera tributaries from Burundi is considered the "source of the Nile" – the southernmost source in the Nile catchment area.

*Preceding pages: Bananas, the main dietary staple of the region, on sale at the market in Bukoba. Left: Farther to starboard! A boatman directs his companions.*

## Buhaya

The mountainous land west of Lake Victoria has long been desirable for settlement. Bantu tribes had migrated into the area and farmed the land, particularly focusing on the cultivation of bananas. Some were also experts at iron-production.

Legends tell of the god-like Chewzi, who came here 400 or 500 years ago and set themselves up as rulers over the farmers. Whether these stories served the privileged classes as an excuse for their leading role in society or whether a cattle-breeding tribe did, in fact, come down from the north to subjugate the locals remains a matter of speculation. In Ugandan Ankole they are called Hima, Tutsi in Rwanda and Burundi, Hinda or also Hima in the Tanzanian parts of this area.

The people in the northwestern tip of Tanzania call themselves Haya and were divided up into different kingdoms even into the colonial period. Land ownership, cattle-breeding and the cultivation of coffee were royal privileges. It may well be that the Hinda upper class brought with them not only the big long-horned cattle, but also the *Robusta* coffee which has been cultivated in this area since time immemorial. The cattle appear to serve less

**LAKE VICTORIA (WEST)**

0   10   20   30   40   50 km

for the production of meat and milk than simply as a demonstration of power and luxury. When the rinderpest swept through East Africa in 1890/91 and killed off 90-95 % of the livestock, it was a hard blow for the upper classes in Haya land (*Buhaya*).

### Coffee is Chewed, Not Brewed

You can see them hanging on market stands and kiosks all over Haya country, strung up on long cords: little triangular brown packets, made of dried banana leaves. No tourist would guess that there are coffee beans wrapped up inside of them. The small dark-brown or black beans come from the coffee berries of the *Robusta* variety (*Coffea canephora*) and are boiled in an herbal brew in a covered pot for 24 hours. Then the beans are allowed to dry on a special tray next to the fire for several days.

For centuries it has been the custom to chew these beans; this keeps people awake and enables them to tell stories for hours on end.

The traditional Haya family offers guests a few of these *emwaani* (coffee beans for chewing) in a woven dish. Before helping yourself, the laws of etiquette dictate that you "purify" your hands with a bundle of bleached papyrus fibers.

Biting open the hard shell surrounding the coffee bean and removing it from your mouth, you then chew the rest slowly and thoroughly, before swallowing.

### 183 Times Banana

The Haya have 183 individual words just to describe the various types and varieties of local banana varieties, as well as the different ways of preparing them. Cooking-bananas, or plantains, are their dietary staple, the Haya's daily bread. These bananas are never eaten raw; they are peeled and cooked, becoming soft and mealy, but never sweet.

Bananas for the traditional beer-brewing are picked before they are ripe, then artificially ripened in a pit of smouldering charcoal for several days. The fruit is then peeled or left unpeeled, depending on the kind of beer being brewed. Then men crush them with their bare feet in huge wooden troughs. The liquid pressed in this way is mixed with water, passed through a sieve and, after the addition of roasted millet (sorghum), left to ferment for several days: the *pombe* is ready.

Banana schnapps, *rubisi*, is also made; women drink it from smaller, men from larger gourds.

One certain kind of banana is used only for roasting: a tasty snack for guests. On the other hand, those bananas which become sweet and soft when ripe are eaten fresh, just as they are in Europe. They are often used as food for children or for older people who are setting off on a trip.

### Modern Kagera

It was European missionaries who after 1892 began spreading not onlly their Christian faith, but also the use of coffee, that commodity so sought after on the world market; it was they who brought *Arabica* coffee (*Caffea arabica*) to Buhaya. The rinderpest had already robbed the upper classes of their status symbols, and the legends of the heavenly origins of the kings were faltering. In addition, the colonial rulers were weakening their positions by encouraging coffee cultivation. A new era dawned: Haya territory flourished on the basis of the mixed cultivation of bananas and coffee, a method still used by smallholders today.

*Right: Women pick coffee beans on a typical banana-coffee plantation.*

The coffee boom and the above-average number of schools helped the area to make notable progress in the first half of the 20th century, but when coffee prices sank on the world market, the country stagnated economically. East African political developments in the 1970s brought some hard knocks to the *West Lake* region, as it was then called. Idi Amin, then dictator in Uganda, declared war on Tanzania, allegedly because of the placement of colonial frontiers. In 1890, Germany and Great Britain had determined that the border between Uganda and Tanzania should lie at a latitude of 1° south, with the Kagera river forming the boundary only for a short stretch in the far west. In 1978, Ugandan troops occupied the entire Ugandan/Tanzanian border zone along the Kagera river. The Tanzanians retaliated by marching into Uganda in 1979 and reclaiming the disputed territory. The region has been pointedly renamed **Kagera**.

Even though both of its western neighbors, Rwanda and Burundi have had no conflict with Tanzania, the civil war which has been seething thre for decades has not been beneficial to the region, Tanzania included. The country has repeatedly taken in hundreds of thousands of refugees, many of them choosing to stay in the country. Out of protest against the rulers at the time, Tanzania closed its border to Burundi in 1996.

Through no fault of its own, the Kagera region is ending up on the political scrap-heap, becoming a victim not only in economic respects, but also in terms of health. AIDS is making a devastating sweep through the entire area, probably as a result of the war.

### BUKOBA

Five times a week, always at night, two reliable ferries make the run between the largest Tanzanian town on Lake Victoria,

Mwanza, and the capital of the Kagera region, **Bukoba**, with a stopover in the port of **Kemondo**. There are also regular flights between Bukoba and Mwanza. Traveling by road here takes a lot of time, not only because the poor condition of the roads prevents rapid progress, but also because there aren't many long-distance buses: only one a week to Kigoma and one to Ngara, via Biharamulo and Lusahunga respectively. For Uganda, take the bus to the border town **Mutukula**, where you can change to Ugandan buses.

Bukoba lies in a picture-book setting: a broad, sandy beach adjoined by low, green marshland and intensively cultivated gardenland. Here, there are also a few buildings still standing from the German colonial period. The treetops teem with pelicans, marabou storks and egrets, while the papyrus plants house weaver finches.

The town center, about 2 miles (3 km) from the port, rises up from the gardens, framed against a semicircular backdrop of steep granite cliffs, and consists of an architecture of astounding unity. Many buildings were erected by Asians in the 1950s and have their own brand of morbid charm. Indian temples, mosques, and conspicuous modern Christian churches vie with one another. While things are leisurely along most of the streets, the busy little **market** indicates the town's significance.

**Kagera Region**

Banana and coffee plantations are found wherever there is sufficient rainfall: on the mountain crests and near the lake. South of Bukoba, mountain ranges extend at a short distance from the lake shore. On their heights lie plantations, gardens and villages, and even several tea plantations; some of the slopes have been reforested with pines, eucalyptus and grevillea (silk oaks); and grassland has taken over in the valleys.

About 25 miles (40 km) farther west, in the **Karagwe** district (district adminis-

tration in **Kayanga**, with a larger market town in **Bugene**), a chain of mountains ranges in a north-south direction, attaining heights of more than 5,500 feet (1,700 m). The Kingdom of Karagwe was once located here. Speke paid his respects to the Hinda King Rumanyika in 1860; and Stanley saw the royal treasure chamber in **Bweranyange** in 1876. Today, it is difficult to make out even the slightest trace of its history.

Kagera is densely settled in its fertile areas; however, nature reserves have also been established in some of the more remote parts of the district. The **Minziro Forest Reserve**, near the mouth of the Kagera, is an area of wood- and marshland with stands of the rare lowland podocarpus trees. It has a continuation in Uganda's **Sango Bay Forest Reserve**. The trees and avian life here are unique.

*Above: Colonial-era house in the center of Bukoba. Right: Milk owls generally relax in trees during the day.*

The game reserves of **Ibanda** in the north and, especially, **Burigi** in the south are too dry for farming and infected by tse-tse flies. Neither of the reserves is developed for tourism.

### Biharamulo

The main road proceeds south from Bukoba through the damp, productively farmed territory along Lake Victoria; numerous villages line the road. But the country becomes drier and lonelier south of **Ruiga Bay**, which is visible in the distance from the road. Only a few charcoal burners go about their work in the bushland. Forest covers the slopes of the smaller chains of hills.

After this, the varied landscape of the Burigi Game Reserve seems a wide frontier belt, devoid of any human life – that, at least, is the impression you glean when you drive across 25 miles (40 km) of it, following the main road. The northernmost stands of *miombo* forest are found here.

The scene changes beyond that: a wide-open hilly countryside dotted with fields, which is the land of the Zinza.

The district town, **Biharamulo**, lies a bit off the main road. There is no running water here and no electricity: Biharamulo district is one of the poorest in the country.

A shady avenue lined with mango trees leads to a hill about half a mile (1 km) away, which commands good views of the lands around. In the year 1890, this was an ideal spot for the German **boma**, which served as a station between the lake area and Burundi. With Dutch help, it was expertly renovated more than 100 years later; today, it's used for government meetings. When the few guest rooms are not being used officially, the lucky tourist may find lodging here.

There is an important traffic junction about 25 miles (40 km) further south, at **Lusahunga**, from where a good road leads to the Rwanda border and **Rusumu Falls** on the boundary river Kagera (58 miles/93 km). It is 230 miles (370 km) of

lonely roads to Kigoma on Lake Tanganyika, 250 miles (400 km) to Tabora. The civil war in Rwanda and Burundi have caused the border areas to grow desolate.

## RUBONDO ISLAND NATIONAL PARK

Biharamulo is a good point of departure for a visit to **Rubondo Island National Park**. It lies in the hard-to-reach southwestern corner of Lake Victoria and belongs to that category of national parks in which non-motorized safaris take place. Hiking and boating are the order of the day. There are about 30 miles (50 km) of hiking trails on this 92-square-mile (240 sq. km) island of **Rubondo**, and if it is not too difficult in this wilderness, you can even strike off cross-country. Three-fourths of the island is forest – rainforest, *miombo* forest, also wooded savannah – and the rest is grassland, partly marshy, with large expanses of papyrus swamp, ideal country for waterbuck and sitatunga (*Tragelaphus spekii*).

211

Rubondo was already declared a nature reserve under the German colonial administration. At that time the inhabitants, just like the ones living on the neighboring island **Maisome**, were forced to move to the mainland. But later, farmers and fishermen began to return to the island. The inhabitants of Rubondo were forced to leave yet again in 1964 to make room for animals: between 1964 and 1967, rhinoceroses, giraffes, chimpanzees, roan antelopes and Colobus monkeys were reintroduced on the island, and settled in well – all but the rhinos, who presumably fell prey to poachers. Beyond that, elephants, hippos, crocodiles, buffalo, several varieties of monkeys, dikdiks and many other mammals appear to be quite at home here, as there are neither lions, leopards nor hyenas. Birdlife is particularly abundant, among their numbers are countless migratory birds.

The park administration has boats, with which you can make excursions to the bays and smaller islands and watch the numerous waterfowl; additionally, fishing is allowed. Secluded beaches entice you to swim.

Campsites and bandas are provided to self-caterers for overnighting. **Rubondo Tented Camp**, a luxury-tented camp, was newly opened in 1997. Park headquarters, lodging and a landing-strip for small planes are at **Kageye**, on the east side of the island.

It is a two-hour boat ride to Kageye from **Nkome**. This port town on the southern edge of Lake Victoria is serviced three times a week from Mwanza by a scheduled ship of the Tanzanian Railway Company (TRC). Depending on which route you take overland from Mwanza to Nkome, you face a trip of approximately 125 miles (200 km), via **Geita**. There is a ranger station for the national park in Nkome.

*Right: A regular sight in Rubondo National Park – two bull hippos in combat.*

From Biharamulo, there are daily buses to **Nyamirembe**, 37 miles/60 km distant, the terminus for the weekly TRC ship to and from Mwanza). Either from here or, better yet, from **Muganza**, 12.5 miles (20 km) further north, you can have yourself brought over to the island by boat (about 2 hours from Nyamirembe; about 20 minutes from Muganza). In this case, you'll land on the west side near the ranger station **Mlaga**, from where it's about 5 miles (8 km) to **Kageye**, to the headquarters, on the east side of the island. This part of the journey is on foot, if you have not ordered a transfer in advance.

### From the Zinza to the Sukuma

A bus runs daily from Biharamulo to Mwanza; allow eight or nine hours for the 143-mile (230 km) ride. The road is infrequently used in its western segment, in the Kagera Region; few people live here in the rocky hill ranges, in the scant remains of *miombo* woodlands, or in the bushland. Sacks of charcoal wait by the roadside for the few passing cars. But everywhere that the farmers can find enough water they grow corn, vegetables, bananas, cotton and, in the river valleys, rice, as in **Buziku**.

The closer you get to the border of the **Mwanza Region**, the lusher the landscape becomes. The market town **Buseresere** stretches out in all directions, and on market days, people come from near and far – mostly on foot. In the hill-country to the east, Germans discovered gold in the 19th century; it is still mined at several sites in Geita District. The little district town of **Geita** has a provincial air, but the larger town of **Sengerema**, 50 miles (80 km) further on, has a nearly metropolitan flair; you can sense the proximity of the leading city of **Mwanza**.

The regional capital lies on the other side of the **Mwanza Gulf**, a narrow

waterway which cuts into the interior some 37 miles (60 km) from the southern edge of Lake Victoria. Car ferries cross it at two points. In twenty minutes' time the ferry takes you from the **Kamanga** peninsula to Mwanza, landing you right in the middle of town (from Sengerema, it is 22 miles/35 km to the ferry landing). It is 40 miles (64 km) from Sengerema to Mwanza, if you take the **Busisi-Kikongo** ferry (7.5 miles/12 km from Sengerema), and then turn north at Usagara into the Shinyanga-Mwanza main road in order to get to downtown Mwanza.

South of Usagara, you head off into the neighboring region **Shinyanga** through the wide, almost flat Sukuma country, as far as **Mabuki**, on an excellently broad and well-drained road. The steppe-like country, often devoid of any tree, has partially result from being used for so long as grazing-land for the cattle herds of the Sukuma, which are, with more than two million members, the largest tribe in Tanzania. Following the rinderpest epidemic in 1890/91, bushland be-

came widespread. During the colonial period, it was deliberately cleared in places to make room for cotton cultivation on the one hand and to check the spread of tse-tse flies on the other. Nowadays, you will again find huge herds of cattle in this region.

## MWANZA

Mwanza is built on more than seven hills: countless rocky ridges of rounded, grey blocks of granite subdivide the town in such a way that it does not look its size of at least 250,000 inhabitants. There is nothing off-putting about the many rocks; in fact, they are rather decorative. Many have such curious shapes that they appear to be sculptures. And green peeks through everywhere: bushes, dark green groves, bits of fields, flowering gardens. At the same time, houses and huts grow up the cliffs out of the valleys. The water in the lake and bays surrounded with gentle green complete the pleasant picture of the city's setting.

213

An odd little helter-skelter pile of granite juts up out of the water and papyrus grass next to the landing dock of the Kamanga ferry: **Bismarck Rock**. Gigantic stone blocks tower on the peninsula **Capri Point**, adjoining to the south. Here the infrequently traveled roads, shade-trees and panoramas of bays and islands invite you out for a walk.

Confined by the **train station** in the south, the **market** in the east and the **port** in the west, the town center is uncomplicatedly small and is broken up by rock-groupings covered with greenery. In the north, on the far side of a small river, you will find hospitals, the fishing harbor and the road to the airport, which is 6 miles (10km) away.

The city is important because of trans-shipment and processing of various commodities, especially the major agricultural product grown in large parts of the surrounding countryside: cotton. Fish, livestock and farm-produce of the region, like corn and cassava, also find buyers here, in this center of population. The influx of new inhabitants is considerable, but only a very few find jobs. There are a considerable number of beggars in the streets.

### Mwanza as Center of Transportation

Mwanza is Tanzania's economic center on Lake Victoria and with that, also the most important hub of transportation. The water in the harbor is deep enough for larger ships; the TRC runs ferries to Bukoba (only at night), to Nyamirembe (during the daytime, with many, many stops along the southern shore of Lake Victoria) and to Nansio (Ukerewe Island). In 1997, only freighters were running to Uganda and Kenya. The railway – there has been a branch that turns off from the *Central Line* in Tabora since 1928 – runs to Dar es Salaam four times a week; it takes almost two days for the 764-mile trip (1226 km).

People prefer to fly the long distance to the metropolis (flight time is about 1 hour and 20 minutes); Air Tanzania operates scheduled flights to Dar es Salaam for every day of the week, some days more than one flight. Planes also fly to Kilimanjaro Airport (Arusha/Moshi) three times a week; and there is one flight a week to Entebbe (Uganda) and one to Kigali (Rwanda). Additional flight destinations include Arusha and Bukoba.

In 1997, Mwanza's leading position as a transportation center was improved by the addition of a fast transit to Kenya: the road to Mwanza from **Sirari** on the Kenyan/Tanzanian border was completely asphalted (only the last 20 miles/30 km before Mwanza are still full of potholes). The southward stretch of road, towards Shinyanga, also looks promising: road construction is underway to widen and pave the road. Bus trips to Arusha are still uncomfortable, albeit interesting, passing through a wide range of different landscapes of Tanzania. The trips lead you either via Bunda, Musoma and Ikoma through the Serengeti and the Ngorongoro areas (foreigners pay US $25 at each of the park gates), taking about 18 hours, or via Shinyanga, Singida and Babati, taking a minimum of 24 hours.

### Saa Nane Island

Small for a nature reserve, but lushly green, is the island of **Saa Nane** in the Gulf of Mwanza. From the eastern part of the peninsula Capri Point (next to **Tilapia Hotel**), you can reach it in ten minutes in a motorboat belonging to the nature reserve authorities. There are departures several times a day (every two hours), and you can shorten your wait by having a look into the little **Museum of Natural History** opposite the landing dock.

It is a bit misleading that the island is termed a game reserve. As far as big

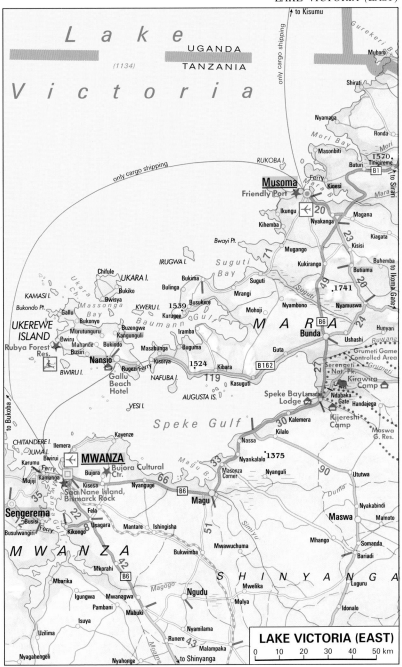

*L a k e*

UGANDA

TANZANIA

*(1134)*

*V i c t o r i a*

to Kisumu

only cargo shipping

*Gurekeri B*

Muhoro

Shirati

Nyamaga

Ronda

*Mori Bay*

*Mori*

*RUKOBA I.*

Masonbiti

Buturi

**1570**

Timgireme

B1

to Sirari

only cargo shipping

**Musoma**

Friendly Port

Ferry

*Mara*

Kirlesi

Ikungu

20

Nyakanga

Magana

Kihemba

Mugango

Kiagata

Kisisi

*Bwayi Pt.*

*IRUGWA I.*

*Suguti Bay*

Suguti

Kukirango

Buhemba

Butiama

23

Chifule

*UKARA I.*

Bukima

Bulinga

Mrangi

Mohoji

Nyambono

Nyamuswa

**1741**

20

Bukiko

Busukere

**1539**

Kurugee

71

64

*Suguti*

Hunyari

to Ikoma Gate

*KAMASI I.*

*Ukara Ch.*

Bwisya

*KWERU I.*

*M A R A*

B6

24

*Massonga Bay*

Bukondo Pt.

Gallu

Bukonyo

Buzengwe

Iramba

Bunda

Ushashi

*Ruwana*

**UKEREWE ISLAND**

Murutunguru

Kangunguli

*Baumann Gulf*

Buguma

Guta

Grumeti Game Controlled Area

Bwiru

Mahande

Bukindo

Masabunga

Kisorya

B162

Serengeti Nat. Pk.

*Grumeti*

Rubya Forest Res.

Busiri

**Nansio**

Rugezi Ferry

**1524**

Kibara

Kirawira Camp

*BWIRU I.*

Gallu Beach Hotel

*NAFUBA I.*

119

Kasuguti

Ndabaka Gate

Handajega

2

*YESI I.*

*AUGUSTA IS.*

Speke Bay Lodge

Lamadai

Kijereshi Camp

*Maswa G. Res.*

to Bukoba

*Speke Gulf*

30

Kalemera

Kilalo

*CHITANDERE I.*

Ilemera

Kayenze

Nassa

*JUMA I.*

Bwirui

Nyankalalo

**1375**

Ututwa

Karumu

**MWANZA**

Bujora Cultural Ctr.

Masonza Corner

Nyanguli

90

Ferry

Bujora

*Magu B*

Nyakabindi

Mamoto

Mujiji

Kamanga

33

*Duma*

Kisesa

Nyanguge

66

B6

**Magu**

**Maswa**

Saa Nane Island, Bismarck Rock

Fela

*Simiyu*

**Sengerema**

Busisi

22

Usagara

Mantare

Ishingisha

51

Mhango

Somanda

Busulwangiri

Ferry

Kikongo

Bukwimba

Mwawuchuma

Bariadi

35

*M W A N Z A*

Mkorahi

42

B6

Bukwimba

*S H I N Y A N G A*

Luguru

Mbarika

Igungwa

*Magogo*

Mwanagwa

**Ngudu**

Mwelika

Malya

Idonalo

Pambani

Mabuki

Nyamilama

Isuya

Uzilima

Runere

43

Malampaka

Nyagahengeli

Nyahonge

*Moame*

to Shinyanga

to Kisumu

**LAKE VICTORIA (EAST)**

0   10   20   30   40   50 km

game is concerned, it has little in common with the marvelous Tanzanian game parks which are more familiar to most tourists. This, by contrast, is a kind of **zoo** and amusement park in a lovely, natural setting with rocks, trees and grassland. The cages are clean, but confining and unimaginative, with one lion, leopard and chimpanzee apiece. This is astounding, considering the amount of knowledge researchers have collected, especially in Tanzania, about the behavior and needs of wild animals. Wildebeest, zebras and a pair of crowned cranes are better off: they run free.

However, foreign visitors should keep in mind that a safari in a national park is beyond the financial means of the average Tanzanian, the more so if he wants to take the whole family. In this zoo, adults and children have a chance to observe

*Above: The Tilapia Hotel before a backdrop of cliffs on Capri Point in Mwanza. Right: Thousands of lizards dwell on Saa Nane Island.*

"their" famous wild animals at close quarters. Nearly 20,000 visitors to the park have been counted each year; it's an especially popular weekend outing. There are many picturesque picnic spots between rocks, bushes and trees, and drinks and snacks are available at a small kiosk.

If you prefer peace and quiet, it is best to go over to the island on a weekday, if school classes don't happen to be on their way over, as well.

It is well worth taking along a pair of binoculars, not only because of the panoramic view of parts of the town that you have during the crossing, but also because of the absolutely incredible profusion of birdlife which is naturally indigenous to the island.

### Bujora, a Cultural Center

At the Mwanza bus station or along the main street, you can always find small buses toward Musoma, with which you can reach **Kisese**, 15 miles (25 km) dis-

tant, traveling through lively suburbs and past industrial locations. The rather flat countryside is intensively farmed, lower-lying fields are rice-paddies. Thousands of marabou storks perch in the trees in these fields. To the north, on a clear day, you can sometimes see as far as Lake Victoria. In that direction, a conspicuous, low range of hills with countless remains of rounded granite blocks is also visible from afar. On one of the hills farther back, there is a whole "wall" of radio transmitters – greetings from modern Tanzania.

The half-hour hike from Kisese to **Bujora** on the hill in the foreground leads you both into the present and into the past. In the Sukuma language *Bujora n'hingo* means "to strangle" – not a particularly complimentary name for a village. But it has been a long time since people were attacked and killed in this area. Up until a short time ago, this place was the seat of a Sukuma king.

The history of the Sukuma is similar to that of the Haya in the west: in that great expanse of land south of Lake Victoria, in roughly the same area that is now designated Mwanza and Shinyanga Regions, there lived small groups of Bantu tribesmen. Some 300 to 500 years ago, cattle-breeders came in from the area northwest of Lake Victoria, mingling with the local population. These cattle-breeders developed into a ruling caste, whose power was balanced out in the beginning, because the kings were elected. Their position underwent some weakening during colonial times.

The Germans had already seen that the dry land of the Sukuma was well suited to cotton cultivation. After the Sukuma realized that they were only being exploited as a cheap labor force on the Europeans' plantations, they began to plant their own fields with cotton and formed cooperatives in order to process and market their own product.

Knowledge and practices of ancient cultures is easily lost when new ways of life take over. The Canadian David Clement came to Bujora in Sukuma land as a

217

priest of the Order of the White Fathers. He did bring the Christian faith, but his interest lay also with the culture of the Sukuma.

With his help, the members of his parish founded a **cultural center** in 1954. It mattered a great deal to Father David Clement that Christian liturgy be linked with Sukuma traditions. He wanted to avoid the error of simply copying the European-American rituals in church matters.

The result was a church the likes of which had never been seen before: a modern building, but with stylistic elements and painting of the Sukuma culture. The church music is not hymns or chorales, but African music played on traditional African instruments. Mass is held every Sunday at 11 am.

In 1968, they built a museum on the church property. By now, they have **archives** for the Sukuma culture, a **royal pavilion** facsimile, and a **dancing pavilion**, in which works of art and craftsman's tools are exhibited. The **medicine man's house** contains collections of herbs and other articles of magic. A Sukuma **farmhouse** presents information about the traditional way of life, which is gradually disappearing. A **blacksmith's** huts impart the process of African iron extraction and iron forging. An additional pavilion is planned which will display a collection of all the magic tricks of the Sukuma **rainmakers**.

In addition, a **research project in African medicine** is being undertaken.

The most spectacular event is the annual June Corpus Christi celebration, **Bulabu Festival**, for which more than 10,000 participants convene a whole week long, coming mainly out of Sukuma land. This is traditionally a time of thanksgiving for the Sukuma, and the famous groups *Bagalu* and *Bagika* compete in dancing. The cultural center is not sufficiently large to accommodate all of this, and the events have to move to the stadium.

The **Bujora Cultural Center** is much more than just a collection of museum buildings: it also houses a **craft center** for wood-carving, knotting carpets and traditional ceramics, but also for such modern techniques as welding, baking, sewing, to name a few. Of course, they are pleased to see visitors, who not only acquaint themselves with the museum, but also purchase souvenirs in the **shop** or take refreshment in the **restaurant**. On the grounds there is also a **campsite**. The premises and bandas can be rented for study groups and other meetings. Interested parties can attend dance-workshops. It is possible to book dance-group performances.

### Ferry Crossing from Mwanza to Nansio

The Kerewe are closely related to the Sukuma; and they have their own realm on the largest island in Lake Victoria, **Ukerewe**. At least once a day, one of the TRC ferries runs from Mwanza to the largest town on the island, **Nansio**.

Even if you don't want to spend much time on the island, the boat trip alone, which takes about two and a half hours, is itself a pleasant experience. You can always go sit in front of the television below deck ...

On relatively clear days, there is always land in sight during this passage. Impressive is the scenery of the bizarre granite rocks of the hills of Mwanza, while the ferry glides out slowly into the gulf. After 45 minutes, these steep cliffs have been left behind, the eastern bank becomes flat and green, with no sign of a sandy beach.

Pelicans move out in front of the ship, and terns seek food on tiny floating islands of water hyacinths. It is worth it to

*Right: There's plenty of room for pelicans on Africa's biggest lake.*

have a pair of binoculars along for bird-watching.

**Speke Gulf** extends more than 60 miles (100 km) to the east, its distant eastern shore invisible to the naked eye. However, single granite rocks emerge from the lake's surface; at times, they seem lined up, reminding you that the landscape of rock-covered hills which you know so well from the mainland is also present here, sunk beneath the shallow lake water. The white spatters that adorn these rock tips indicate their popularity with the birds.

Traditional small, flat-bottomed fishing boats, with pointed prows and sterns, and larger wooden barges cross the ferry route. The latter turn out to be dhows; their sails in fact differ very little from those seen on the Indian Ocean. When Speke and Stanley explored Lake Victoria in the 19th century (Stanley circumnavigated it in 1876 with the *Lady Alice*, the dismantled boat he had lugged along with him all the way from the coast), sails still seemed to be unknown here. These

"modern" ships were first introduced in the late 19th century, with the increase of caravan traffic to the lake region, and by 1895, the first steamer crossed the lake. All of these boats did their bit to make overland caravans with carriers superfluous around the lake. Now, at the dawn of the 21st century, dhows are still indispensable for most of the cargo transport on the largest lake in Africa. Perhaps this ecologically friendly method of transportation is, after all, the best way to move on into the future.

## UKEREWE

The skyline of Ukerewe is a group of spiky hills in a green landscape. The highest of these,, **Kuruego Hill**, measures 4,285 feet (1,306 m) above sea level. That is only 564 feet (172 m) higher than the surface of Lake Victoria – high enough here, however, that this rise can be used as an outlook over almost the entire island and the surrounding water. The Kerewe show their respect to this

spot, named **Handebezyo,** by keeping up a small **museum**.

The inhabitants are proud of their island. On less than 173 square miles (450 sq. km) 200,000 people make their home, astoundingly populous for a country that lives from farming and fishing. This is made possible by ample precipitation; only the smaller neighboring island of **Ukara** receives more rainfall. The Kerewe farm their land with great diligence. Wherever you look, you see smal green plots of land, beds, gardens, and orchards. On many beaches, you can also see *dagaa* fishermen at work during the season.

In **Gallu Beach Hotel** in **Nansio**, only ten minutes from the landing dock, petroleum lamps and water-bucket-showers

*Above: The fishermen's boats lie near the ferry dock at Kisorya. Right: Wild buffalo in the grassy plains south of Bunda indicate the proximity of the Serengeti – wild animals don't always observe national park boundaries!*

are a matter of course. Apart from several guest-houses, it is the only hotel on the island. You can also pitch your tent there. The house dates from the 1970s (renovated in 1995), when an *ujamaa*-settlement was put up in **Gallu**, on the northwest tip of the island.

The roads are elementary, and there are hardly any buses. You can organize a taxi if you want to see the most important stone testimony to the past, much of it European: the neo-Gothic, 100-year-old Catholic church in **Kagunguli**; East Africa's first cotton gin, dating from 1904, in **Murutunguru**; or the chief's residence in **Bukindo**, which was erected by Italians in 1928. Of the German **fort** in **Hamuyembe**, at the west end of the harbor, only a few ruins remain.

The natural surroundings are even more alluring: **Rubya Forest Reserve**, a pine forest and its beaches in the southwest of the island; bird colonies on **Kiregi Island**; and other secluded islands and sandy bays for swimming, which are best reached by boat.

The eastern tip of the island ends at the village of **Rugezi** with monumental granite rocks near the landing for the car-ferry to the mainland. Pick-up trucks take 30 minutes from Nansio. The crossing of **Rugezi Channel** to **Kisorya** takes only a few minutes. If you arrive on the last afternoon ferry, be prepared to stay overnight at a very simple guest-house.

### From Bunda to Mwanza

It is only 75 miles (120 km) from the ferry landing in Kisorya to the district town **Bunda**. Buses, however, take 3-4 hours, since apart from passengers, they also have freight loads to transport, such as sacks of corn sent into town by the farmers, or oilcake from cotton gins, which is sold as cattle fodder. The cattle on the green grassland near Lake Victoria look very well fed.

In places, you overlook the wide expanse of Speke Gulf south of the road: on the banks large papyrus swamps, in the water whole groups of granite islands.

Only a few miles away from the lake, the countryside is already fairly dry savannah, with extensive cotton plantations sporadically breaking up the monotony. Shortly before Bunda a huge, modern cotton gin gives some indication of just how important the cultivation of cotton is in this area.

The steep rocks of the **Ushashi Mountains** limit **Bunda** at its eastern side. In a southerly direction, they abruptly make way for a seemingly endless grassy plain, which gives over into the western corridor of the **Serengeti** a bit further on. While cattle still graze near the mountains, you can also see wildebeest, gazelles or zebras further south.

Here, you pass the approach to **Ndabaka Gate**, the west entrance to Serengeti – the only one so near an paved road. From here, it takes about three hours to **Seronera**.

Two overnighting possibilities are provided near the park entrance. One is the **Kijereshi Tented Camp**, a little way outside the park boundaries; the other is

North of Nyamuswa you pass through **Butiama**, Julius Nyerere's home village. You meet up with the main road again at an important interchange, 42 miles (67 km) past Bunda: it is 53 miles (85 km) northeast to Sirari on the Kenyan border, 12.5 miles (20 km) northwest to **Musoma**.

## MUSOMA

With its population of about 80,000, **Musoma** is much smaller than Mwanza, and the town center around the market and bus stop appear unassuming, but this regional capital is actually quite an extensive place. It spreads along two larger bays of the **Mara** river delta, which stretches quite a long way back into the hinterland.

The port in the east services only freight ships. It links Musoma with Mwanza, Bukoba, Kisumu (Kenya). Passenger ferries, such as the one to **Kinesi** on the opposite side of **Mara Bay**, depart from the small beach at the fish market near the town center.

A striking hilltop borders the town center to the west. The terrain beyond leads to the second bay and the choicer parts of town under shade trees: regional administration, villas, post office, police station.

The lake shore is interspersed with rocky outcrops. The luxurious **Peninsula Hotel** operates a campsite on a sandy beach right on the lake near the town; the hotel itself is located 1.5 miles (2 km) farther away, near the lake.

Transport by road is particularly plentiful: small buses often make the run to Sirari on the Kenyan border; a direct bus goes to Nairobi daily. Buses to Mwanza are frequent: you can reach Arusha by bus three times a week, passing through the Serengeti and the Ngorongoro area. The **airport** is located immediately south of the town center, and has daily flights to Dar es Salaam.

**Speke Bay Lodge**, right on the shore of Lake Victoria.

As far as **Magu**, the good main road winds alongside the lake, which is never very far away. However, potholes make the last 20 miles (30 km) to Mwanza a torture.

### From Bunda to Musoma

North of Bunda, the asphalted Mwanza-Musoma main road crosses the wet, intensively cultivated fluvial plain of the **Suguti** river; as long as the bridge is closed, traffic has to make its way through a ford.

From Bunda, a side road offers an alternative easterly route through the mountains, through the hilly, fertile interior towards the north. In the village of **Nyamuswa**, a route branches off to the Serengeti; from there to **Ikoma Gate** it is about 80 miles (130 km) on a sand track.

*Above: The Goliath heron seeks cover in high stands of papyrus grass.*

222

## BUKOBA
### Accommodation
*BUDGET:* **E.L.C.T. Conference and Training Centre**: Aerodrome Rd., near lake, modern guest quarters, canteen; Box 98 Bukoba, tel. (66) 23121, 20954. **Lake Hotel**: near lake, colonial building, in need of renovation, restaurant; Box 66 Bukoba. **New Upendo Lodge**: in garden, between Jamhuri and Independence streets, new, restaurant; Box 631 Bukoba, tel. (66) 20620. **Coffee Tree Inn**: Jamhuri St., near stadium, spacious rooms, in need of renovation, restaurant; Box 412. **Kahawa Guest House**: behind the cathedral, good value; Box 1263 Bukoba, tel. (66) 20304. **New Banana Hotel**: Zamzam St. clean, expensive. **New World Guest House**: Near stadium, clean, good value. Several cheap *gesti* near bus stand.

### Restaurants
**Lake Hotel**: Popular meeting place, good food. **Corner Cafe**: In center, Kashozi Rd., across from Lutheran Church.

### Transportation
*PLANE:* **Precision Air** to Mwanza: We/Sa/Sun. *BOAT:* to Mwanza Mo/We/Fr (9 pm): **M.V. Victoria**, passenger ferry, 1st & 2nd class cabins, 2nd & 3rd class seats; Tu/Su: **M.V. Serengeti**, car ferry, also takes passengers. Harbor 2 mi/3 km SE of town center. *BUS:* daily service to Mutukula on the Ugandan border; once a week to Kigoma and to Ngara (near the Rwandan border), via Biharamulo and Lusahunga.

## BIHARAMULO
### Accommodation, Restaurant
*BUDGET:* Near the bus stand: rather simple *gesti*.
### Transportation
*BUS:* Daily service to Mwanza and Nyamirembe; Biharamulo twice, Kigoma once a week.

## RUBONDO ISLAND NATIONAL PARK
30 mi/50 km of hiking trails, car and boat rental from park authorities; swimming; fishing by permit.

### Accommodation
*LUXURY-TENTED CAMP:* **Rubondo Tented Camp**: reservations: Flycatcher Safaris & Hotels, Haile Selassie Rd., Box 591 Arusha, tel. (57) 6963, fax: (57) 8261. *BUDGET:* **Bandas**. *CAMPSITES:* booking through park authorities; bring your own equipment and food.

### Transportation
*PLANE:* Airstrip at Kageye.
*BOAT:* From Mwanza by TRC ferry or, by car, to Nkome; from there, 2 hours by boat to park headquarters at Kageye.

## MWANZA, BUJORA
### Accommodation
*MODERATE:* **Tilapia Hotel**: nice setting at Capri Point peninsula, restaurant, swimming pool, luxury boat for excursions; Box 82 Mwanza, tel. (68)

50517, fax: (68) 50141. **Tema Hotel**: 5 mi/8 km S of Mwanza; Box 786 Mwanza, tel. (68) 41988, fax (68) 42377. *BUDGET:* **IKO Hotel**: Capri Point, new, green surroundings; Box 2469 Mwanza, tel. (68) 40900. **Lake Hotel**: Near station, a bit old, restaurant; Box 910 Mwanza. **Christmas Tree Hotel**: Off Karuta St., near bus stand, restaurant, well-tended, new; **Annex Zimbabwe Hotel**: Near bus stand, Karuta St., some rooms have toilet & showers, clean, good value; Box 90 Mwanza. Many cheap *gesti* E of bus stand: **Victoria Hotel, Annex Victoria Hotel, Zimbabwe Guest House** etc. There are many older hotels in the downtown area; new hotels are springing up near Lumumba/Karuta/Kenyatta Sts. *CAMPSITE:* **New Blue Sky Campsite**: Station Rd., S of station, Box 6419 Mwanza. **Bujora Cultural Centre**: 17 mi/27 km E of Mwanza, 1 mi/2 km N of Kisese, signposted; Box 76 Mwanza.

### Restaurant
**Tilapia Hotel**: Breezy rooftop restaurant next to lake, good meals. **Kuleana Pizzeria**: Post St., next to New Mwanza Hotel, snacks; **Four Ways Inn**: Popular garden restaurant at corner Kenyatta/ Station Rd. **Sitar**: Lumumba St., near river, good food. **Chake Chake**: Lumumba St. near Karuta St., good value.

### Transportation
*PLANE:* Several flights a day to Dar es Salaam; daily flights to Kilimanjaro, several flights a week to Bukoba, Musoma, Kigali, Entebbe, Nairobi and others. *BOAT:* Five boats a week to Bukoba, four to Nkome, one a week to Nyamirembe; one or two a day to Ukerewe. *TRAIN:* Tabora/Dar: four times a week. *BUS:* Daily service to Arusha, Musoma, Singida, Tabora, Biharamulo; buses run to Arusha via Serengeti three times a week.

### Travel Agencies
**Four Ways Travel Service**: Across from Four Ways Inn, Box 990 Mwanza, tel. (68) 40653. **Mansoor Travel & Tours**: Bantu St., Box 2860 Mwanza, tel. (68) 50234.

## UKEREWE
### Accommodation
*BUDGET:* **Gallu Beach Hotel**: Nansio, 15 min. walk from harbor, near beach, restaurant, boat hire, campground; Box 2657 Mwanza. **New Kilakabila Guest House**: 10 min. walk from harbor, new, Box 57 Nansio/Ukerewe, tel. 93.

## MUSOMA
### Accommodation
*MODERATE:* **The Peninsula Hotel**: 1 mile/2 km from center, near lake, new, restaurant; Box 440 Musoma, tel. (675) 2526, fax 2720. *BUDGET:* **Hotel Orange Tree**: On the way to the harbor, fine, clean rooms, restaurant; tel. (675) 2353.

## THE LAUGHING HYENA

For whatever reason, there are certain animals that have, among humans, an undeservedly bad reputation. Among these are spiders, snakes, and sharks, as well as the hyena. People say all kinds of nasty things about this animal, and it's commonly depicted as a treacherous, cowardly, filthy scavenger. For a long time people thought that it was a hermaphrodite, because the reproductive organs of male and female hyenas bear an outward resemblance to each other: to many human observers, this fact seemed to confer upon the animal a touch of immorality. All of this is an example of the way that people tend to judge animals superficially, by human standards, without really knowing their true nature. Thus are born prejudices which are not so easy to eradicate.

*Fisi* is the Kiswahili word for hyena; the spotted hyena (*Crocuta crocuta*) is especially widespread in Tanzania. It isn't exactly a favorite animal of the Africans, either. It doesn't have the streamlined form of the leopard, nor the black-and-white stripes of the zebra's shining hide, nor the playful elegance of a herd of Thomson's gazelles. Such beauty is not conspicuous in the hyena, an animal about the size of a sheep, whose shoulders stand higher than its rump. Its back slopes from its massive head down to its scrubby tail. The stubbly hairs on its back and the undefinable brownish-gray fur with the irregular dark blotches give the predator a somewhat untidy apperance. Hyenas are nocturnal hunters, but you can sometimes see solitary ones during the day, walking on their toes, propelling its seemingly uncoordinated body

*Preceding pages: Every woman has her own individual way of wearing her kanga. Three young cheetahs gang up on a baby impala. Right: Hyenas and lions share the same kill.*

forward as it mistrustfully surveys its surroundings. Seeing one thus, many people find it more repulsive than in any way "nice" or "cute." No, it isn't easy for the hyena to find human friends.

A spotted hyena's life begins in isolation, in a small den where the female hyena goes to gives birth to one or two young, rarely more. There the baby hyenas remain for about two weeks, until the mother takes them to the pack's common den. In the first six months of their lives, the hyenas are nourished exclusively from their mother's milk. The milk is of such high quality that high-performance dairy cows would be jealous: it contains four times as much protein and fat as the best Holstein's. To be able to produce it, the hyena mother has to search intensively for food. Her main diet consists of the animals that live on the savannah, but large insects will do if nothing else is available. Since hyena packs have marked territories and the den is located within the territory, the female hyenas are forced to follow the wandering grazers of the savannah, such as gnus (wildebeest) and zebras. Hyenas can devour up to 25 percent of their own weight at one time. They are excellent food-utilizers. The animals even crush and eat bones of their prey with their powerful molar teeth and completely digest them.

The spotted hyena covers many hundreds of kilometers a month in search of food and returns, well-nourished, to her den. Here the young wait patiently for their own mother – they can hold out for up to five days – watched over by other adults. All of the young animals in the pack live together in the common den, but every hyena mother nurses only her own young. At the age of six months, the young hyenas gradually start eating solid food, but they are not weaned until they're about one and a half.

A pack of hyenas can number up to 80 individuals and defends a territory of 30 to 40 square miles (75 to 100 sq. km).

The common den is located at the center, usually a slight elevation with a number of entrances leading to a subterranean labyrinth. Territorial boundaries are marked with glandular secretion and excrement that looks white as chalk – as a result of the calcium ingested from the bones the hyenas consume.

Female hyenas are larger and, on average, 13 pounds (6 kg) heavier than the males. Each gender has its own hierarchy in the pack, but, on the whole, the females dominate.

Hyenas were once considered to be exclusively scavengers. They were often seen around the carcasses of animals that had already been feasted upon by lions. People could easily believe that a lion could kill wildebeest, zebras and giraffes, but didn't think that a much smaller hyenas was able to do the job. This was a gross underestimation of their strength and hunting skills. A single hyena can easily overcome a medium-sized gazelle. Spotted hyenas, in groups of three, hunt every kind of large savannah animal you

can imagine, and, when they've eaten their fill, they quite often leave the lions a part of the spoils – thus saving the lives of many a young lion. Furthermore, hyenas primarily hunt weak and sick animals, thus helping to guarantee that the main stock of the population is strong and healthy.

Anyone camping overnight in the Tanzanian wilderness can't miss the ghostly "song" of the hyenas, which can be heard for up to 3 miles (5 km). Their long, cat-like cries, "coughing" and famous "laughing" are all means of communication, even warning signals. This "song" may not exactly sound like music to human ears! Hyenas don't care what tourists think of their concert – they can't imagine that many people have been frightened by it. For them, their voices are an expression of cunning and teamwork. They are certainly satisfied with their physical beauty. And the human view of the lion as being the king of the animal kingdom? The hyena can only laugh; for in his eyes, the lion is more a beggar!

## THE LIFE OF YOUNG ANIMALS

Many species of fish have mouths that are made for more than just eating: for a number of cichlids (*Cichlidae*), the mother fish's mouth serves as a nursery. All the cichlids in Lake Nyasa, as a matter of fact, are *mouth-brooders*. Once the female has laid her eggs – usually in a flat pit, which the male prepares for her with the help of his mouth and fins on a sandy part of the lake floor – she grabs the fertilized eggs, taking them into her mouth, and keeps them there. Throughout the gestation period she keeps turning them over carefully, making a kind of "chewing" motion. As one can imagine, it's not particularly easy for her to eat during this time. In her mouth, the eggs grow into larvae which develop into young fish. After two or three weeks, sometimes longer, the moment arrives: mother opens the door of the nursery, and the small fish swim out into the unknown. In the first few days, they find themselves in a new and dangerous world; but if they seem to be in danger, their mother opens her mouth invitingly, and the brood of children obediently returns home. The mother even worries about inquisitve youngsters who stray too far afield: if one happens not to return, she will searchit out and catch it.

The image of being stuck in the mouth of a large feline predator may disturb most people, but it certainly doesn't bother a lion cub. Lionesses can carry their young so carefully in their huge jaws that the lion cub must feel as comfortable in this position as on a swing at a playground, although, just as a precaution, he remains completely motionless. David Livingstone, as a grown man, supposedly survived such a "lion transport" without any severe injuries, which would seem to demonstrate that the jaws of a

*Right: A baby leopard can get away with quite a bit with his mother.*

"big cat" can be used very sensitively indeed.

Humans are usually enraged when they hear that male lions can be inexorably cruel, biting all of the pack's cubs to death and even devouring them. No one likes to think that the "king of the beasts" is capable of this kind of cannibalism. However, you have to look at leonine behavior and habits a little more closely to understand when and why this happens. Lions live in a kind of "extended family" within a certain specific territory. Heart of the pack are the females, more or less related to each other. An average pack includes between five and ten lionesses and their cubs, with, in addition, two or three male lions who are responsible for siring new young and generally protecting the territory. They continue to perform this function until a stronger male from outside the pack arrives to challenge their position. If a newcomer is able to drive away another lion "leader" and take over his position in the pack, he will not tolerate the presence of his predessor's offspring, and will be compelled to kill them. Many lion mothers try to hide these cubs from the new despot, but to no avail: it's the law of nature that the stronger and more successful should propagate the species. After losing their young, the lionesses quickly come into heat again, so that they can bear new cubs to the new masters of the pack. These baby lions are willingly accepted by their fathers. They would never even think of killing their own progeny.

Some of the demands placed on many newborn baby animals seem remarkable. In the huge, wandering herds of wildebeest, most of the calves are born – by the thousands – within a short period of time. Calves are born in the middle of the herd; in the broad expanses of savannah where the wildebeest dwell, this seems the best-protected place for both mother and baby. Only a few short hours after its birth, a gnu calf is already able to follow

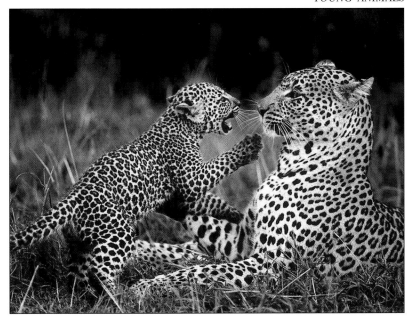

its mother swiftly on its thin, unsteady legs. After three days – at the latest – it can keep pace with any animal in the herd; and after ten days, it's already eating grass, although it continues to nurse from its mother for the next four months or so.

Other herd animals of the great savannah, such as impalas or Thomson's and Grant's gazelles, separate themselves from the herd when they want to give birth, and find places to conceal their offspring in open country. The mother is very careful to eradicate from her calf all telltale traces of its recent birth: she licks it off thoroughly, and either eats the placenta or moves the calf far enough away from it so that this evidence, a tasty tidbit for vultures or other predators, doesn't lead them to her offspring to vultures or predators. Then – she leaves it. The calf follows its instincts: it doesn't make a sound and stays motionless. Thanks to the thorough ablutions of its mother, it is almost completely odorless; furthermore, it is so well camouflaged by

its hide that it is extremely difficult to see between the clumps of grass. The mother has no trouble remembering where her calf is hidden, and, after grazing herself, she returns there several times a day to nurse her baby.

Ostrich even develop into veritable actors to protect their young from predators. If, when an ostrich family is out for a walk – mother in the lead, the young birds in the middle and father bringing up the rear – the parents sense the approach of an enemy, mother and offspring secretly slink away while the ostrich father gives a remarkable show of his acting talents. He shows the approaching predator that he is a sick bird, limping conspicuously, letting a wing droop, and generally drawing the hungry enemy's attention to himself. The robber imagines that his prey is already within reach, but now father ostrich shows the stuff of which real ostriches are made. He is one of the best long-distance runners on the savannah, and is quickly able to leave his enemy in the dust behind him.

AAAH!! MAMA !!!!
MIE NIMECHOKA NA HUO
UGALI KWA MAHARAGE KILA SIKU!!!
SIKU YA IDDI TU!!!
ND'O TULIKULA WALI
NA KUKU BAAASI !!!!

BABA YAKO AKIJA,
MWAMBIE HIVYO HIVYO!!!
UMESIKIAEEE!!

SI ATAKUWA
AMELEWA?

© — DAN KYUNGU—bsm 80'

## CARTOONS – MIRROR OF TANZANIAN SOCIETY

In the period immediately following Tanzania's independence, most citizens were a long way from seeing their own lives as a part of the nation's destiny. Many regions were not only remote, but also isolated both linguistically and culturally, and people didn't hear much about what was going on in other parts of the country. However, in the 1960s and 70s Julius Nyerere, teacher and president of the young socialist state, strongly promoted school education and the consistent use of Kiswahili as the national language, and Kiswahili has since become a link between the many local languages and cultures of Tanzania. The literacy rate grew far more rapidly than in most

*Above: Only gruel and beans, day in and day out, because Daddy drinks up all the money. Right: The debtor promises to pay back the money little by little – just like the country of Tanzania.*

other African countries; the Tanzanians became ardent newspaper readers, and have remained so.

In the 70s and 80s, most people took little notice of what went on in the *Bunge* (parliament). Of course, some newspapers reported about such things, but the people had other worries, and it was these that cartoonists tended to target. *Matatizo*, "Problems," was one comic strip popular in this period: it features *Karikenye*, a quick-witted young man, who, shaking his head disbelievingly, is the witness of a range of problems in contemporary daily life. For example, in one strip he applies for a job and presents his diploma to the head of the Personnel Department – but the man in question is far more interested in knowing what tribe he's from and which football team he prefers.

Alcoholism, its causes and consequences, is an inexhaustible subject for cartoonists. In one cartoon, a mother walking down the street with her five children points to the corner bar: "Your father lives over there at the end of the month and leaves all of his money there!"

Mothers, and the way they manage to keep control of their lives, are another constant theme. For instance: six children swarm around their mother as she stirs the cooking pot. One child complains that they have to eat the same food every day: *ugali kwa maharage*, gruel and beans. "You should tell your father that!" she answers. "He is drunk when he comes home!" another child counters (see illustration at left).

At the end of the 70s and the beginning of the 80s, there was a shortage of food and consumer goods, which drove many mothers to resort to rather unconventional measures: "Now stop complaining about school! What is it good for? Can you eat your school?" And she instructs each of her children to stand in line for sugar, milk and soap. "And not one of you is to come back empty-handed!" The black market is booming: *Karikenye* watches as a piece of soap is sold on a street corner for the equivalent of a worker's daily wage.

If you don't have money, you borrow some and hide from your creditors. A father says to his small son, who is playing in front of the house, "If someone comes and asks you where I am, tell him I'm away on a trip!" The creditor comes along and asks the son, "Is your papa at home?" "He's away on a trip!" "When will he be back?" "Don't know. I'll ask him!" and the boy runs into the house.

Another debtor has more confidence as he complains to his creditor about the latter's persistence. "Man, don't make a big thing out of it! I'll pay you your money back, little by little! Our country is also up to its ears in debt and promises to pay it all back little by little! How dare you insult me every day and humiliate me on a public street, just because of a couple of shillings!" (see illustration at right). Here, offhandedly, the government's habit of repaying its debts to its international creditors slowly, if at all, is presented as normal, and therefore acceptable. But politicians' mistakes have rarely been a subject for cartoonists in the early years of Tanzania's independence. Cartoonists may poke fun at the free beer handed out during election campaigns, and have gradually started to target the empty promises of district candidates, as well as the wealth they have accumulated since the last election. But their criticism remains general and doesn't get personal.

After the socialist Nyerere era came to an end in 1985, there followed two consecutive terms of the Zanzibarian Mwinyi. *Ruksa* (permission) was the magic word: anything was permissible if it made you rich. Egotism and political separatism created plenty of problems: Zanzibar took it upon itself to join the Organization of Islamic States, as if it wasn't even a part of Tanzania! One cartoonist depicted Mwinyi standing, shaking with

fear, his hands raised in supplication, before the old master (*mzee*) Nyerere, stammering, "*Mzee*, we... we... we've gotten stuck." Another cartoon shows Nyerere holding up a collapsing house labeled "Tanzania" with his own hands, calling out orders to *Ali* (Mwinyi) as to how to repair it.

In the 90s, cartoonists have a much franker approach. speak with absolute frankness. President Mwinyi, Foreign Minister Diria and other high government officals are being evaluated by the school system, *Shule ya Tanzania*, which grades them in such subjects as "empty promises," "lies," "democracy," "management" and "parading around." According to these ratings, Diria was absent 99% of the time, while Mwinyi scores 90% for both empty promises and lies.

Today, people judge the government harshly, to the point of unfairness. Once, it was more usual to complain about conditions in general or take the blame on oneself. Now, however, Tanzanians are more outspoken and don't shrink from pointing fingers at those responsible.

## KANGA - A FASHION AND A STATEMENT

*Kanga* is the Kiswahili word for guinea-fowl, an attractive bird, about the size of a chicken, whose soft black feathers are sprinkled with round white polka-dots. *Kanga* is also the name of the brightly colored, patterned cotton cloth worn by women in East Africa, who wrap them around their bodies in an imaginative and individual manner. *Kanga* are always purchased in pairs, two connected pieces of cloth of the same size (1 m x 1.50 m), with the same pattern. You just have to cut them apart and hem them, and then they're ready to wear. Colors and design may change rapidly, but the basic, traditional principles of the design generally remain the same: a rectangular frame surrounds a large area, usually with a large, eye-catching motif smack in the middle. This could be a big mango, an airplane, a hen, an imaginary flower, or even simply a huge, monochrome circle – or, in short, just about anything else you can think of. Under this distinctive central image there is usually a saying in Kiswahili, and sometimes in English.

A *kanga* doesn't have to be a "dress"; in fact, it generally functions as an outer garment. It also fills a number of purposes. It looks attractive, provided you understand how to wear it elegantly. It protects its wearer from the elements, notably cold and dust. It can be skillfully wound around one's head into a decorative turban, with which the other matching *kanga* is worn around the hips. Mothers wrap their babies in a *kanga* to carry them more easily – as if in a knapsack. The tip of a *kanga*, tied into a tight knot and pushed into the "waistband" of a *kanga* wraparound skirt, is an effective,

*Right: Kangas may be industrially mass produced, but each woman still wears hers with a distinctive style (here, on the east coast of Zanzibar).*

and theft-proof, wallet. The possible applications are virtually endless. Yet there's also another very important reason to wear a *kanga*: by doing so, a woman can demonstrate her opinions, secret wishes and unsayable ideas in public, on the open street. *Kangas* are most often worn as wraparound skirts, which means that the central picture and the saying are clearly visible from the back, there for everyone to read without revealing his or her curiosity to the wearer. The woman next door will surely understand if her neighbor appears in a *kanga* stating, "Mind your own business!" or, "Every day you talk as if you were standing before a large assembly, but only the entrance to your hut is listening."

What does the guinea-fowl have to do with the history of fashion in East Africa? In the 19th century, Zanzibar became a crossroads of international trade. All of East Africa was eager for goods from the far corners of the globe. Merchants and traders from Europe, America and Asia merchants had long sensed this, and reacted quickly. Their new products, industrially manufactured textiles, delighted the Africans. A *marikani* (cloth produced in America), for example, was considered to be much finer than homespun cloth, fabrics made of bark or flax, or even leather clothing. Anyone who owned foreign fabric raised his or her social status, as well.

As early as the 16th century, Portuguese merchants were trading in Mozambique in small squares of cloth the size of handkerchiefs. These were a convenient way for Africans to transport gold dust. Such cloth, whether handkerchief, kerchief or scarf (the Portuguese word is *lenço*), was delivered in the form of a bolt of fabric, from which the squares could be cut individually.

By the middle of the 19th century at the latest, creative ladies from Zanzibar came up with the idea of buying one long section of fabric with six or twelve of the

square patterns, cutting the fabric only once and sewing the two narrow sections together, so that what started as a long, narrow piece of fabric became a rectangular cloth twice as wide. It became the fashion to wrap oneself coquettishly in this cloth, continually changing the manner of draping to vary the effect. These fashionable cloths were known as *leso*. Seeing this trend, European merchants, advised by Indian traders, subsequently developed a new product: large rectangular pieces of cloth that no longer had to be sewn together.

When, in 1890, a merchant introduced a fabric with white polka-dots on a dark background, surrounded by a border with a repeating patter, it was called *kanga* - guinea-fowl. The pattern has changed many thousands of times since, but the name has endured. For the double cloth, the term *leso* is still common.

About 20 years later, *kanga* design saw an innovation – probably introduced to boost sales – that was so successful that it, too, has remained a standard feature of modern kangas. In the inner square, beside the central image, there now appeared a saying in Kiswahili. This trend may have started with women from the more educated upper classes, who initially commissioned *kangas* with lines of erotic poetry. Today, the printed sayings cover the whole spectrum of human sentiment, knowledge, wisdom and everyday humor: sexual hints, expressions of anger, pleas for forgiveness, defense against rumors, and a whole range of other things. Not uncommonly, the inscription is so cryptic or elliptical that only a few close friends of the wearer can fully understand the meaning. *Kangas* also make wonderful presents for different occasions – at which time it becomes very important to find an appropriate saying.

The patterns of the *kangas* change very rapidly – who, after all, wears yesterday's fashions? Yet many saying remain significant, and ambiguous, such as *Dunia ya jana si la leo* – yesterday's world is not today's world.

## BAO – A GAME WITHOUT LIMITS

All Africa is addicted to the game of *bao*. It is played all over the continent, under different names and according to different rules. Merchants and traders carried the game to every country around the Indian Ocean, and slaves from West Africa brought it to the Caribbean. *Bao* is ancient: in Egypt, archaeologists have found game boards carved into the stones of the great pyramid of Cheops and the temples of Karnak. In the coffee-houses of 19th-century Egypt, the custom was that the loser had to pay for the coffee that was consumed during a game. In pre-colonial Tanzania, losing a game could be quite a costly expierence. The Sukuma called the game *Isolo*, and tribal chiefs were known to lose their entire property, complete with all their villages and their inhabitants, to their opponents.

The Kiswahili word *bao* simply means "board." In East Africa, one usually uses a wooden playing board with either two or four rows of eight depressions (*mashimo*, or, in the singular, *shimo*) carved into its surface. Pebbles or seeds about the size of beans serve as the playing-stones (*kete*, also the word for cowrie shells, which were once used as money).

At the start of a game of 16-hole *bao*, the two players each have 18 *kete* in groups (*mtaji*, or, literally, "capital") of three pieces each, distributed among any of the *mashimo* in the player's own row; consequently, on each side of the board, six *mashimo* are filled and two remain empty.

After it's been decided who starts, the first player scoops up all the *kete* from any one of his *mashimo*, and distributes them one by one, counterclockwise, in the next (three) *mashimo*. This clearing

*Right: Spectators can also get drawn into a bao game.*

up of the board and redistribution is called *takata* (literally, "becoming clean").

If the last *kete* falls into an empty *shimo*, it's the other player's turn; if not, the first player can continue. If he has, for example, dropped his third *kete* into a *shimo* with three *kete*, he then takes all four *kete* out of this *shimo* and places them one by one into the next four *mashimo*. The player continues to repeat the *takata* until his last *kete* falls into an empty *shimo*: *kete imelala*, "the *kete* has gone to bed," is the appropriate term. Now the second player can, in turn, start his own *takata*. When he, too, reaches the point at which his last *kete* "sleeps," it's the first player's turn again.

Each player carries out two such *takata* – after which the game really begins. If, during the following *takata*, the last *kete* happens to fall into a *shimo* which contains a single *kete*, the player is lucky. He has won a "house" (*nyumba*)! It doesn't even matter if this *nyumba* is on his own side of the board or on his opponent's side: the "house" belongs to the person who won it, and the stones in it cannot be removed. On the contrary: whenever a new distribution round "crosses" the house, another *kete* has to be deposited here. Thus the number of stones in the house continues to increase throughout the game, constituting a strong advantage for the house's "owner."

After these first two opening rounds, the "cashing in" begins: now each player tries to end his *takata* by placing his last *kete* in an empty *shimo* on his own side of the board – if it's worth it. It's "worth it" if the *shimo* across from it contains is a "fat" *mtaji* – in other words, as many *kete* as possible. The more *kete* in the opponent's *shimo*, the better: for the player takes all these *kete* away from his opponent and puts them aside.

Naturally, you can't always cash in like this, and it's just as important to build additional *nyumba* and fill more

*mashimo*, interfering with your opponent's chances of building his own *nyumba* or cashing in (for, as mentioned above, once you have a *nyumba*, it can never be taken away from you).

The winner is the one with the most *kete* from cashing in and from the contents of his *nyumba*.

*Bao* is played at incredible speed. The players have to keep count with lightning speed and stay absolutely on the ball. If you know the basic rules, just watching is fun.

The game is much more complicated on the more common 32-hole board. Here, in his *takata*, each player moves only on his own two rows of the four-row board, which means he has two times eight *mashimo*. Each player begins with 24 *kete*; he distributes 20, in groups of two, on his side of the board, while saving four for the rest of the game. After each player has ten filled and six empty *mashimo*, the game can begin.

Each player can choose whether to do his *takata* clockwise or counterclockwise. In any case, at the start, he takes an

additional *kete* from his reserve and continues to distributes his *kete*, as usual, until he arrives at an empty *shimo* and it's his opponent's turn. As in the 16-hole version, each player carries out two *takata* and then begins to build houses and engage in another form of cashing in. As long as he has *kete* in reserve, each player begins his *takata* with one extra *kete* from this reserve.

The cashing in is decided in the two middle rows, those bordering on the opponent's *mashimo*. If, in a *takata*, a player puts his last *kete* in a *shimo* in his front row which already contains a single *kete*, then that player can take the *mtaji* from his opponent's *shimo* opposite him, in the front row on the other side of the board (unless, of course, it's a *nyumba*). He takes all of his opponent's *kete* out of the *shimo* and distributes them on his own side, starting with the *shimo* next to the one in which he has just placed his last *kete*. A player always has the choice of moving clockwise or counterclockwise. Got it?

237

## PREPARING FOR YOUR TRIP

### Getting There and Away

All visitors to Tanzania need a valid passport. Citizens of Scandinavia, including Iceland and Finland; the Commonwealth countries; the Republic of Ireland; several island-states in the Indian Ocean and the Caribbean, and several African countries can enter Tanzania without a visa. Everyone else has to have a visa; these are available at Tanzanian High Commissions, embassies and consulates, and are issued for stays of one to three months. Since 1996, it's also been possible to get your visa when you enter Tanzania at the Tanzanian-Kenyan border at Namanga, as well as at the airports of Dar es Salaam, Zanzibar and Kilimanjaro. To avoid hold-ups upon entry, however, it's best to obtain your required visa beforehand.

The visa is valid for a single entry to Tanzania. If you wish to cross the border several times, you have to apply for a special permit from the Department of Immigration (in Dar es Salaam, on the corner of Ghana and Ohio Streets).

When you arrive, a health official will check your passport; if you're coming from a country where yellow fever occurs, you must prove that you've been vaccinated against this disease.

You can bring in personal travel equipment – camera, film, binoculars, etc. – as well as 200 cigarettes, 1 l of alcoholic beverages and 250 g perfume duty-free. To bring in valuable items such as radios, video cameras, musical instruments, ad the like, you may have to pay an import tax. You may even be asked for a customs bond to ensure that you take the goods with you again when you leave the country.

You may neither bring Tanzanian currency into nor take it out of the country.

If you leave Tanzania on an international flight, you'll have to pay an airport tax of 20 US$; by ship, there's a harbor tax of 5 US$.

### Money

The currency, Tanzanian shillings, is usually abbreviated Tsh. Since this currency cannot be brought in or taken out of the country, you have to exchange all your money in Tanzania, and, when you leave the country, either leave your Tanzanian shillings there, or exchange them back into another currency. You can, however, bring in as much foreign currency as you like.

You can exchange cash or travelers' checks at banks or – often at better rates – at Forex offices (authorized exchange offices), which exist in Dar es Salaam, Zanzibar, Arusha and Moshi. Each of these cities has several different Forex agents, so it may be worthwhile to check their different exchange rates. For smaller denominations (1 to 10 US dollars, for example), you often get a much lower rate than for larger sums. Larger hotels, especially in the tourist areas, will accept foreign money, normally US dollars – make sure to check the exchange rates!

Foreigners have to pay entrance fees and for other services in the national parks and other reserves in US$. Harbor tax, at the bigger ports along the Indian Ocean as well as on the large lakes, is US$ 5 for foreigners; airport tax amounts to US$ 20 for international, Tshs. 1,000 for domestic flights.

There are still hotels, especially on Zanzibar, which ask foreigners to pay their bill in US$. Evidently, not everyone is yet aware that the Tanzanian government officially forbade this compulsory payment for overnight accommodations in foreign currency in 1996.

Change, especially banknotes in US dollars, often seems to be in rather short supply; you'll be better off keeping smaller bills and coins with you, so you can pay the exact amount required.

An increasing number of hotels, travel agencies and shops in larger centers, especially in tourist areas, accept credit cards. However, it can happen that you have to pay an additional percentage on your bill (some credit card companies also require this for international transactions).

Travelers' checks are best exchanged in banks; they are rarely accepted as payment. Eurocheques are not known in Tanzania.

## Luggage

On safari vehicles and on domestic flights in smaller aircraft, there is usually a luggage allowance of up to 33 pounds (15 kg); soft-sided suitcases or travel bags are preferred. When you travel in Tanzania by public transportation (mainly buses), you will soon understand how advantageous it is to pack light and portable: you can then safely stow your bag under your seat or up on the narrow luggage rack. If your pack is too large, it will be stowed up on the roof of the bus (sometimes for an additional charge) among such other cargo as smoked fish, oil cans, or live goats. Most hotels, even the smallest guest houses, offer laundry services (some of the luxury-tented camps even provide it free of charge), which also helps you to keep your luggage to a minimum.

## Health Precautions

Ideally, you shouldn't think about inoculations only because you're going to Tanzania; you can pick up the following diseases all over the world: polio, tetanus, hepatitis, diphtheria, typhoid fever. The length of a vaccination's effectiveness varies depending on the invidual vaccination.

Anyone traveling to or through Tanzania for a longer period of time should also get a yellow fever inoculation, which is good for ten years. At least two to three months before your departure to Tanzania, you ought to consult a tropical disease specialist who can tell you which precautions you should take at the moment. You can't necessarily get all the vaccinations you need all at once; for some diseases you need several shots at certain set intervals.

Malaria is an almost ubiquitous threat in Tanzania. The best protection is not to let yourself be bitten by the *Anopheles* mosquitoes which transmit the disease. They generally "hunt" during and after sunset, into the night. Thus, it's best to sleep under a mosquito net (most of the simple guest houses have them; they're less common in more expensive hotels, although air conditioning is not a guaranteed method of keeping mosquitoes away); wear long-sleeved or -legged clothing to protect your skin; and apply plenty of insect repellent. Malaria tablets don't afford complete protection from infection, but they do ensure that, even if you do catch malaria, it will be a less severe case than you might otherwise have. You'll need a doctor's prescription for malaria tablets; your tropical disease specialist will know which ones to use. Take the tablets regularly, starting a week before you travel, and continue until four to six weeks (the approximate incubation period for malaria) after returning home. If you have caught malaria (high fever, headaches), try to bring the fever down, take a large dose of malaria tablets (consult your doctor at home before you leave about which ones), and see a local doctor immediately. Every doctor in Tanzania has plenty of practice in treating malaria.

There is, as yet, no prophylactic measure you can take against shistosomiasis or bilharzia. You risk catching this in the habitats of a certain kind of water snail: stagnant fresh water with lush growth on the shores, especially in the vicinity of human settlements. Hypercautious travelers don't dare to swim anywhere in the country, but there are certainly sections of the large lakes that aren't dangerous; when in doubt, ask the locals. And always purify your drinking water, be it taken from lakes, rivers or even the tap.

*Ukimvi* is the Kiswahili word for AIDS: The Tanzanian government has launched various information campaigns: in some parts of the country, such as in Rukwa Region, you'll find that every room, even in the simplest guest house, is equipped with free condoms. Some travelers, worrying that they could be infected with HIV if they were to require treatment at a Tanzanian hospital and be injected with an insufficiently sterilized needle, carry a few disposable syringes in their luggage.

Your travel first-aid kit should include malaria tablets, insect repellent, disinfectant, stomach medicine, salt tablets, sunscreen, band-aids, and, if you want, disposable syringes.

### Climate / When to Go

Tanzania is in the tropics: in the lowlands and by the ocean, expect it to be very hot and very sunny. Even though temperatures in the mountainous parts of the country are lower, the sun there has the same or even greater intensity as it does at sea level.

The main tourist seasons are June-October and December-March.

The worst of the rainy season is between March and May/June. Although it doesn't rain constantly during this period, the ground is in many places so wet, or even washed away, that progress is impossible even in a four-wheel-drive vehicle. Several rivers rise so drastically that ferries have to discontinue service (at, for example, Rufiji and Kilombero). In some parks, the lodges and campgrounds are closed (Selous, Ruaha, and others). And even for snorkelers and divers, visibility during the rainy season is poor.

The cool, dry period in June and July is very pleasant; in the mountains, at night, it can become cold. From now until November, temperatures increase constantly and it remains dry. During this period, the roads are at their best; many trees lose

their leaves; the grass is shorter; and in all the parks, the animals collect around the slowly dwindling watering-holes.

Precipitation during the lesser rains in November/December is generally low, yet enough to freshen up nature. The rain sets the great migrations of the Serengeti area in motion; now, until March, is the best time to watch them. In February, in many parts of the country, visibility is extraordinarily good on some days.

### What to Pack

On safari in jolting jeeps or trucks, or on tours in rattling buses, light, durable cotton clothing stands up the best. Because of the heat, garments should be loose and comfortable; because of insects, UV rays, and good manners, clothes should cover your body sufficiently. Make sure to protect your head from the heat of the sun!

During the cool season, June through August, in the mountain areas (around Arusha, Ngorongoro, Njombe, Mbeya, for example), you'll need warm, windproof clothing, sturdy shoes, and socks. Do not underrate the danger of catching cold in over-airconditioned rooms.

Those who climb Mounts Meru and Kilimanjaro dress no differently from anyone else making a similar mountain excursion anywhere in the world. Many a mountaineer lightens his luggage, after the climb, by giving away equipment he no longer needs. Some tour agents even lease mountaineering equipment and clothing.

### TRAVELING TO TANZANIA

### By Plane

The following airlines offer regular flights to Tanzania (where the international airports are at Dar es Salaam, Kilimanjaro or Zanzibar): Air Tanzania; Aeroflot, Air France, Air India, Air Zimbabwe, Alliance Air, British Airways, Egypt Airlines, Ethiopian Airlines, Gulf Air, Kenya Airways, KLM, Precision

Air, Royal Swazi, Swissair, Zambia Airways. Many tourists, especially those coming from Europe, opt to fly to Kenya (Nairboi, Mombasa) because of the cheaper airfares and greater choice of flights; from there, they continue by bus (or, from Mombasa, by hydrofoil) to Tanzania.

### By Boat

From **Kenya**, the new, fast and reliable hydrofoil *Sepideh* plies the route Mombasa-Tanga-Pemba-Zanzibar-Dar es Salaam twice a week.

From **Congo** (formerly Zaire), ferries cross Lake Tanganyika between Kalemie and Kigoma.

From **Zambia**, there are two ships a week from Mpulungu to Kigoma

From **Malawi**, there is at least one boat a week from Nkhata to Mbamba Bay.

From **Mozambique**, there is irregular boat service between Pemba (Mozambique) and Msimbati (Mtwara Region).

### By Rail

TAZARA (Tanzania-Zambia Railway) operates express trains twice a week from Kapiri Mposhi to Dar es Salaam.

### By Bus

**Kenya**: There are several buses a day from Nairobi to Arusha (thence to Moshi or Dar es Salaam); there's daily service on the routes Nairobi-Musoma-Mwanza and Mombasa-Tanga.

**Uganda**, **Rwanda**: Local Ugandan and Rwandan buses run as far as the border-towns; from there, you can change to local Tanzanian buses.

**Malawi**: Buses run from Lilongwe to Dar es Salaam.

### By Car

Upon entering Tanzania, cars with non-Tanzanian license plates are charged at least 60 US$. Later on, in the parks, foreign cars have to pay significantly higher fees than Tanzanian ones do.

### Closed Border

In 1996, political disagreement between Tanzania and Burundi led to the closing of their common border.

The border crossing between Kenyan Maasai Mara Game Reserve and Serengeti National Park is also closed.

## TRAVELING IN TANZANIA

### By Plane

**Air Tanzania**, ATC House, Ohio Street, Dar es Salaam, tel. 51-110245-8, with twelve other offices throughout the country. **Coastal Travels**, Upanga Road, Dar es Salaam, tel. 51-37479. **Precision Air** (AICC, in Arusha, tel. 57-6903; in Dar es Salaam, tel. 51-30800) can book regular or charter flights to the major cities or to tourist highlights in the parks, along the coast, or on the islands (Zanzibar, Pemba, Mafia). Charter flights only through **Air Zanzibar** (Zanzibar, tel. 54-32512); **Tanzanair** (office at the Sheraton Hotel, Dar es Salaam, tel. 51-113151); **Zan Air Ltd.**, (Zanzibar, tel. 54-33670). The domestic airport in Dar es Salaam is located next to the international one. At Arusha, the domestic airport is some 5 km west of the city; some domestic flights also depart from Kilimanjaro airport (45 km east of Arusha).

### By Boat

**Mainland-Zanzibar/Pemba**: There are about a dozen different hydrofoils every day between Dar es Salaam and Zanzibar; at least five a week from Zanzibar to Pemba and back; and two a week from Tanga to Pemba. In addition to the rapid vessels, there are also older motor vessels which do take passengers and are cheap. These, however, are mainly used for cargo, and because of the time they need to load and unload, their schedules are somewhat unreliable.

**Dar es Salaam-Mtwara**: The ferry *Canadian Spirit* operates once a week; it has three different passenger classes, but no cabins. You have to pay for the total passage (Dar-Mtwara) in advance, however, if you only want to cover part of the tour (e.g., Dar-Mafia), the purser will reimburse you before you leave the ship.

**Dhows**: Work on these small freighters is very hard, the trip dangerous, and space scarce: therefore harbor authorities generally don't allow dhows that are used for cargo transport to take tourists, even if captain and crew have no objections. However, a chartered dhow is another matter: if the winds are favorable, these are a slower but far more attractive alternative to motorboats as a way to get to secluded beaches, islands, or diving or snorkeling spots.

**TRC ships**: On Tanzania's three large inland lakes, Victoria, Tanganyika and Nyasa, the Tanzanian Railways Corporation operates ferries for passengers and cargo. For travelers with plenty of time, this is one of the nicest ways to get to see remote and extremely beautiful parts of the country. Headquarters: TRC Marine Division, Box 235 Mwanza, tel. 68-40438/41.

### By Train

There are two independent railway systems in Tanzania, each with a different size gauge. Advance reservations for first- and second-class tickets are highly recommended. The Kiswahili word for "station" is *stesheni*.

The **TRC** is the authority for the railway network which dates mainly from the colonial era; its stations are located near city centers. Trains run between Dar es Salaam and Kigoma (about 40 hours) four times a week; from this "central line," two lines branch off at Tabora, one going to Mwanza (four times a week), the other to Mpanda (three times a week). Three classes are available; there are sleeping cars in first class. There's one passenger train to the north, with once-weekly service between Dar es Salaam and Moshi. On this leg, buses are faster and run very frequently.

The **TAZARA** (Tanzania-Zambia Railway), built by the Chinese in the 1970s, connects Dar es Salaam with Zambia; its most-frequented route is Dar es Salaam-Mbeya (three local trains and two express trains per week). Its stations are generally located a few miles out of town.

### By Bus

Comfortable, big overland buses run frequently on the few well-asphalted roads. Some drivers of smaller buses see these roads as invitations to hot-rod. All the rest of the roads in Tanzania – that is, the majority – don't permit fast driving. Sand or gravel roads, rocky or muddy in stretches, and filled with potholes, combined with antique buses (which frequently break down along the way, only to be repaired on the spot with admirable dexterity) and the time-consuming process of loading and unloading a lot of bulky luggage, make for average speeds of around 12 to 20 mph (20-30 km/h). Take this as a rule of thumb, and don't be too quick to believe the bus agents' assertions about arrival times! A town's central bus stops are called *(basi) stendi* in Kiswahili.

### By Daladala or Truck

The more sparsely an area is populated, the less sense it makes to have a public bus system. In such regions, every existing vehicle can be enlisted as a form of all-round transport: *matatu* or *daladala* (collective taxis or service taxis), pick-ups, trucks – anything, in short, on four wheels. Passengers pay the driver the equivalent of a bus fare.

### By Rental Car

In light of the difficult road conditions, it is advisable to hire a car with a driver, who will, in addition, be familiar with the language and the country. Most of Tanzania's car rental companies are based in Dar es Salaam. In remote areas, you have little chance of finding a rental car.

## By Motorbike, Bicycle

Rental motorbikes are a very popular mode of transport on Zanzibar (though the bikes are often in rather poor condition). You can get rental bicycles quite cheaply in many towns (but not in Dar es Salaam); don't expect fancy mountain bikes but rather sturdy Chinese push-bikes. If you want to take a longer bike or motorcycle trip through Tanzania, you'll need – besides perfect physical condition (look out for difficult stretches of sand, mud and potholes!) – knowledge of Kiswahili and local etiquette, plenty of time, and adequate equipment. Riding bikes in national parks is prohibited.

## By Taxi

Always negotiate fares before getting in.

## Hitchhiking

Hitchhiking is uncommon. In Tanzania's many remote areas, nearly every vehicle does double duty as "public transportation," and anyone who rides, pays.

## PRACTICAL TIPS
### Accommodation

The number of hotels in Tanzania has soared within a very short time, and standards have improved remarkably. Hotels of the upper price category (called *LUXURY* in the guideposts at the end of each chapter) – above US$ 150 for a double room – meet international standards and are priced accordingly. *LUXURY-TENTED CAMPS* are an ideal combination of the advantages of a small, high-quality hotel and the grand experience of intimate closeness to the wilderness. Prices are high, but fair: the camps' remoteness makes logistics difficult and expensive; and the price includes full board as well, in some cases, as drinks and laundry service.

The *MODERATE* category (about US$ 30 to 150 for a double room) has taken incredible strides during the 1990s, especially along the coast and in Zanzibar, but also in several regional capitals. Individualists will be glad to know that this price category now includes a number of small hotels with a distinct personal touch.

The *BUDGET* category comprises a wide choice of inexpensive hotels, from run-down large, old establishments (about US$ 25 for a double room) up to a *nyumba ya wageni* (guest house, also called *gesti*) without electricity, where a guest may have to draw his own water from the well (from about US$ 2). The *gesti* have improved tremendously in quality throughout the country, especially the renovated or newly-built ones: many of them boast at least a few rooms with their own bathroom and toilet; almost all of them have mosquito nets; linen is generally clean; foam mattresses keep away bedbugs and other pests; and, at US$ 5-10 for a double, they offer good value for money. Some of these *gesti* have a bar, a restaurant, and/or a TV, and thus are a focal point for locals in the evenings until late into the night: wear earplugs!

*CAMPSITES* in the national parks often lie in beautiful landscapes; sometimes, they are nothing but a fairly flat spot in the wilderness, offering no services whatsoever, although some of them do at least have latrines (for prices see "National Park Fees").

Private campsites outside the parks are often a lot better equipped, and are available for around US$ 5 per person.

## Begging

In most areas, begging is not much of an issue, but in larger cities (Dar es Salaam, Mwanza, Arusha) you see beggars sitting along the sidewalks. A clever way to obtain some money in a country with a high unemployment rate is to render a small service that was not asked for (such as giving instructions to a driver parking a car) or that is usually free of charge (such as stowing luggage on the roof of a bus). Rarely does it happens that someone – usually a younger person – asks directly, "*Naomba hela*," "I beg for money," and as often as not an older person may then reprimand the would-be beggar for his behaviour.

## Comportment

In Tanzania, people spend a lot of time and patience creating a harmonious atmosphere with another person before getting down to the business at hand. Tanzanians are delighted when they encounter a foreigner who is familiar with the appropriate formulas and formalities (see also "Guests and Hosts," p. 39).

Decent, clean clothing is a must everywhere, not only in the Muslim coastal areas. If you're making an official visit (village headman, offices, churches, etc.) be sure that you are well turned out from head to toe!

Polite Tanzanians will conceal their annoyance if an insensitive visitor unwittingly but unthinkingly abuses or takes advantage of the hospitality they so freely grant. A Tanzanian saying suggests that after three days one should hand a hoe to such a guest, to remind him that work has to be done in the fields...

The presence of a foreigner in a remote village is a rare and generally welcome sensation. However, as a stranger, it's your responsibility to make your stay a harmonious one by following the proper etiquette: Make yourself known to the village headman and ask for permission to hike in the area, camp, and the like.

## Crime

*Pickpockets:* Large crowds of people and a slightly disorderly atmosphere are the preferred working conditions of pickpockets worldwide, in Tanzania as everywhere else. When traveling overland, keep travel documents and money hidden away close to your body. In hotels, leave your valuables at the reception desk. At small guest houses, guests are handed a padlock with which to secure their rooms.

*Hold-ups:* Deserted streets and areas (including the national parks in the north), and, particularly, beaches and extensive bungalow complexes around Dar es Salaam and Zanzibar are not really safe – and not only at night: the number of daylight incidents is increasing. Always inform yourself on the spot about the security in a given place.

## Drinking

In most restaurants you'll find boiled drinking water standing in pitchers on the tables, or you can ask for some. Drinking water in plastic bottles is widely available, as are soft drinks – although not always chilled. Besides cola-type drinks and lemonades, *Tangawizi* is very popular, a sweet soft drink spiced with ginger. *Bia* (beer), in bottles, is also consumed in large quantities. For weekends and festivities, but also on weekdays, there's also the local millet- or banana beer, called *pombe*.

Always purify water from the tap or from natural bodies of water before drinking! It's safe to drink tea (*chai*) – you get it practically everywhere.

## Eating

You can find international cuisine in the big hotels. Especially along the coast and in larger cities, there are plenty of restaurants offering a variety of dishes that reflect the influence of Arabian, Indian, European and Chinese immigrants.

In small, local restaurants, you can generally find the menu and price-list on a large board hanging on the wall inside, inviting you to get to know a number of local dishes. The most common staples are rice (*wali*), maize porridge (*ugali*) or plantains (*ndizi*). Along with these, you order side dishes – people often order only one – such as *maharag(w)e*, beans; *mchicha*, spinach; *kabeji*, cabbage; *viazi*, potatoes; *samaki*, fish. *Nyama* means "meat"; you can get *nyama ya ng'ombe*, beef; *nyama ya kuku*, chicken; or *nyama ya mbuzi*, goat. Fish and meat are usually served in a small bowl, together with *mchuzi*, gravy. Extras include *chapati*, flat, pancake-like bread; *slesi* or *mkate*, bread; *(m)andazi*, deep-fried, sweet, doughnut-like cakes; *sambusa*, deep-fried crispy pastry filled with vegetables or meat. On the tables, you generally find a small plate with *chumvi* (salt), *pilipili* (hot peppers) and *limao* (lime/lemon) for additional seasoning.

People eat with their right hands or with cutlery. Soap and water for washing your hands is usually available in one corner of the dining hall. As in any restaurant anywhere in the world, not everything on the menu is always available. If there's no one else in the restaurant, it's wise to ask in advance whether they're serving at all: *Kuna chakula?* Is there anything to eat? If so, *Chakula gani?* What kind of food? *Bei gani?* What's the price?

## Electricity

230 volts, alternating current, 50 hertz. Power outages are not infrequent events, especially in towns that aren't hooked up to the national power network. Lodges and hotels in the wilderness usually operate their own generators, which may get switched off at night.

## Hours of Business

Banks: Mon-Fri 8:30 am until 12:30 pm, some until 4 pm; Sat 8:30-11:30 am; Forex offices are often open later than banks. Government offices are officially open Mon-Fri 7:30 am-3:30 pm. You cannot always count on the officials' being there for the whole day. Shops in towns open at about 9-10 am and close by 5-6 pm, and some have a lunch break; on Saturdays, they're only open in the morning, and on Sundays they're closed. Roadside stands often close at sundown; along busy streets or bus stations, you'll always find a few shops open.

## National Park Fees

It takes a considerable amount of money to protect huge areas of unspoiled nature. Most of the people who want to see Tanzania's natural beauty are foreign tourists. For them, special tariffs apply (as compared to Tanzanian residents). Tariffs as of January 1, 1997:

Fee for one entry within 24 hours:

1. *Northern Circuit* (Kilimanjaro, Arusha, Tarangire, Lake Manyara and Serengeti National Parks; Ngorongoro Conservation Area): 25 US$.

2. *Southern Circuit* (Ruaha, Mikumi and Udzungwa National Parks; Selous Game Reserve) and Katavi and Rubondo Island National Parks: 15 US$.

3. Mahale Mountains NP: 50 US$.

4. Gombe Stream NP: 100 US$.

Camping fees: in a Public Campsite (open to anybody), per person/24 hours: 20 US$; in a Special Campsite (booked for one person or one party only), per person/24 hours: 40 US$.

Huts: Mountain huts along Kilimanjaro's Marangu Route are 40 US$ each; on Mount Meru, 20$. In the other parks, 20-30$.

Guide fees: according to type of service/duration of tour, 10-20 US$.

There are additional charges for motor vehicles and accident insurance, rescue fees for mountain tours, and permits for fishing or filming, among others.

## Photography

Photographing military facilities or people in uniform is prohibited. Most Tanzanian men, women, and children like having their picture taken – as long as one has first made sure to establish the proper atmosphere of mutual trust (see also "Comportment"). Often, many *wazungu* (white people) are in too great a hurry and, because of their haste, forfeit their chance to take a photo of a Tanzanian. At any rate, respect any rejection! People who allow themselves to be photographed sometimes impose conditions: they ask for money (the Maasai, who have frequent contact with tourists, nearly always do this) or to have the photo sent to them. Such a photo is always highly appreciated!

## Public Holidays

January 1: New Year's Day; January 12: Zanzibar's Day of Revolution; April 26: Union Day of Zanzibar and Tanganyika; May 1: Workers' Day; August 8: Farmers' Day (often called *nane nane* after the date, 8/8; sometimes, July 7 or 7/7, *saba saba*, the date of the founding of TANU, is also celebrated as Farmers' Day); December 9: Independence Day; December 25 and 26: Christmas. Flexible Muslim holidays: Id el-Fitr (end of Ramadan); Id el-Hajji (pilgrims' festival); Maulid (the Prophet's birthday). Flexible Christian holidays: Good Friday, Easter Monday.

## Safari, Organized in Tanzania

While many tourists book their safaris well in advance of their departure, there are others who prefer flexibility and don't decide what kind of tours they want to go on until they get to Tanzania. Like-minded individualists tend to meet up in Arusha and go off together to look for an appropriate agent; conversely, an agent may collect a number of individual clients to form a safari group. Agents in Moshi and those from the Marangu hotels specialize mainly in Kilimanjaro climbs; agents in Dar es Salaam often cater to tourists to the *Southern Circuit*. The information offices of the TTB (Tanzania Tourist Board) keep updated lists of licensed tour operators in their files.

The easiest way to compare different agents' safari offers is to ask for the rate per person per day (at a given group size), and then establish details about exact routing, time schedule, how many game drives are included, how many service personnel come along (only driver? driver and cook?), name and kind of overnight places, quality and size of car/plane, nature of camping equipment and food. Too, you should ask about safety and security, which is important on tours to remote places (does the car have a radio? is there a watchman at the camp-site?); fees (is everything included, or will there be additional charges for guides, security or other "extras" along the tour?).

A warning against extremely cheap offers: if an agent's daily rate is rather near to the high daily park/overnighting fees (see "National Park Fees"), caution is indicated: in such a case, it seems virtually inevitable that either the park authorities or the tourists will be cheated. Ask precise questions about details (Where exactly is the camp? Is there water for washing?). Question travelers coming back from a safari about their experiences.

## Shopping

Popular souvenirs include *Makonde* carvings and other woodwork; basketwork and raffia work; mats; woven articles; *kanga* and *kitenge* (brightly-colored cotton cloths which women wear as outer garments, see p. 234); soapstone carvings; articles made of used tin cans, such as toys or oil lamps; Maasai jewellery; and more. Take your time, and bargain until you've negotiated a good price.

## Telephoning

When calling Tanzania from abroad, dial the international country code for Tanzania, 255, then the two-digit city or regional area code (no "0"), then the number. Within Tanzania, dial "0" before the area code if you're making a long-distance call. For an international call out of Tanzania, dial "00} before the international country code. Cardphones of different companies, including the national Telecom company, have been installed in several cities. Make sure you've got the right card for the card phone you're. Telecom offices sell only Telecom cards; you can also place calls there for cash. The number of private mobile phone users is growing steadily.

## Time

Tanzania is 3 hours after Greenwich Mean Time, 2 hours after Central European Time. **Note that** in Tanzania,

"0:00" means 6 am/pm, about the time of sunrise/sunset. Many departure times are written the Tanzanian way: *Saa* (clock) *moja* (one) *asubuhi* (morning) means 7 am; *saa moja jioni* (evening) is 7 pm. When you're traveling overland in Tanzania, it is wise to learn by heart the Kiswahili numbers 1-12, the times of the day (*asubuhi* - morning, *mchana* - day, *jioni* - evening, *usiku* - night), and the days of the week, otherwise you might find that the one bus of the week, which you had intended to take, already left six hours ago...

### Tipping

Safaris: Drivers, guides, cooks and porters know very well that the tourist has paid about 100 US$ a day, often even more, for his trip. They receive only a minimal portion of that money from their employers, although they have to toil the whole day long. For such demanding work, a tip of US$ 5-10 per day and person is a fair amount. In high-class restaurants and hotels, the service charge is included in the bill. 10% tips are recommended in restaurants.

### Women Traveling Alone

will have no problem in Tanzania, especially if they're as independent as Tanzanian women, who can climb atop the highest truck without any help, bargain adroitly about the transport costs of whatever cargo they have with them, and simultaneously look after a couple of kids.

### ADDRESSES

#### Diplomatic Representation in Dar es Salaam

**Canada**: Canadian High Commission, Mirambo St., Box 1022 Dar es Salaam, tel. 5120651-4. **Denmark**: Royal Danish Embassy, Ghana Ave., Box 9171 Dar es Salaam, tel. 51-46318. **Finland**: Embassy of Finland, NIC Investment House, 9th Floor, Box 255 Dar es Salaam, tel. 51-46324. **Great Britain**: British High Commission, Azikiwe/Samora Ave., Box 92000 Dar es Salaam, tel. 51-26901-4. **India**: High Commission of India, NIC Investment House, 11th Floor, Wing A, Box 2684 Dar es Salaam, tel. 51-33754. **Japan**: Embassy of Japan, Upanga Rd., Bos 2577 Dar es Salaam, tel. 51-31215-9. **Kenya**: High Commission of the Republic of Kenya, NIC Investment House, 14th Floor, Box 5231 Dar es Salaam, tel. 51-31502. **The Netherlands**: Royal Netherlands Embassy, New ATC Town Terminal Building, Ohio St./Garden Ave., Box 9534 Dar es Salaam, tel. 51-46391-4. **Norway**: Royal Norwegian Embassy, Mirambo St., Box 9012 Dar es Salaam, tel. 51-46443. **South Africa**: South Africa Embassy, Mwaya St. (Msasani), Box 10732 Dar es Salaam, tel. 51-66559. **Sweden**: Embassy of Sweden, Extelecoms Building, Samora Ave./Bridge St., Box 9274 Dar es Salaam, tel. 51-23501-2. **U.S.A.**: Embassy of the United States of America, 36, Laibon/Ali Hassan Mwinyi Rd., Box 91123 Dar es Salaam, tel. 51-66010-15.

#### Tanzanian Embassies Abroad

**Canada**: 50 Range Rd., Ottawa, Ontario KIN 8J4, tel. 613-232 1500-9. **Great Britain**: 43 Hertford St, London WIY 8DB, tel. 71-499 8951. **South Africa**: Box 56572, Arcadia 0007, Pretoria. **Sweden**: Oxtorgsgatan 2-4, S-103-89 Stockholm, tel. 8-244870. **Switzerland**: 47 Avenue Blanc, CH-1201 Genève, tel. 22-731 8920. **U.S.A.**: 2139 R Street, NW, Washington D.C., 20008, tel. 202-939 6125-7.

#### Tourist Information

**Arusha**: TTB (Tanzania Tourist Board), Boma Street, Box 2348 Arusha, tel. 57-3842-3. **Dar es Salaam**: TTB, Samora Avenue, UNESCO House, Box 2485 Dar es Salaam, tel. 51-113144. **Zanzibar**: Zanzibar Tourist Corporation, downtown information office: Creek Rd; main office: Livingstone House, Box 216 Zanzibar, tel. 54-32344.

**TANAPA**; Tanzania National Parks, Box 3134 Arusha, tel. 57-3471, 3181.
**TAWICO**; Tanzania Wildlife Corporation, Box 1144 Arusha, tel. 57-8830-1.

## GLOSSARY

Pronunciation of Kiswahili vowels (long or with emphasis/short): "*a*" as in f**a**r/b**u**s; "*e*" as in s**a**y/t**e**n; "i" as in b**ee**/p**i**n; "o" as in f**ou**r/p**o**t; "u" as in z**oo**/b**u**ll. Kiswahili "*th*" resembles English th in **th**ick; Kiswahili "*dh*," English th in mo**th**er. Words are accented on the second-to-last syllable.

How are you?(sing./pl.) . . . . . . .
. . . . . . . . . *hujambo/ hamjambo?*
I am/we are fine . *sijambo/hatujambo*
What's the news? . . . . . . *habari gani?*
What's your news? . . . . *habari yako?*
What's today's news? . *habari za leo?*
...new at home? *habari za nyumbani?*
...new at work? . . . . . *habari za kazi?*
(answer is always) Good! *nzuri* or *njema*
Hello! (casual) . . . . . . . . . *jambo!*
How are you? (casual) . . . . . *habari?*
Come near (welcome)! . . . . . *karibu!*
please; thank you . . . *tafadhali; asante*
Mr.; sir . . . . . . . . . . . . . *bwana*
Mrs.; ma'am . . . . . . . . . . *mama*
honorable old man . . . . . . . . *mzee*
Greeting, old man . . . *shikamoo, mzee*
(answer) . . . . . . . . . . *marahaba*
Goodbye . . . . . . . . . . . *kwa heri*
person; people . . . . . . *mtu; watu*
man; men . *mwanamume; mwanaume*
woman; women *mwanamke; wanawake*
child; children . . . . . . *mtoto; watoto*
My name is . . . . . . . . . *ninaitwa*
What's your name? . . *unaitwa nani?*
I come from . . . . . . . . *ninatoka*
Where do you come from?
. . . . . . . . . . . . *unatoka wapi?*
England, France . *Uingereza, Ufaransa*
English person, people . . . *Mingereza,*
. . . . . . . . . . . . . . *Waingereza*
English language . . . . . *Kiingereza*
America; Canada . . *Marekani; Kanada*
American, Canadian . . . . . . . . . .

. . . . . . . . *Mmarekani; Mkanada*
Have a good trip! . . . . *safari njema!*
I am traveling by ... *ninakwenda kwa ...*
airplane . . . . . . . . . . . . *ndege*
railway, train . . . . . . . . *reli, treni*
bus; ship; boat . . . . . *basi; meli; booti*
bicycle; motorcycle . . *baiskeli, pikipiki*
I walk . . . . *ninakwenda kwa miguu*
left; right . . . . . . . . *kulia; kushoto*
straight on . . . . . . *moja kwa moja*
slowly; quickly . . . *polopole; haraka*
from, to . . . . . . . *kwenda, kutoka*
departure; arrival . . *kuondoka; kufika*
ticket; price (of passage) . *tikiti; nauli*
1st/2nd/3rd class . . . . . . . . . . . .
. . . . . . *daraja la kwanza/pili/tatu*
I want to buy . . . *ninataka kununua*
How much is it? . . . *ni shilingi ngapi?*
1, 2 . . . . . . . . . . . . . *moja, mbili*
3, 4 . . . . . . . . . . . . . . *tatu, nne*
5, 6 . . . . . . . . . . . . . *tano, sita*
7, 8 . . . . . . . . . . . . . *saba, nane*
9, 10 . . . . . . . . . . . . . *tisa, kumi*
11; 12 . . *kumi na moja; kumi na mbili*
20; 30 . . . . . . . . *ishirini; thelathini*
40; 50 . . . . . . . *arobaini; hamsini*
60; 70 . . . . . . . . . . *sitini; sabini*
80; 90 . . . . . . *themanini; tisini*
100; 423 . . . . . . . . . . *mia (moja);*
. . . . . . . . . *mia nne ishirini na tatu*
1,000; 10,000 . . *elfu (moja); elfu kumi*
expensive; cheap . . . . . *ghali; rahisi*
big; small . . . . . . . . *-kubwa; -dogo*
just a little . . . . . . . . . . *kidogo tu*
I have small luggage . *nina mzigo mdogo*
I want; I don't want . *ninataka; sitaki*
yes; no; perhaps *ndiyo; hapana; labda*
yesterday; today; tomorrow . *jana; leo;*
. . . . . . . . . . . . . . . . . *kesho*
Monday, Tuesday . *Jumatatu; Jumanne*
Wednesday, Thurs. *Jumatano,Alhamisi*
Friday, Saturday . . *Ijumaa; Jumamosi*
Sunday; publ. holiday *Jumapili; sikukuu*
What's the time? . *saa ngapi sasa hivi?*
Do you have a room? . . . . . . . . .
. . . . . . . . . . *Kuna chumba hapa?*
with shower and bath . *selfcontained*
toilet; bath . . . . . . . . *choo; bafu*
single room . . *chumba cha mtu mmoja*

double room      *chumba cha watu wawili*
Please, show me      *tafadhali, unionyeshe*
Is there water? . . . . . . . *kuna maji?*
breakfast . . . . . . . *chai ya asubuhi*
food; help yourself! . . . . . *chakula;*
. . . . . . . . . . . . *karibu chakula!*
market . . . . . . . . . . . . . . *soko*
police, doctor . . . . . . *polisi, daktari*
danger . . . . . . . . . . . . *hatari*
Just a minute! . . . . . . . *ngoja kidogo!*
Stop! . . . . . . . . . . . . *simama!*
Excuse me! . . . . . . . . *samahani!*
It doesn't matter! . . . . *hamna shida!*
OK . . . . . . . . . . . . *sawasawa*

## AUTHORS

**Elke Frey** is a freelance tour guide for study groups and writes books and articles about her favorite travel destinations. She studied geography and geology. Contrary to the general trend in travel fashions, she prefers to travel slowly, preferably on foot or by bike. Her first encounter with Tanzania was in 1985, during a cycling trip through wild landscapes and on indescribably bad roads, but accompanied at every turn by the natural charm and warmth of the Tanzanian people. As a tour guide who has worked all over the world, she finds Tanzania a veritable magnet. She is also the author of the *Nelles Guide Sri Lanka* and co-author of the *Nelles Guide Norway*.

**David Kyungu** is a Tanzanian journalist and cartoonist. As a child, he grew up with the problems of his young, newly-independent country. Always fond of drawing, he invented the cartoon character *Karikenye* while he was still in school. He calls himself a "product of Julius Nyerere," born into a difficult period of transition into a new African future. He has made a number of documentary films about contemporary Tanzanian themes, including *AIDS* and *German Guest Workers in Tanzania*. His contribution to the *Nelles Guide Tanzania* is the feature "Cartoons – Mirror of Tanzanian Society."

## PHOTOGRAPHERS

**Angermayer**, Toni                                55
**Archiv für Kunst und Geschichte**,
    **Berlin**        26, 29, 31, 35, 52, 143, 199
**Berger**, Rudolf H. (Tierbildarchiv
    Angermayer)                          46/47, 213
**Birkmann**, Anneliese (Archiv Amberg)
                                                            147
**Braunger**, Manfred              30, 40, 70,
                                              90/91, 128
**Brehm**, Dr. Hermann (Silvestris)      57
**Credner**, Barbara              42, 129, 138
**Degen**, Marcus                                197
**Dennis**, Nigel (Silvestris)                69
**Fiebig**, Hartmut                          76, 78
**Frey**, Elke        118, 142, 146, 152, 156,
            157, 159, 168, 173, 175, 176,
            180/181, 202/203, 210, 216, 220
**Heine**, Heiner (Silvestris)              209
**Jafferji**, Javed      8/9, 12, 15, 33, 37, 48,
        61, 64, 72, 85, 92, 96, 99, 100, 101,
        104, 105, 107, 111, 117, 122/123, 124,
            150/151, 161, 162, 217, 224/225
**Janicke**, Volkmar E.                    16, 131
**Joerissen**, Heinz                          25, 163
**Kisbye**, Henrik                          132, 133
**Kyungu**, David                            232, 233
**Lahr**, Günther        10/11, 17, 41, 44/45,
                            58, 60, 63, 71, 75, 211
**McCullagh**, Paul (Silvestris)          219
**Pölking**, Fritz (Tierbildarchiv
    Angermayer)                  24, 136, 194,
                                226/227, 231
**Reinhard**, Hans (Tierbildarchiv
    Angermayer)                                222
**Schink**, Hans-Christian              43, 84
**Schwarz**, Berthold      38, 59, 79, 81, 102
**Villeret**, Laurent      cover, 97, 103, 172,
            185, 187, 191, 196, 204, 235
**Willetts**, Duncan (Camerapix)        106,
                                        221, 229
**Wisniewski**, Winfried (Silvestris) 23, 53
**Wirz**, Dominique              18, 65, 177,
                                182, 184, 195
**Wurschi**, Gunther          115, 139, 160,
                                    167, 237
**Ziesler**, Günter (Tierbildarchiv
    Angermayer)                            21, 54.

# Explore the World

## NELLES MAPS

## AVAIBLABE TITLES

Afghanistan 1 : 1 500 000
Australia 1 : 4 000 000
Bangkok - *Greater Bangkok,
Bangkok City* 1 : 75 000 / 1 : 15 000
Burma → *Myanmar*
Caribbean Islands 1 *Bermuda,
Bahamas, Greater Antilles*
1 : 2 500 000
Caribbean Islands 2 *Lesser Antilles*
1 : 2 500 000
Central America 1 : 1 750 000
Colombia - Ecuador 1 : 2 500 000
Crete - Kreta 1 : 200 000
China 1 - *Northeastern*
1 : 1 500 000
China 2 - *Northern* 1 : 1 500 000
China 3 - *Central* 1 : 1 500 000
China 4 - *Southern* 1 : 1 500 000
Dominican Republic - Haiti
1 : 600 000
Egypt 1 : 2 500 000 / 1 : 750 000
Hawaiian Islands
1 : 330 000 / 1 : 125 000
Hawaiian Islands 1 *Kauai*
1 : 125 000
Hawaiian Islands 2 *Honolulu
- Oahu* 1 : 125 000
Hawaiian Islands 3 *Maui - Molokai
- Lanai* 1 : 125 000

Hawaiian Islands 4 *Hawaii, The
Big Island* 1 : 330 000 / 1 : 125 000
Himalaya 1 : 1 500 000
Hong Kong 1 : 22 500
Indian Subcontinent 1 : 4 000 000
India 1 - *Northern* 1 : 1 500 000
India 2 - *Western* 1 : 1 500 000
India 3 - *Eastern* 1 : 1 500 000
India 4 - *Southern* 1 : 1 500 000
India 5 - *Northeastern - Bangladesh*
1 : 1 500 000
Indonesia 1 : 4 000 000
Indonesia 1 *Sumatra* 1 : 1 500 000
Indonesia 2 *Java + Nusa Tenggara*
1 : 1 500 000
Indonesia 3 *Bali* 1 : 180 000
Indonesia 4 *Kalimantan*
1 : 1 500 000
Indonesia 5 *Java + Bali* 1 : 650 000
Indonesia 6 *Sulawesi* 1 : 1 500 000
Indonesia 7 *Irian Jaya + Maluku*
1 : 1 500 000
Jakarta 1 : 22 500
Japan 1 : 1 500 000
Kenya 1 : 1 100 000
Korea 1 : 1 500 000
Malaysia 1 : 1 500 000
West Malaysia 1 : 650 000
Manila 1 : 17 500

Mexico 1 : 2 500 000
Myanmar (Burma) 1 : 1 500 000
Nepal 1 : 500 000 / 1 : 1 500 000
Trekking Map *Khumbu Himal /
Solu Khumbu* 1 : 75 000
New Zealand 1 : 1 250 000
Pakistan 1 : 1 500 000
Peru - Ecuador 1 : 2 500 000
Philippines 1 : 1 500 000
Singapore 1 : 22 500
Southeast Asia 1 : 4 000 000
Sri Lanka 1 : 450 000
Tanzania - Rwanda, Burundi
1 : 1 500 000
Thailand 1 : 1 500 000
Taiwan 1 : 400 000
Uganda 1 : 700 000
Venezuela - Guyana, Suriname,
French Guiana 1 : 2 500 000
Vietnam, Laos, Cambodia
1 : 1 500 000

## FORTHCOMING

South Pacific Islands
Trekking Map *Kathmandu Valley /
Helambu, Langtang* 1 : 75 000

*Nelles Maps in european top quality!
Relief mapping, kilometer charts and tourist attractions.
Always up-to-date!*

# Explore the World

*Nelles Guides – authorative, informed and informative.*
*Always up-to-date, extensivley illustrated, and with first-rate relief maps.*
*256 pages, appr. 150 color photos, appr. 25 maps*